" It is the law of life which has yet to be broken, that a nation can only earn the right to live soft by being prepared to die hard in defence of its living."

Lord Wavell

HISTORY OF THE 12TH NORTHAMPTONSHIRE BATTALION HOME GUARD

1940 — 1944

By Lt.-Colonel L. E. BARNES, M.B.E.

The Naval & Military Press Ltd

Published by

The Naval & Military Press Ltd

Unit 10 Ridgewood Industrial Park,
Uckfield, East Sussex,
TN22 5QE England

Tel: +44 (0) 1825 749494
Fax: +44 (0) 1825 765701

www.naval-military-press.com
www.nmarchive.com

DAWN ON THE WESTON FRONT, 1940

(Photo: J. Wright)

Introduction

This short history of the 12th Northamptonshire Battalion Home Guard (The Borough Battalion) has been written as a small tribute to all those good fellows who served in its ranks during the Second World War. Many hundreds received their first military training in the Battalion and passed from us to the Regular Forces. Some, alas, will never return, having made the supreme sacrifice on battle-fields in all parts of the world. It is also an attempt to acquaint the Citizens of the Borough with the efforts that were made for their protection during those hectic years, and to leave behind for future generations some slight record of our activities in the years of our existence. No one is more aware of the shortcomings of this book than myself. I have tried to make it as accurate and as comprehensive as possible, but should there be omissions I would ask for the indulgence of its readers. In conclusion, if those who peruse it get half as much enjoyment from reading it as I have got from writing it, they will enjoy themselves a hell of a lot.

CONTENTS

	Page
L.D.V. — HOME GUARD	11
EARLY DAYS OF THE NORTHAMPTON L.D.V.	17
ORGANISATION, RE-ORGANISATION AND STILLL MORE RE-ORGANISATION	25
EXERCISES, SCHEMES, ETC.	30
BATTALION PARADES AND SPECIAL OCCASIONS	44
WEAPON TRAINING	52
THE HOME GUARD AND THE CIVIL DEFENCE	61
ROAD BLOCKS, VULNERABLE POINTS, ETC.	69
THE FEEDING OF THE HOME GUARD, AND WEEK-END CAMPS	73
BATTALION HEADQUARTERS	77
A DREAM OF ST. PETER'S BRIDGE, NORTHAMPTON	85
ROUND THE COMPANIES:	
A Company	92
B Company	103
C Company	106
D Company	110
E Company	115
F Company	119
G Company	120
H Company	124
The Battalion Band	126
Northampton Post Office Company	127
MEMBERS OF THE BATTALION SERVING AT THE STAND DOWN	129
RECORD OF OLD MEMBERS WHO JOINED H.M. FORCES	143
OLD MEMBERS KILLED OR DIED ON ACTIVE SERVICE	145
RECORD OF SERVICE OF OLD MEMBERS:	
Battalion Headquarters	147
A Company	151
B Company	156
C Company	161
D Company	166
E Company	170
F Company	171
G Company	173
H Company	176
MEMBERS OF THE HOME GUARD WHO DIED WHILE SERVING WITH THE 12th BATTALION	177
INTERESTING FIGURES OF THE BATTALION	178
A MESSAGE FROM HIS MAJESTY THE KING	179
SPECIAL ORDER OF THE DAY by The Commander-in-Chief, Home Forces	180
MESSAGE TO ALL HOME GUARDSMEN from The Commander, East Central District	181
FAREWELL MESSAGE from the Colonel of the Northamptonshire Regiment	181
FINALE	182

ILLUSTRATIONS

DAWN ON THE WESTON FRONT .. .. *Frontispiece*

AN EARLY PARADE OF THE BATTALION. .. *Facing page* 12

THE SPIGOT MORTAR near St. Peter's Bridge .. ,, ,, 16

THE SPIGOT MORTAR IN ACTION .. .. .. ,, ,, 32

WEAPON TRAINING: THE LEWIS GUN .. .. ,, ,, 48

STEN GUN PRACTICE ON THE R.E.M.E. RANGE ,, ,, 64

ANNIVERSARY PARADE, COUNTY GROUND, 1943 ,. ,, 80

THE END OF THE "BATTLE" (County Ground) .. ,, ,, 96

THE NORTHOVER .. .. ,, ,, 97

THE SMITH GUN .. .. ,, ,, 112

THE DESPATCH RIDERS .. .. ,, ,, 113

WIRING PARTY (Abington Park) .. .. .. ,, ,, 128

ST. PETER'S BRIDGE .. .. ,, ,, 129

WALL CLIMBING (Crispin Street) .. .. .. ,. ,, 144

ROAD BLOCK (Abington Park) .. . .. ,, ,, 145

CAMOUFLAGE SUIT .. .. ,, ,, 160

HOME GUARD FETE FOR HOSPITALS, 1944 .. ,, ,, 161

THE BATTALION BAND .. .. ,, ,, 176

REMOVING THE BLACK-OUT FROM MANFIELD
HOSPITAL .. .. ,, ,, 177

THE LAST OF THE HOME GUARD, December, 1945 ,, ,, 184

CHAPTER ONE

L.D.V. — HOME GUARD

IN the Spring of 1940, with the German invasion of Norway, Holland, Belgium and France, we were introduced to a new type of warfare as distinct from that of 1914—1918 as the latter was distinct from the Boer War. By the use of paratroops, fifth columnists and fast-moving armoured columns, the Germans completely transformed the character of war. It was evident to all that this country of ours was not after all so immune from attack as we had all supposed. The English Channel and the Straits of Dover, though still invaluable and " worth a £ a pint," did not present the same bulwark as hitherto. A new method of defence had to be found to combat this possibility of an airborne invasion. No longer was it necessary to guard and defend only the coasts of these islands, but every square mile must be watched, for attacks were liable to begin in districts far removed from the shores. In Holland the main attack came from the air at Rotterdam, right in the heart of the country. To maintain a force large enough to protect the whole of these islands would have absorbed all our man-power, a man-power which at that time was so urgently needed in the factories, first to replace the losses of material that the British Army had sustained on the Continent and secondly to obtain parity and then superiority over the Germans in weapons, tanks, planes, etc., so essential in present-day warfare. It was clear that a system had to be found, one that could maintain and increase the flow of munitions and provide the food needed by the people, and at the same time make adequate provision for the defence of the land. And so the L.D.V. came into being, whereby an army of men was trained who would work at their normal occupations but, should the country be threatened, would lay down their tools and take their place in the firing-line in the defence of the country against the enemy invader. This characteristic of the L.D.V., later the Home Guard, was maintained to the end, and never did their training and operational duties interfere with the war production. All was accomplished in the spare time of its members.

It was on the evening of May 14th, 1940, with the news from Europe getting blacker and blacker that the voice of Mr. Anthony Eden, then the Secretary of State for War, came on the air.

"In order to supplement, from sources as yet untapped, the home defence of the country, it has been decided to create a new force to be known as 'Local Defence Volunteers.' This force, which will be voluntary and unpaid, will be open to British subjects between the ages of seventeen and sixty-five years of age. The period of service will be for the duration of the war Volunteers accepted will be provided with uniforms and will be armed.

"Men of reasonable physical fitness and with a knowledge of firearms should give in their names at their local police stations. The need is greatest in small towns, villages and less densely populated areas. The duties of the force can be undertaken in a volunteer's spare time. Members of existing Civil Defence Organisations should consult their officers before registering under this scheme.

"The Force will be under the command of the General Officer, Commanding in Chief, Home Forces."

The result of this announcement was astounding. In a few days well over a million men had responded and enrolled. It is characteristic of the British that they are always at their best when the situation is at its worst, and this was undoubtedly one of the reasons for the response, but the chief one to my mind was the opportunity it gave, so badly wanted by every patriotic man, particularly the old soldier, to play his part, and at last to feel that he could do something to help his country in its hour of dire need.

And so all over the British Isles from Land's End to John o' Groats the L.D.V. came into being and speedily commenced its duties. As far as towns like Northampton were concerned these duties fell into two categories, (a) to watch by stationary or moving patrols or both, the ground immediately round the boundaries of the Borough and open spaces within it and (b) to provide guards for the vulnerable points in the town itself. Armed with nothing but a stick and a stout heart, perhaps with a loaned shot-gun here and there, or a revolver, a relic of the last war dug up from a bottom drawer, we went out on our Observation Posts. These were " the cap and walking-stick " days, and for some months from dusk to dawn these posts were manned and the skies, our skies, anxiously watched. If you look round our countryside you will see that every mile or so there are places where aeroplanes can land. At this time our role was almost purely observational. Information of any enemy landings had to be obtained and passed on rapidly to the Regular Forces, so that the latter could get quickly to the seat of danger and prevent a trickle becoming a flood. With the lack of arms our role could be nothing more than observation, but there is no doubt that this was well done. From church towers and from every point of vantage during those summer and autumn months of 1940 lonely vigil was kept throughout the land, and had enemy paratroops descended from the skies they would have been quickly observed and reported upon by the ever-watchful L.D.V.'s.

The Germans endeavoured to counteract the L.D.V. movement by a declaration that all its members without uniform captured with arms in their hands, would be shot as franc-tireurs. I am sure that this did not worry us much; in fact, we were rather pleased that our activities had attracted the notice of the Bosches, and we hoped that they were anxious about us. Nor did the lack of uniforms perturb us unduly; but what we did demand was weapons and ammunition. Uniforms could wait, but our demand for weapons could not. I can scarcely believe the story that in those days one enthusiastic L.D.V. sold his wife for twenty rounds of small arms ammunition. But it is true that members were prepared to go to almost any length to obtain this.

However, after a period of the usual grousing, especially from the old soldier, one bright day, arms arrived; not enough, certainly, for one per man, but enough to enable all patrols and guards to go to their posts armed, and with sufficient ammunition to last about five minutes if they were careful. It is no secret now that all these weapons had been rushed over from the U.S.A., and these arms issued in 1940 were carried by us throughout our years of service until the Stand Down at the end of 1944. None of us who served will ever forget the rifle with the red band. To the uninitiated it may be explained that the American ammunition was of a different calibre to ours, so that only American ammunition could be used in these rifles, and therefore to prevent confusion it was necessary for them to be plainly marked. Hence the red band. The Home Guard, particularly those serving in 1940, will always cherish in their hearts a warm spot for the U.S.A. for their generous help in providing them with arms at a time when they were so badly needed.

AN EARLY PARADE OF THE BATTALION.

As time went on, the Home Guard became better equipped for their job. Denims, overcoats, steel helmets, grenades, etc., arrived, very often in driblets to the accompaniment of grousing from the unfortunates. But considering the state of the Regular Army after Dunkirk, it must be admitted that the Home Guard did not do so badly. In those days members wore the badge of the regiment with which they had served in the last war, but in April, 1941, an instruction was issued that they should henceforth wear the badge of the County Regiment. By this time, too, the Home Guard had evidently done quite a lot of walking, for the first notice about the repair of boots appears.

As the months rolled by we became inundated with weapons of all types—Northovers, spigot mortars, Smith guns, and anti-tank two-pounders. Each of these had its devotees, but if a " Gallup ballot " was held, I believe that the spigot would secure first place as the most effective sub-artillery weapon, for its simple mechanism, its accuracy and the devastating effect of its fire. In fact, during the later stages of the War we had far too many different kinds of weapons and not enough of one particular kind. We always felt that an ideal weapon for the Home Guard would have been the two- or three-inch mortar, one far more mobile and easier to handle than the sub-artillery ones in our possession. The Sten gun was a godsend to us, as it enabled every man to have a personal weapon and was especially suitable for street fighting and house clearing where the ranges were short. In the last year of our existence there is no doubt that we were well-armed, not perhaps in the manner that we would have liked, but still armed, so that we could have put up a really good show if called upon to do so.

From time to time the role of the Home Guard changed, although always maintaining its local character. This was one of the main differences from the Territorial Army. We were not asked to defend the whole of Britain, but our own particular bit of country, whose surface and pecularities we knew by heart. In 1940 when observation was of paramount importance, posts were established on the outskirts of Northampton. A ring of road-blocks were made, supported by rifle-pits to hold a section of men. An instruction issued at this time stated that rifle-pits constructed by the Home Guard should be protected by barbed wire to prevent cattle or sheep from either falling into them or trampling down the sides. The intention of these road-blocks with their rifle-pits was to deny the roads to the enemy and also to prevent his access to the town. A year or so later this system of small isolated posts on the outskirts of the town was abandoned, and the Home Guard concentrated in Defended Localities in the town itself at important cross-roads and river bridges. Here, well wired in and with a sufficient garrison, the Companies and Platoons could be expected to hold out for a lengthy period. There was much heart-burning at the time at this change, and the thought of giving up the old L.D.V. posts and with-drawing into the town itself, forced upon us by the Higher Authorities, did not meet with anything like approval, especially from A and D Companies, who were very reluctant to give up their posts at Buttocks Booth and Weedon Road. But looking back and reflecting, there is no doubt that the alteration gave the Battalion a much better chance of survival in the case of an enemy invasion by fit, well-armed and well-trained men. This involved the complete overhaul of the defence scheme, and the situation had to be reviewed. The position of the civilians in the areas which were likely to be subjected to heavy shelling was considered very deeply and it was decided that families should be evacuated to other houses in the locality. This was a matter for the Police, and householders were warned of the plan. In no circumstances whatever was this to be published in the local Press. Those evacuated were to be told that this, far from constituting an exception to the general Stand Firm Policy, was intended to make it easier for that policy to be carried out. It was dictated purely by military necessity to facilitate the defence, was of a local and temporary nature, and was for the protection of the civil population. And so the Defended Localities came into being and as far as possible preparations made for their defence. This was the reason for those enthusiastic wiring parties on the Racecourse and in Abington Park and other places that attracted the attention of so many of the inhabitants.

In February, 1942, a radical change occurred in the constitution of the Home Guard. The old "housemaid's clause" of a fortnight's notice on either side came to an end. Members of the force had now to be in for the duration, which, after all, was what the majority of the members had joined for. There was to be a maximum of 48 hours of duty per month, and men already serving had to make up their minds by February 16th whether they were prepared to serve under the new conditions. As was to be expected there were practically no resignations from our Battalion, but many employers, chiefly the Municipal Authorities, were most concerned with the position of their employees in the Home Guard. All these members appeared to be the most valuable men, who could not be spared under any circumstances. How flattered these men would be if they had only known what their employers felt about them! It is difficult to imagine what some people thought would have happened if the enemy had appeared round Northampton. They evidently presumed that life would have gone on as usual, whereas to all who had had any experience of war it was plain that normal life would have been suspended and there would have been none of those activities so typical of Northampton life; there would have been no Saturday market, no shopping in the town centre, no Friday pay day, no time for church services, no opening of public-houses, no functioning of schools; in fact, there would have been a cessation of our normal activities, so that the land could be rid of the enemy in our midst. When this is fully realised it is difficult to understand how application, among others, could be made for the withdrawal of a valuable member who at such a time would be urgently needed for the repelling of the enemy, on the grounds that he would be required to "assist in the removal of objects belonging to the Mayor, Corporation and Burgesses of Northampton to a place of safety." As if such objects mattered when our very existence might be at stake. However, Lieut.-Colonel T. E. Manning with his customary suavity and tact overcame all these difficulties by the promise that these members would not be available for Home Guard duties until released by their civil employers. Knowing most of these Home Guards personally I have a pretty shrewd idea of what would have happened if the Huns, for example, had got as far as Weston Favell. On the other hand, it is only fair to state that most of the employers grasped the possible situation and readily gave permission for their men to be available straight away. Among these were the Custom and Excise Authorities, who realised that in such circumstances there would have been no great rush by the inhabitants to pay their taxes.

At the same time, compulsion for the Home Guard came into being. This was received with mixed feelings. There were many among us who desired that the force should continue on a voluntary basis, a band of keen volunteers, eager and anxious to play their part in the defence of their homes. They were afraid that the old spirit of comradeship that had played such a large part in the building up of the 12th Battalion would be lost with the introduction of men who in 1940 had not the same desire. On the other hand, there was no doubt that there were many men "dodging the column," and this was particularly felt in the villages, where the contact between individuals is closer than in the towns. However, whatever our thoughts, men started to be directed into the Battalion, and we received our quota via the Labour Exchange. The fears that the spirit of the Battalion would be changed proved to be groundless, for the early lot of directed personnel soon settled down in their Companies and proved a very helpful acquisition, relieving considerably the older members from duties that were becoming onerous. As time went on, we began " to reach the bottom of the pint pot " and the directed personnel became of a very indifferent quality. Some of them were unfit physically, while many others had not the slightest interest in the defence of their country. They had no public spirit whatsoever and their only purpose in life seemed to be getting as much money as possible. They were merely names on the Platoon rolls and were a confounded nuisance to all who had the job of trying to get them on parade. Finally I went to the Labour Exchange and implored them not to send us any more of this class, as I felt, together with all the Company Commanders, that we were better without them. All this time we had worked in complete harmony with the Labour Exchange Authorities, who were only too willing and anxious to do all they could to assist us. Particularly should I like to pay a tribute to Mr. Walter Greenfield, himself a Home Guard since the earliest days and a valuable member of H Company, for his very hearty and cordial co-operation. Without him matters could never have proceeded in the smooth manner in which they did, and we were indeed fortunate in having such an understanding person to deal with. The difficulties of the Labour Exchange were many. As one who was in close contact with them for some years, no one realises this more than I do. Besides having to find personnel for the Home Guard they were also responsible for the direction of men to fire-watching on business premises, etc. It is no criticism of their efforts when I express the view that there were far too many young men doing this job, who imagined that they were fulfilling their duty to the community by fire-watching for one night a week, a duty that usually resolved itself into sleeping on the premises. I always felt that these should have been replaced by older members of the population, thereby releasing them for a more active role either in the Home Guard or the Civil Defence. However, despite my representations, nothing matured and these younger men, who ought to have felt shame when they saw the older Home Guards going out to stand all night on their Observation Posts, continued their dormant duties to the end.

While on the subject of fire-watching, in June, 1942, we received an instruction from the Sub-District to carry out fire-watching on 136 requisitioned premises in the town, which had recently been vacated by the Regular Forces. We felt that it was not right or fair to call upon the Home Guard for this, especially as it would have absorbed all our strength and would have washed out all training. In addition, in the early days an undertaking had been given to us that we should not be required to do compulsory fire-watching. We suggested that the keys of these premises should be given to the Street Wardens, who could then act as supervisors. In the end this scheme was adopted, and with the exception of two or three premises on the Market Square, which, on an alert, were looked after by members of B Company, we heard no more about fire-watching and another difficulty had been overcome.

After this digression, now to return to our real activities. In the Summer of 1942, Sub-District Reserve Companies had been formed, and as always the lot fell upon the 12th Battalion to form the one for this district. The Home Guard in two years had made remarkable progress, but it could not stand still. It must either go backward or forward; there is no alternative for an armed force. And so the Home Guard, or part of it, assumed a more mobile role. This Company was composed almost entirely of the younger and fitter members, and those who were immediately available in case of necessity. They were to proceed by transport anywhere in the County of Northamptonshire to deal with an emergency.

In 1944 the chances of invasion were much less than in the past. The Field Army had turned from its defensive role to a contemplated offensive overseas. When this came about the Home Guard had to assume the major responsibility of protecting these islands against sea-borne and air-borne raids. This was all that the enemy could hope to attempt at this stage; the landing of groups of men with the object of sabotage and destruction, and with the intention of dislocating communications and attacking vulnerable points. Looking back, it was astonishing that the enemy failed to interfere with the preparation and mounting of such a difficult operation as D Day. To meet this possible menace the role of the Home Guard was again altered and the principle of mobility extended. With the exception of the Keep Company (F Company) all the companies had to be prepared to take on a mobile role. During the weeks before D Day, railways, roads, and vulnerable points were patrolled and guarded during the nights to prevent any sabotage of communications so necessary for the successful invasion of the Continent. With the invading armies firmly established in Normandy the work of the Home Guard was virtually at an end. The possibility of enemy action in this country had almost completely gone. The culminating point was the announcement of the Minister of War that compulsory attendance was no longer to be enforced. The impression created by this broadcast was that there was no further use for the Home Guard, and so it proved, for soon after came the Stand Down throughout the British Isles. There were many who felt, and I must say that I was one, that this Stand Down came at the wrong time. The older L.D.V. members particularly wanted to see the job through and would have preferred to have kept on, with some lessening of duties, until the war with Germany was over. However, the powers-that-be decided otherwise and so on December 5th, 1944, the Home Guard stood down, and for all practical purposes came to an end.

Thus ended the existence of the greatest unpaid Army that this country has ever seen. Formed in the fateful days of May, 1940, when we were probably in greater peril than ever in our history, with no organisation, no equipment and no weapons, it had developed through the years into a well-organised and well-trained force. I have heard from many of its members expressions of regret that no opportunity had occurred for it to go into action and so prove the value of its existence. Although many of the old soldiers no doubt would have liked to have had one more crack at the Hun, we have to remember that fighting cannot take place without casualties, and had enemy action taken place in this country, there would have been gaps in our ranks to-day, besides loss of life among the civilian population, men, women and children. That we have been spared all this, we should be grateful. Hitler's secret weapon was to paralyse a nation. This the Home Guard helped to prevent, by standing ready through those critical years to play its part manfully in defence of this country of ours. In the words of Milton: " They also serve who only stand and wait."

THE SPIGOT MORTAR NEAR ST. PETER'S BRIDGE

CHAPTER TWO

EARLY DAYS OF THE NORTHAMPTON L.D.V.

Your danger is as you have seen,
And truly I am sorry that it is so great.
But I wish it to cause no despondency,
As truly I think it will not,
For we are Britons.
It is no longer disputing, but out
Instantly all you can

CROMWELL.

IN common with the rest of the country, the response of Northampton to Mr. Anthony Eden's broadcast was excellent. In the course of a few days, upwards of two thousand men of the town had visited the old Police Station in Dychurch Lane and signed on for the L.D.V. Then, if the Police had nothing against us, we were enrolled. Although so many joined up, particularly the old soldier, it was surprising that every able-bodied man at this time of danger did not come forward, anxious to strike a blow in the defence of his home and family, and if we were to go down, at any rate to go down fighting. In time of trouble there are some people who wring their hands, while others shake their fists. Those who enrolled were certainly not content to wring their hands. Judging by the events in Europe it is clear that had we been vanquished, the British race as we know it would have been wiped out of existence and for at least a hundred years we should have been Nazi slaves. The " Voelkischer Beobachter " proclaimed at this time: " The settlement with England will be terrible. The British will be exterminated. No stone will be left standing on the other in the Island Empire." The L.D.V. were full of defiance.

It is only right and fair at this juncture to say that among those volunteering for the new force were several who were already serving in the A.R.P. By an understanding with Mr. John Williamson, the Chief Constable and Civil Defence Controller, these were not permitted to join. Obviously it would have been unwise to interfere with one organisation already built up and functioning successfully, in order to build another. Later in this book I deal more fully with the relations between the Home Guard and the Civil Defence.

Major-General Sir Hereward Wake was appointed Commander of the Northampton County L.D.V. The county was split into divisions, coinciding with the Police divisions, and Major T. E. Manning, a very popular choice, was given the command of the Northampton Borough Division. With affairs getting worse and worse on the Continent, it was imperative to get going quickly, as observation was becoming urgent. Part of the Offices of the British Legion at 4 and 5, The Arcade, were placed at our disposal, and it was here that the L.D.V. had its origin in Northampton. The Staff consisted of the Commander, the Second-in-Command (the author of this record), and Mr. A. W. Gardner, later to be appointed Quartermaster, who came along voluntarily at this time to render what assistance he could. There, with sleeves rolled up and with a pencil in one hand and a burning brow in the other, we toiled to get the organisation going. I am afraid that the bulk of the work fell upon T.E.M., but Gardner and myself backed him up to the best of our ability. Owing to the time factor, which necessitated quick organisation, it was decided that the speediest and easiest method was to build up on the Ward system. The town was divided into four Groups—North, South, East and West, with various Works Companies, who would operate under Divisional Headquarters.

North Group: Kingsley, Kingsthorpe and St. George's Wards.

East Group: Weston, St. Michael's and St. Crispin's Wards.

South Group: Delapre, South and St. Edmund's Wards.

West Group: Castle Spencer and St. James' Wards.

Here is the first list of Commanders of the Northampton L.D.V.:—

NORTHAMPTON BOROUGH DIVISION L.D.V.

Division Commander - Major T. E. Manning.

Second-in-Command - Major L. E. Barnes.

NORTH GROUP

Group Commander - - - - - N. P. Andrews.
Second-in-Command - - - - - P. Hutton.
No. 1 Company: Kingsley - - Leader: R. E. Corsby.
No. 2 Company: Kingsthorpe - ,, J. V. Collier.
No. 3 Company: St. George's - ,, H. G. Oates.

EAST GROUP

Group Commander - - - - - W. Care.
Second-in-Command - - - - - S. H. Barber.
No. 1 Company: Weston - - Leader: F. W. Freestone.
No. 2 Company: St. Michael's - ,, C. C. Oakey.
No. 3 Company: St. Crispin's - ,, Major H. St. J. Browne.

SOUTH GROUP

Group Commander - - - - - A. MacFarlane.
Second-in-Command - - - - - O. J. Hargrave.
No. 1 Company: Delapre - - Leader: L. W. Lucas.
No. 2 Company: South - - ,, P. C. Williams.
No. 3 Company: St. Edmund's - ,, H. G. Beers.
No. 4 Company: Stimpson's Mill ,, S. B. Patrick.

WEST GROUP

Group Commander - - - - - Major R. Manning.
Second-in-Command - - - - - A. S. Baxter.
No. 1 Company: Castle - - Leader: J. S. Mennell.
No. 2 Company: Spencer - - ,, P. G. Jones.
No. 3 Company: St. James' - ,, C. Phillipson.

DETACHED WORKS COMPANIES

Electric Works - - Company Commander: Captain F. H. Holder.
Second-in-Command: Lieut. H. L. C. Jennings.
Northampton Gas Coy. Company Commander: Captain N. C. Batten.
Second-in-Command: F. Cole.
Northampton Borough Company Commander: Inspector F. T. Lea.
Transport Second-in-Command: H. Cattell.
Northampton Borough Company Commander: L. H. Brown.
Water Department Second-in-Command: R. Reynolds.
Express Lift Company Company Commander: V. Amberg.
Second-in-Command: F. H. Salter.
G.P.O. Company - - Company Commander: W. R. Morton.

It is interesting to note that of the above, some retired quite early in our career, but the majority continued until the Stand Down. Only three— Major A. MacFarlane, Lieutenant L. W. Lucas and Major W. R. Morton— served in their original capacity throughout the whole of our existence.

Soon after this first list of Commanders was published other Companies were formed. The L.M.S. Railway joined up with E. W. Powell as Commander and R. J. Marfleet as Second-in-Command, while the United Counties Bus Co. formed a unit under J. H. Mills.

On Sunday, May 26th, 1940, the first parade of the Northampton L.D.V. was held at the rear of the Drill Hall, Clare Street. In order to simplify matters on this initial turn-out, only those who had previous service were asked to attend, and nearly 500 paraded. What a collection of old sweats! Some had already served in two wars and here they were turning up for a third. Typical of these was my old friend and colleague, Bill Langton, who had gone out with the Northampton Volunteers in the Boer War, had served all through the 1914—1918 War, and was with me for so many years in A Company of the 4th Northamptons (Territorials). It would be interesting to ascertain how many of these originals continued to the end. There were some among us that Sunday morning with a heart that was willing but with flesh that was weak. It was not easy for men over the sixty mark to perform their day's work and then go out on patrol all night. Many, however, did until they found the strain too great and made way for younger men. One cannot too highly commend the action of these older men, whose spirit and patriotism led them to perform these all-night duties during the Summer of 1940. Although some were forced to drop out, the majority of those present at the first parade were with us on that dismal afternoon on the Market Square on December 5th, 1944. This I am perfectly certain of, that during the whole of our life the old L.D.V. members were always the backbone of the 12th Battalion.

As one's mind goes back, one cannot help contrasting these two parades— the first with its eagerness and its expectancy of the unknown future, the second with its atmosphere of gloom—with the feeling that this organisation of ours, which had been built up with such pains and such labour by all its members, was now like the old soldiers to fade away. Now it is all over and passed, I can say how miserable I felt on that Stand Down afternoon, and it was only by an effort that I was able to say a few words of thanks and farewell.

So much for reminiscences, and back to that never forgettable first parade. Things proceeded quite smoothly, men fell quickly into their Groups, Companies were organised and section leaders appointed. So that on the next evening, May 27th, 1940, the first patrols went out to their duties round the town.

During the week previously the Commander and myself had made a reconnaissance of the outskirts of the town to decide on Observation Posts. Our main object was first of all to see that the whole of the area was covered by observation, while at the same time to keep the number of Posts to a minimum, so that the duties did not come round too frequently and so impose too big a strain upon the members. So on this memorable night of May 27th we first went out and manned the Observation Posts round Northampton. We must have presented a queer spectacle as we proceeded on our way, a motley crew in caps and raincoats with an L.D.V. armband, armed chiefly with sticks. It was reported that some even took umbrellas in case the weather was unkind. Those early nights of watching were a trial to everyone. There had been no time to arrange shelters, and the patrols were awake most of the night. As time went on, things became better; huts and tents were put up, so that those not actually watching could get a little sleep in the hours that they were off duty. But in the early days there were no luxuries like this, and men spent practically the whole of the night walking about. Only those who have been out all night know how cold it can be even in summer, especially in the hour or so before dawn. But the job was done, and no enemy paratroops could have landed round Northampton without being quickly observed and their whereabouts immediately reported. I include the list of Observation Posts so that all who stood out in those early days can ruminate on the long, cold, but happy nights they spent, and can recall memories of all the good fellows who kept watch with them.

Observation Posts:

Windmill Inn, Welford Road.

Boughton Green Reservoir.

Kingsthorpe Lodge (Golf - Course).

Buttocks Booth Lane.

Weston—East of the Headlands.

Water Tower, Abington Mill.

Rushmere Road.

Electric Light Works.

Hunsbury Hill.

The Tip, Weedon Road.

Hopping Hill, Rugby Road.

During the Summer there were several occasions when the message "Extra vigilance" came through, indicating that enemy landings were considered likely. Those were anxious times for the officers who were on duty all night when these messages were received. All patrols "Stood to" for the hour before darkness and for an hour before dawn until an hour after.

By June 30th, 1940, it had been possible to absorb the non-Service volunteers, so that the strength of the Battalion was now 2,109, made up as under:—

Headquarters Group with H.Q. Platoons	618
North Group	436
East Group	320
South Group	264
West Group	206
L.M.S. Railway Group	265

In those days, records, receipts for arms and equipment, written orders and red tape mattered not at all. Nothing mattered except that the L.D.V. had to be out on their Observation Posts with the least possible delay, as the landing of enemy troops by parachute was considered to be an imminent danger. We might be invaded at any moment. If the Hun came we were to fight him with anything we had in our possession, which was not a great deal, a few rifles and a little ammunition, pieces of lead piping, knives, cheese-cutters, home-made bombs, and anything else we could think of. "Many would probably be killed, but some would survive, and as in these islands there was nowhere to run, we were to stand and fight. Peril might descend upon us from the skies at any time when we were on our Observation

Posts." In a situation like this we had to get on with the job. Naturally, things did not always go too smoothly, mistakes were made, as was to be expected, but the tact and smiling countenance of T.E.M., together with the forbearance of the Group Commanders, overcame most of the difficulties and the Battalion soon settled down into a well-organised unit.

There were many problems with which we had to deal. " What happened to the men who had no rifles or uniform? Were they to assemble? What happened to them if they were on the Observation Posts? " This was one of the queries put up by a Group Commander. We answered this to the effect that there was always a certain amount of work to be done by people who did not need arms—first-aid work, messengers, etc.—while many could render assistance to the Police by helping to control the civil population. At this time, too, there was a strange reluctance among the Higher Authorities to give the L.D.V. the old-fashioned army designations such as lieutenant, sergeant, corporal, etc. Instead of which they were named platoon leaders, section leaders, sub-section leaders, all of which was confusing, and there was a natural diffidence on the part of these individuals to give orders without a clear definition of their right.

There was also the difficult question, " What happens to the L.D.V. when the Regulars arrive? " The L.D.V. Commanders had no official Army status, and without this it was unlikely that the Regulars, even an N.C.O., would take orders from any " leader " of the L.D.V., whatever his position. The position was not clarified until early in 1941, when officers of the new force were given commissions and the good old Army names of sergeant-major, sergeant and corporal adopted. It was then made clear that Home Guard officers had authority in the Field over all ranks junior to themselves, and this greatly eased the situation and the Home Guard knew where they were.

The signal that enemy troops had landed in the locality was to be the ringing of the church bells. Whether this would have been effective or not it is difficult to say, as no practice or rehearsal was allowed. This was unfortunate, as no method can be judged until it is tried out. There were practice calls on the sirens; why not at least one test alarm for the Home Guard? While the church bells would probably have worked well in the villages, where the Observation Posts as a rule were not far from the church, the feeling was that in the towns there would have been much delay. Later on a knocking-up system was introduced in the event of a local raid, but this method again was unsatisfactory. From time to time the calling out of the Home Guard occasioned Commanders many headaches, as it was obvious that speed was the essential factor in dealing with any enemy landing. We could never understand the ban put upon the use of the sirens, for here was an ideal method for the purpose. Surely it was not beyond the wit of man to introduce a different note or succession of notes on the siren, or if this was impossible, then a long continuation of the blast would have had the desired effect. This view was put forward at conference after conference but nothing was done, and to the last the matter remained very far from satisfactory.

However, in the early days we went ahead with the plans for the church bells, and the following arrangements were made:—

St. Mary's Church, Far Cotton	Volunteer Frisby to ring.
All Saints' Church - - -	Mr. Atterbury.
St. Peter's Church - - -	Rev. W. R. M. Chaplin.
St. Edmund's Church - -	Rev. Denny.
St. Matthew's Church - -	Key with A.R.P. Warden in crypt.

St. Alban's Church -	-	-	Church porch always unlocked and bell rope left hanging.
Kingsthorpe Church	-	-	Rev. M. L. Couchman, or steeple keeper, Mr. G. Parker.
Holy Trinity Church	-	-	Rev. D. M. Forrester, or Verger, Mr. F. Whiting.
St. Sepulchre's Church -	-		Mr. G. Arnold.
Dallington Church -	-	-	The Vicar or Mr. B. L. Smart.
Christ Church -	-	-	Rev. A. W. P. Jaggard or Mr. Crane.
St. Michael's Church	-	-	Rev. W. D. Saunders or Mr. Goodman.
St. Lawrence's Church -	-		Rev. J. N. E. Wareham or Mr. G. Allen.

On Friday evening, June 14th, 1940, a test alarm was arranged by Sir Hereward Wake, the County Commander, to take place throughout Northamptonshire, when at a specified time the church bells would be rung for a period of ten minutes, and all L.D.V.'s would proceed to their posts. This exercise would have been invaluable, but at the last moment, however, a ban was put upon the bells, with the result that its chief value was destroyed. Instead, the bells were " presumed " to have been rung at eight o'clock, and notwithstanding the unsatisfactory nature of the call-out, over 75 per cent. of our Companies turned out within half an hour of the " Alarm." The exercise showed that the communications were quite good; by car drivers, motor-cyclists and pedal-cyclists, messages very soon reached Headquarters, while the use of the Police boxes on the Borough boundary was also a means of quick communication. This was the first turn-out of the L.D.V. and showed that in the evening time, at any rate, the new force would be out quickly and in good strength.

In those 1940 days the L.D.V. poorly armed and equipped could not be a real fighting force. In this district this responsibility lay with the I.T.C., commanded by Lieut.-Colonel A. St. G. Coldwell, who had always a Company " Standing to " and ready to proceed by bus to deal with any emergency. It was the duty of the L.D.V. to observe and report any landing as quickly as possible, and as the test showed, this would have been accomplished. As time went on and arms became available, we became more self-reliant and felt confident of dealing with small bodies of the enemy, while hoping to delay and contain larger numbers of the Hun until the arrival of the Regulars. In August, 1941, the I.T.C. left the Barracks, and the 12th Battalion, with the help of various small detachments of Regular units in the town, became solely responsible for the defence of Northampton. The chief of these detachments was the Technical College Troops under Major Hague, who had two Companies of 120 men in each to render us assistance. Later, when a new defence plan was drawn up, they were detailed to hold the Keep with F Company. There were generally Regular troops in the neighbourhood, but as these were part of the Field Force they were liable to be moved at a moment's notice. Close liaison, however, was maintained with all Regulars who were stationed in the district, and they were informed of all our dispositions. It is pleasing to record that throughout the whole of our existence our relations with the Regular Forces were most cordial, never once did they fail to assist us in every way possible, and I am certain that had we had to fight, that we should have battled side by side in the greatest cameraderie.

On those Summer and Autumn evenings one could see the Home Guard proceeding to their Observation Posts an hour or so before dusk. There they watched all night until 6 a.m. when, with a feeling of relief that another night had passed without anything happening, they trudged wearily homeward. A change, a wash and shave, a hurried breakfast, and so to another day's work. A typical example of these enthusiasts was W. H.' R. Stubbs, a wholesale greengrocer by trade, who often left the Observation Patrol in the early hours of the morning to catch the 4.30 a.m. train to London for Covent Garden. Back again in Northampton in the evening, he was on parade at 7 p.m. for training. In the factories, in the offices, and on the railways of Northampton were toiling men who had spent the previous night watching on Hunsbury Hill, Rushmere Road, Buttocks Booth, or one or other of the various Observation Posts round the town. Great was the keenness and enthusiasm in those days; rarely was a man missing from his post, and if through illness or working overtime one was unavoidably absent, there was always a volunteer to fill the gap. During those long nights many were the yarns of the last war spun by the old soldier, who always found an attentive audience among those too young to serve in 1914. I should not like to vouch for the truth of all those stories; indeed, as I stood with them on various posts I heard some rather tall ones, but they certainly increased the prestige of the old 'un in the eyes of the recruit, who no doubt thought that they were in the company of some of the finest soldiers in the land. Which was all to the good.

Speaking personally I found a cycle very handy on those nights for visiting the posts. The Commanding Officer and myself on alternate nights visited the men standing out. Starting out at dusk I found that I could just finish the round of the town by dawn. Not that I was riding all the time, for there were chats on each post, and old friends with whom I had served in the last War, dug up reminiscences of the past, which usually began something like this: "Do you remember, sir, when we were on the Somme?" or recollections of Ypres, where your trenches often went up in the air twice nightly. I found the nights most interesting, and there was always the humorous side. On one pitch-black night I disturbed the slumbers of a cow peacefully sleeping on a footpath in Delapre Park, by a flank attack with my cycle. On another misty night, near Duston Mill, I lost my bearings and both cycle and myself disappeared in one of the many streams that abound in that neighbourhood. Fortunately there were no spectators to witness my effort to retrieve my steed from the bottom of a five-foot brook. But these little incidents only served to give an added interest to life.

Men naturally were not on duty every night, not the same men, the average being once every four nights. But there were other duties to be performed, for training was going on practically every evening of the week and on Sunday mornings. There was little difficulty in the teaching of musketry, for there were plenty who had been instructors in the last war, and with a little rubbing off of the rust and a little looking up in the manual they were soon giving the benefit of their knowledge to the recruit, who was only too eager to learn all he could of the rifle. This eagerness led to one or two incidents, amusing now but rather perturbing at the time. So anxious was the youngster to know how the rifle was loaded, and so keen was the old soldier to show him, that strictly against orders, I am afraid that many rifles were loaded and unloaded on the Observation Posts. As inevitably happens on these occasions, for no reason at all the rifle sometimes goes off. One bullet, it was alleged, passed over Cheyne Walk from the direction of the South Bridge, while a police constable on the Boughton Green Road averred that a bullet missed his helmet by a hair's breadth. There were no doubt other unrecorded incidents of a like nature. However, no permanent injury was done and the Home Guard was gradually learning its job.

On October 15th, 1940, with the days shortening it was obviously impossible for the Home Guard to be on watch at dusk and dawn without seriously interfering with their civilian occupations, and patrols were therefore discontinued during the winter months. There was also the improbability of any enemy landings during this time. An anxious period had passed. It is idle, perhaps, to surmise what would have happened in the months immediately after Dunkirk if Hitler had decided to invade, but there is no denying that this was the time that gave him his best opportunity, which, fortunately for us, he did not take.

The initial troubles of the Home Guard were over. The winter provided a breathing space for the overhaul of the organisation that had taken place so hurriedly, while weapon and tactical training went on apace, so that a very different proposition awaited the Hun had he attempted any action after those early days. The Home Guard in 1940 had fulfilled its purpose and had not been found wanting.

CHAPTER THREE

ORGANISATION, RE-ORGANISATION AND STILL MORE RE-ORGANISATION

S already stated in another Chapter, on the formation of the L.D.V. we became the Northampton Borough Division with Groups and Companies and Works Units. Throughout our existence there were constant changes, most of them enforced by the military situation, so that right up to the last year of our existence the 12th Battalion never settled down to a smooth and placid life. Probably no other Battalion in the Home Guard saw so many alterations as ours. The only thing that did not change in those years was the spirit of the men.

On July 30th, 1940, the L.D.V. changed its name to the Home Guard, and with this a re-naming took place. The Northampton Borough Division became the Northampton Borough Battalion with Companies instead of Groups and Platoons instead of Companies. Some months later, on March 5th, 1941, the Battalions in the County of Northamptonshire were numbered from east to west, and we became the 12th (Northampton Borough) Battalion, Northamptonshire Home Guard, a title we retained until the end.

Platoons were numbered as follows:—

A Company	-	Nos.	1, 2, and 3.
B Company	-	„	4, 5, and 6.
C Company	-	„	7, 8, 9 and 10 (Abington Mill).
D Company	-	„	11, 12, and 13.
E Company	-	„	14, 15, 16 and 17.

The A Company Mobile Platoon under Captain G. F. Devaliant was transferred to Battalion Headquarters with the title of No. 3 H.Q. (Mobile Platoon).

The titles of the Headquarters Platoons were changed as under:—

Electric Light Works Platoon became No. 1 H.Q. Platoon.

Gas Company Platoon	„	No. 2	„	„
A Company Mobile Platoon	„	No. 3	„	„
Borough Water Platoon	„	No. 4	„	„
Express Lift Works Platoon	„	No. 5	„	„
United Counties Bus Co.	„	No. 6	„	„

It will be noted that of the original units the Northampton Borough Transport Platoon had been disbanded. They consisted mainly of drivers and conductors of the Northampton buses and found that their civilian duties made it very difficult to get any system of co-ordinated training, and also there was the fact that on invasion their services might have been required in another capacity. And so, very reluctantly, the Platoon came to an end, although a few of the members joined up in other Platoons.

With the exception of a few minor changes this organisation continued for some twelve months. The Weston Favell Platoon of the 11th Battalion had come under our orders for operational purposes, as they would have worked alongside our No. 7 Platoon at Bushland Road School. The Borough

Water Platoon had ceased to exist as, in the event of enemy action against the town, most of its members would have been required for duties of a technical nature. They had rendered good service in those days of 1940, especially in the guarding of the power-house at Ravensthorpe Reservoir.

In the Spring of 1942 came the change in the Defence System of the town with the creation of Defended Localities. It was now necessary to have a " Keep," which in emergency would be the " last ditch " of the defenders, and so a Keep Company was formed. On June 14th, 1942, the Keep Company, named F Company, came into being. Captain A. S. Baxter, who since the L.D.V. days had been acting as Second-in-Command of D Company, took command of the new Company. No. 9 Platoon of C Company, under Lieutenant C. G. Harris, formed the nucleus, while officers were recruited from other Companies, and most of the Directed Personnel who lived in the centre of the town were posted to the Company. It was not easy in the Home Guard at this stage to form a new unit, for the 1940 members had settled down in their Platoons and formed comradeships and did not wish to be disturbed. However, F Company went to work with a will, gradually built up its numbers, and became a very efficient organisation.

In the following month of July a further change took place. In common with other Sub-Districts throughout the country the Northamptonshire Sub-District was ordered to form a Reserve Company, which would be mobile and would function anywhere in the county. The 12th Battalion was ordered to form this new Company. Coming so quickly after the formation of F Company, this presented the Battalion Commander with quite a headache, especially as the personnel had to be the fittest men in the Battalion and also in Category 1, that is, immediately available when required. It was difficult to see where this new unit was to come from without disturbing the whole of the Companies of the 12th. By this time, as I have pointed out, there was a natural reluctance of members to leave the Platoons in which they had served for some two years. Captain S. B. Patrick, who was Second-in-Command of C Company, was appointed Company Commander of the new G Company, with Captain F. C. Whiting as his deputy. These two immediately got cracking on their uphill task. Obviously the Battalion Mobile Platoon had to form the backbone of this new unit, and led by Sergeant Savage, later to become the C.S.M., they responded excellently. Unfortunately, however, over 250 men were required and the Mobile Platoon could furnish nothing like this number. As Smith guns were to form part of the equipment of this Sub-District Reserve, recruiting was opened at the Armstrong-Whitworth Works, as it was quite reasonably thought that these men would be ideal for the particular job. There was a good response at the Works, but unfortunately many of the men were in Category 2 and therefore not available. However, a Battery was formed and many of the men became enthusiastic gunners, and were a valuable acquisition to G Company. The remainder were formed into a separate Platoon of B Company, and until their disbandment at the end of 1943 were a constant source of trouble. The position got so bad and the Platoon so hopelessly inefficient that this was the only course I could take. It is no good trying to kid yourself that you have a fighting platoon when you have only an ill-trained group of men, incapable of putting up a resistance, and so the Platoon had to go. Volunteers were invited from the other Companies to make up the numbers in G Company, but although a few men transferred, as was to be expected the response did not solve the problem. I then gave Major Patrick the first choice of all the Directed Personnel, and these, together with the lads of 17 who joined, gradually built up the Company until, after an existence of some twelve months, it had reached the strength of 233 and, thanks to the hard work of the Company Commander and Captain Whiting and all the members, it had been welded into a really efficient fighting force.

While the formation of this Company was progressing, the Battalion suffered a severe and unexpected blow by the retirement of Lieut.-Colonel T. E. Manning from the position of Commanding Officer. Always cheery and with an abundance of tact, he had carried the Battalion through those very difficult early days and had moulded the 12th into what we all think was one of the finest Battalions in the Home Guard. As the one who was in closest touch with him in those times, and was aware of the many obstacles that had to be overcome, I know that we owe him a deep debt of gratitude for all his unsparing efforts to get the show going and to make it a success. The success that we attained was due in the main part to the foundations which he had laid. We all regretted his decision, taken on the advice of his medical adviser, and I pleaded with him to take six months' leave, during which time I would carry on, and then with his health improved he could resume where he had left off. But my efforts were unavailing. It is typical of the man that although feeling incapable of carrying the burden of Commanding Officer, yet he should have continued as Intelligence Officer of F Company and have been with us on all our Parades. The officers of the Battalion spontaneously desired to show their deep appreciation of his work, and at a little gathering at the Peacock Hotel on October 9th, 1942, they were able to express their feelings by a presentation of a silver salver as a memento to him of the happy times we had spent under his leadership.

On the writer fell the onus of carrying on. Up to this time I had had a most enjoyable time in the Home Guard. Being somewhat of a free lance, without a great deal of responsibility, had suited my temperament. Acting as the enemy with the A.T.C. Cadets in the early stages, lecturing round the Companies, bombing at Hunsbury Hill, with visits round the Observation Posts, had indeed been a glorious existence. It was, therefore, with many qualms and a certain degree of reluctance that I assumed the mantle of responsibility. None recognised more than myself that I am not a Headquarters soldier, and that I always feel happier " in the Field." Fortunately, a month previously there had arrived in the 12th a certain Captain Barton, who had been posted to us as Adjutant. This was a great stroke of luck, for he turned out to be a great acquisition, and no Commanding Officer could have wished for a better right-hand man. Looking back and reflecting, I believe that it was the knowledge of the ability of Barton that finally influenced my decision.

I had for some time been of the opinion that the organisation of the Battalion, which had by force of circumstances to be so hurriedly carried out in 1940, was cumbersome and not tactically sound. We had no Battalion reserve except a Platoon, and there were a number of " private armies," the Headquarters Platoons, who, had the emergency arisen, would have been fighting isolated battles. It was found, too, on Battalion schemes that the time taken to send out messages to all the Companies and to the Headquarters Platoons was far too long. Consider the time it took, even with duplication of messages, to write and send out a lengthy message to each of seven Companies and to each of six H.Q. Platoons. I therefore decided to form a further Company, " H," to form the Battalion reserve, and to put the H.Q. Platoons in those Companies in whose areas they were situated. This meant that the Electric Light Platoon and the United Counties Bus Platoon would form part of B Company and that the Express Lift and the Gas Company Platoons would go to D Company. As might be supposed, this did not meet with the approval of all concerned, but the changes were carried out and made for the better working of the Battalion. Captain O. J. Hargrave moved over to take command of H Company, while Captain F. H. Holder became Second-in-Command of B Company. In addition, as one of the lessons learnt on the "Eleanor" Exercise, each Company formed a Platoon to act as its Company reserve.

These alterations having been effected, we sat back and hoped that now the 12th was, as we thought, on a sound tactical basis, we could proceed smoothly with the training without any further re-organisation. Alas for our hopes, which in the next few months were rudely shattered by Colonel Short, the Sub-District Commander. Early in 1943 a suggestion was made that the Battalion should be divided. At the time I could see no reason for this, and even when looking back I still fail to see the advantage in this split. We were now well organised, with an excellent Adjutant and Quartermaster, and things were proceeding very smoothly and the training of all ranks was progressing satisfactorily. In addition, in a town of this character it was difficult to make a division from a tactical point of view. However, despite my opposition, the powers-that-be decided that the Battalion must be divided, the only thing that seemed to weigh with them were numbers; our strength at this time was about 2,700. I was requested to submit my proposals. What I was particularly anxious to avoid at this stage was a dislocation of the existing Companies with further re-organisation. My first recommendation was that E Company (the Railway unit) should form a separate Battalion, as its character was naturally different from the rest of the 12th. This suggestion did not find favour, and it was at last decided to combine E and D Companies, together with the Electric Light Works Platoon, to form the new Battalion. A rough line of demarcation was the river, and the new unit, the 15th Battalion, would be west and south of the Nene, leaving the Companies on the north and east in the 12th. As the division had to come, this in my judgment was the best solution and the most satisfactory arrangement, as it caused the least disturbance of our organisation. Major N. P. Andrews, who had been the most efficient and popular Commander of A Company since its formation in 1940, was chosen to command the new Battalion, and much as we regretted losing him from the 12th we felt that no better choice could have been made. And so on July 1st, 1943, we very reluctantly said good-bye to our old friends who had served the 12th so well. It was a matter of great satisfaction to us that the 15th did so well during the eighteen months of its existence, and the feeling between the two Battalions was always of the most cordial nature.

With this break, Major Hargrave gave up his command of H Company and resumed his original position as Second-in-Command of B, which had been rendered vacant by the transfer of Captain F. H. Holder to the 15th. Captain Rex Armitt assumed command of H Company for a time, and then handed over to Major A. W. Blason. H Company had not had an easy time, for there was always the difficulty of numbers, being formed as it was when our strength was decreasing. However, by hard work and enthusiasm the Company was pulled round, and in the last year was working well together as an efficient unit.

Meanwhile we had lost the United Counties Bus Platoon, who had been formed into the 2001 Northampton Home Guard Motor Transport Company, under Major J. H. Mills. In case of invasion this Company had special transport duties to perform.

There is no rest for the wicked, and a few months later another bomb-shell was dropped on the Battalion in the nature of the formation of a new Company to be called the Coastal Reinforcement Company. The Higher Authorities had decided that the Coastal Areas needed thickening up in case of invasion, and the Midlands, being remote from the coast, were ordered to provide Companies who would proceed there if the military situation rendered it imperative. Having learnt by bitter experience the difficulty of forming a new unit by getting volunteers from other Companies, and also wishing at this late stage to avoid more disruption that was inevitable, the policy was adopted of combining No. 2 and 3 Platoons of A Company. This had several advantages. First it gave us approximately the required number of 200, and much as we regretted again disturbing A Company, the other Companies would be untouched. Men who had served together since 1940 would still be together and the skeleton organisation was there and only needed expanding. Lieutenant Frank Jordan was given the Command, with Lieutenant Eric Beeston as his Second-in-Command. These two, with many others, got to work and in a short time the new Company was functioning admirably, so much so that although only formed in December, 1943, a week-end reconnaissance by the Battalion Commander, the Adjutant, the Company Commander, the Second-in-Command, and the Intelligence Officer, Lieutenant A. Holland, was made at Great Yarmouth early in the following February. A few weeks later a further reconnaissance was made by the officers and N.C.O.'s of the Company and at Easter the whole of the men, with one absentee, manned the battle position on the coast both by day and night. But more of this anon, as this journey to Great Yarmouth is worthy of a much fuller description.

This formation of the Coastal Reinforcement Company was the last re-organisation of the Battalion. Besides the defence of the town of Northampton, the 12th had played its part in helping other parts of the country and we hope was a credit to the town.

CHAPTER FOUR

EXERCISES, SCHEMES, ETC.

AS has been pointed out in a previous Chapter, in the early days of the L.D.V. the Battalion, without weapons, could do little more than observational and reporting duties. The I.T.C., who were the only Regulars in the town, were responsible for dealing with the enemy once they had been reported and located by us. In order to test out these arrangements, exercises were held in 1940. With the ready assistance of the Air Force Cadets, who were especially valuable as they had a uniform distinctive from the khaki of the Army, I invariably acted as the enemy. Needless to say, we were rarely successful in overcoming the Regulars and the L.D.V., and on different occasions I have been " killed, wounded or taken prisoner." But I always bore in mind that the object of these exercises was to train the L.D.V., and what happened to us did not matter as long as this training was of value.

Records of these early exercises are scanty and I am relying on memory for much of this description of those days. I remember that in practically the first, we scored our one and only success. This was a scheme planned to take place in the Harlestone Heath, Hopping Hill, Dallington area. Harlestone Heath we always regarded as one of the danger points around Northampton, as it appeared extremely suitable for the dropping of paratroops, both from the fact that it is a wide open space and, via the railway line and road, gives a direct and quick approach to the town. Hence this was chosen for the first try-out. Observation Posts were manned by the West Group, and the I.T.C. as usual were standing by. After lying in hiding for some time we raised large red flags, which were the pre-arranged signal to indicate enemy landing. We estimated in those days that it would take the enemy some fifteen to twenty minutes to land, get their arms out of the containers and organise themselves into their units. I am afraid that we rather under-valued the Bosche, as future events proved they were on the move in very much quicker time than this. And so in order to make the exercise realistic we waited this time before moving off to the town via the long narrow copse afterwards so well known to Home Guards. Any moment as we advanced " in fear and trembling " we expected to be obliterated by the British troops. But nothing happened and we found ourselves in the village of Dallington and on our way to St. James' quite unopposed. What had gone wrong? The L.D.V. observers had seen the dropping almost immediately, had rushed to the Police box and in two or three minutes the report had reached the I.T.C. Here it was that the trouble started. The Company detailed for duty that night had been issued with S.A.A. in case of a real landing. This had to be collected from the men, as of course it was not permissible for ammunition to be carried on exercises, and a careful examination made so that an accident did not occur. All this took time, which naturally would not have happened had real enemy arrived. In addition, when the Company did get on the way the driver of the buses took a wrong turn in St. James', so that it was some 35 minutes before the Company arrived on the scene of operations, too late to be of any effective help. This, our first test-out, was most disappointing, and quite destroyed the confidence of a large number of L.D.V. officers who were watching the show as spectators.

The matter could not obviously rest there. It was essential that the confidence of the L.D.V. be restored. Therefore, soon after, another exercise was planned and this time there was to be no mishaps. The east of the town was chosen for this second exercise and the landings were to take place in the meadows near Weston Mill. Now it is all a thing of the past, I can reveal that this show was stage-managed, and events went as all good exercises should do. Before the day the Platoon Officer of the I.T.C. and myself, as leader of the enemy, made a careful reconnaissance of the ground. I told him my plans, and we decided on a course of action for his men. We even arranged the field in which we were to be scuppered. On the evening all went well, the landings were made and were duly observed in quick time by the L.D.V., the report was rapidly made by means of the Police box, and the I.T.C. were on their way in double quick time. Meanwhile we, the enemy, had proceeded up the valley towards the town and after a feint attack on Abington Mill, which was gallantly defended by the Mill Platoon, we made off in the direction of St. Peter's Bridge. Near here, as arranged, we ran into the Regulars and were completely wiped out. So vigorous was the charge that my A.T.C. Cadets, who of course knew nothing of the arrangements, took to their heels in consternation. And so ended this second exercise, which in the view of the spectators was a complete success. The confidence of the L.D.V. was restored and all went to bed that night very happy, feeling that if the enemy did appear he would be quickly and efficiently dealt with. And whatever the means taken to achieve this result, this was all that mattered.

During the remainder of 1940 several more exercises were arranged to give each Company practice in observing, reporting and, with the arrival of arms, dealing with enemy landings. I well remember a cordon scheme in Major Ray's estate with A and C Companies, one near the Boughton Green Reservoir with the Kingsthorpe Platoon, and another in the snow on a Sunday morning near Weston Favell. On all these exercises we had the hearty co-operation of the A.T.C. Cadets, who were of the greatest assistance in acting as the enemy, and our very best thanks are due to them and to Flight-Lieutenant R. T. Phillips who did all he could to help us. It was a thankless job, acting as " stooges " for the Home Guard and being repeatedly scuppered, but these boys turned out with the greatest enthusiasm time after time, and as the one who commanded them and shared their inglorious fate, I can say we really did appreciate their efforts. All these lads are now in the R.A.F., and we wish them a safe and speedy return. I know that this list does not include all those who turned out on the various schemes, for there was no lack of volunteers, but in the list I have before me the following names appear:—

P. Brewster	G. Cole	W. Facer	J. Shakespeare	F. Barratt
J. Leach	K. Hudson	E. White	A. Chapman	E. G. Weston
S. J. Page	N. Hamp	R. Stevenson	J. Bates	R. Rodhouse

Many thanks to all of you who did your best to make the Home Guard more proficient in those early days.

In 1941, with some arms, at any rate, having been issued, and with all the Battalion equipped with uniform, we became more ambitious in our exercises.

In January, 1941, a Communication Scheme was held in the Battalion, using the A.T.C. Cadets as cyclist messengers, Battalion H.Q. being set up at the Old Police Station in Dychurch Lane. It was found that the use of these messengers was most successful and, had a number of messages to be sent out, a much quicker result was obtained than by phoning; we also learnt the necessity of having a H.Q. of our own. This moving of H.Q. on Action

Stations to a position where we could be with the H.Q. of the Civil Defence did not work in actual practice, and so afterwards we operated from our own H.Q. at the Drill Hall.

TERRIER AND SCORCH EXERCISES

On November 1st and 2nd, 1941, there was arranged the first large-scale exercise for the Home Guard. This took place over the Beds, Hunts and Northants Sub-Area, and tested out the communications and the administrative arrangements of Battalions. No troops were used, as this was really a preliminary for a larger exercise to be held in the month of December. As Colonel Manning was away on this particular week-end, and as in those days we had not an Adjutant, Battalion H.Q. were manned by myself, by Captain Gardner as Q.M. and by Lieutenant Arnold Payne, the I.O., acting as Adjutant. It was a paper exercise, in which almost every conceivable situation that could happen to the Home Guard was put forward for solution. These conundrums had to be solved and token messages sent. In addition we were constantly receiving telephone calls, some genuine and some fake, and during the week-end that the exercise lasted, from 20.00 hours on the Saturday to midnight on Sunday, nearly 100 different situations were presented and considerably over 100 messages sent out. Many of these problems are now hoary, but in those days they were fresh and provoked much thought. We were indebted to Major J. T. H. Pettitt and Captain J. D. Houison-Craufurd, of the 9th Battalion, for acting as Umpires and for producing so many interesting situations, some of which brought out points in administration which at that time had not been considered. As an example of these situations, here are a few:—

(1) X Company reports that his food had been contaminated by gas. Where can he obtain a further supply?

(2) At 06.00 hours Y Company reports that some of his men want to go to work. What is he to do?

(3) Z Company reports that he has no cooking facilities to give the men a hot meal. Can Battalion do something about it?

(4) X Company has taken a supposed fifth columnist. What are they to do with him?

(5) The electric light fails. What plans have been made for carrying on?

(6) Y Company reports that the A.R.P. has asked for 50 men to prevent panic among the civil population caused by bombing. What is he to do?

All these problems and many more had to be solved during that hectic exercise, and proved of great usefulness in the SCORCH Exercise that followed in the next month.

And so we come to that famous Exercise "Scorch," which will never be forgotten by the Home Guard serving on December 5th/7th, 1941. It must indeed have been a humorist who named this, for the night was as unlike "scorch" as it was possible to be, wet and cold and everything that good exercise weather should be. It was the first large-scale operation held in these parts by the Command, and portrayed as close a picture to invasion conditions as it was possible to get. Regular troops, R.A.F. personnel, Home Guard and Civil Defence all took part, while 50,000 troops were used as the enemy with armoured columns, etc. I am not going to enlarge on the results of the exercise and the many lessons it taught, for the battle never reached Northampton, and so we were denied any chance of really functioning as a fighting unit. But the exercise did enable us to get our administration

THE SPIGOT MORTAR IN ACTION.

going. Sleeping accommodation for reliefs and feeding arrangements had to be made, and both these were successfully accomplished. As Dr. Thompson and I made a round of the Platoons, never in war time did I see so much food. One Platoon had a dish of rabbit stew; where the rabbits came from I could have guessed, but discretion being the better part of valour I maintained a discreet silence. " Them that asks no questions isn't told a lie." Anyway, the stew was very good. The Home Guard, true to soldierly tradition, had improvised very well and all Platoons had comfortable quarters more or less. The amount of money that changed hands that night in games of " skill " must have been enormous. Not that feeding and pontoon were the only things that happened on the historic night; observation was well kept and sentries did their job nobly in the wet, while added interest was given by a police message that a certain car was wanted. This gave the Home Guard the opportunity to stop all cars and examine identification cards. However, despite the good that we derived, there was an intense feeling of disappointment that we had not had a chance to show the efficiency of our training.

ELEANOR EXERCISE : July 5th, 1942.

Objects.

(1)   To test the efficiency of the defences in the 12th Battalion Northampton Home Guard Area.

(2)   To test such other Defended Localities immediately outside the Borough boundary.

(3)   To test the Civil Defence services and all organisations connected thereto.

Enemy provided by 9th, 10th, 11th, 13th and 14th Battalions Northamptonshire Home Guard.

GENERAL IDEA

At dawn on July 3rd, 1942, the Germans launched a full-scale invasion of the British Isles. All Home Guard localities have been manned and Civil Defence Services mobilised. Considerable sea-borne landings have been made on the coast of East Anglia, on the South Coast and in the area of the Bristol Channel.

Enemy paratroops have also been dropped in various parts of the country to create diversions. Their main objectives appear to be aerodromes and vital centres of road and railway communications. Information about initial successes have been confused, but serious landings of enemy paratroops and troops landed by troop-carrying aircraft and gliders have been made in the County of Northamptonshire and especially in localities commanding the approaches to Northampton. Sywell Aerodrome had been captured by the enemy.

By 06.05 hours on July 5th the immediate threat to Northampton has increased and by 08.00 hours it is known that large numbers of the enemy (probably in the neighbourhood of 2,500) have successfully concentrated in localities at distances of approximately 5—10 miles from the Borough boundary. There are indications that an early attack will develop against Northampton. Air activity on both sides has been considerable, but the British have so far maintained a degree of air superiority. The town has been heavily bombed and numerous fires have been started.

SPECIAL IDEA

Actión Stations was ordered shortly before dawn on July 3rd, 1942. Northamptonshire Home Guard Battalions were mustered. On July 5th at 06.00 hours reports reached the 12th Battalion that the enemy forces were gradually encircling the town of Northampton. Rumours and reports from civilian sources had enabled the defence to assess the enemy's strength at between 2,000 and 2,500 men. Commander ordered the call-up of Category 2 personnel.

At 08.30 hours on Sunday, July 5th, following an all-night enemy attack on the Borough of Northampton, the position is found to be as follows:—

ST. DAVID'S ESTATE. The area "bombed" is bounded by Boughton Green Road, Harborough Road, Kingsland Avenue.

The housing property has been severely damaged and several unexploded bombs have been detected. The whole area has been evacuated. The Rest Centre at Bective Schools and the Wardens' Post in Cranford Road are out of action. All injured people have been removed and no Civil Defence Services are operating in the area. The Harborough Road has been partially blocked by debris and Debris Clearance Parties are at work. Single line traffic has already been established and it is hoped to clear the road completely by 09.30 hours.

HEADLANDS. The area "bombed" is bounded by Bushland Road, Bush Hill Spinney, Northwood Road, Lindsay Avenue, Norman Road and Wellingborough Road.

The "bombing" in this area has not been severe, but two U.X. parachute mines are in the area, one at the junction of Whiteland Road and Headlands and the other in Beverley Crescent, necessitating the total evacuation of the area. The Rest Centre at Weston Favell School, Bushland Road, and the Wardens' Post at Longland Road are out of action. The casualties were fairly light and have been removed, but there are some fires still burning in house property. It is expected that the crews at work will be recalled at 10.00 hours. The Wardens' Post at the junction of Norman Road and Wellingborough Road is still in operation. Wellingborough Road is clear of debris.

SPENCER ESTATE. That part of the estate adjoining the railway has received severe damage, the area being bounded by Merthyr Road, Gladstone Road, Spencer Bridge Road and the railway. Spencer Bridge Road is blocked by damage to the road and the partial demolition of Spencer Bridge. Several bombs have dropped in the goods siding. The houses have been evacuated as all property requires either demolition or repair. The damage to the road and bridge will take some days to repair. Gas mains, water mains and electricity cables are broken.

———

I have quoted both the General Idea and the Special Idea in full so that all may see a situation that very probably would have occurred had an invasion of these islands been attempted, and a proposition that the Home Guard of Northampton would have had to face up to. To meet such a situation as this the 12th Battalion had spent innumerable hours in learning their weapons, had spent many mornings in trying them out on the ranges and in the bombing pits, had crawled through miles of grass and ditches, had listened to many lectures on the best means of dealing with the enemy, and altogether through much sweat and physical and mental effort had endeavoured to make themselves as fit and as efficient as possible. I sincerely trust that any citizens of the Borough who read this history will ponder over the sacrifices that the 12th Battalion were prepared to make so that the Germans should not occupy this town of ours and bring distress and death to its inhabitants.

To combat this threat to the town we had under our command:—

12th Battalion Northamptonshire Home Guard	1865
E Company, 47 Warwicks, Post Office Unit ...	53
26 Technical Training Group	300
2 A.A. Division Workshop	90
One Section, 443 S/L Battery, R.A.	17

Of these, the 26 Technical Training Group were technical troops who were undergoing a course at the Technical College and were very mixed as regards their training for fighting, the Workshop troops had few arms, and the Searchlight Section were to defend their site on the Billing Road and to help C Company. The Technical Training Group were to assist F Company and thicken up the Keep.

A COMPANY were responsible for the North of the town with Defended Localities at

(1) Kingsthorpe (junction of Harborough and Welford Roads).
(2) East Corner of Racecourse (Kettering and Kingsley crossroads).
(3) Kingsthorpe Hollow (held by the Advance Motor Works with the assistance of the 2 A.A. Division Workshop).

Company H.Q. at 58, East Park Parade.

B COMPANY held the South of the town, particularly the important river crossing at the South Bridge, where they had a defended locality.

Company H.Q. were at Phipps' Brewery.

C COMPANY were responsible for the East of the town with Defended Localities at

(1) North-West Corner of Abington Park, Wellingborough Road and Park Avenue crossroads.
(2) Billing Road (Town and County School).
(3) St. Peter's Bridge over the River Nene on Bedford Road.

Company H.Q. at the Town and County School.

D COMPANY held the West of the town with Defended Localities at

(1) West Bridge at Castle Station.
(2) Spencer Bridge (junction of St. Andrew's Road and Grafton Street).

Company H.Q. at Manning's Brewery.

E COMPANY defended

(1) Castle Station.
(2) Bridge Street Station Locomotive Shed and Midland Goods Station.
(3) Inland Distributing Depots at Old Towcester Road and St. Andrew's Road; to be prepared to disrupt and destroy these on receiving an order from Battalion H.Q.

WORKS PLATOONS:

(1) Gas Works.
(2) Express Lift Co.
(3) Electric Light Works.
(4) United Counties Bus Co.

These Platoons had the job of defending their own works, and also to attack any enemy in their vicinity.

F COMPANY, assisted by the 26 Technical Training Group, were responsible for

(1) The Police and Fire Stations.
(2) The Drill Hall.
(3) The Barracks (assisted by Northamptonshire Regiment details).

BATTALION RESERVE consisted of
(1) No. 3 H.Q. Mobile Platoon.
(2) No. 3 Platoon, A Company.
(3) No. 5 Platoon, B Company.
(4) No. 11 Platoon, D Company.

In addition to these, all Observation Posts had to be maintained, and guards found for various vulnerable places such at Water Works, Wireless Transmitting and Relay Stations, etc.

Arrangements had also been made for feeding, accommodation, taking over houses for defence, evacuation of inhabitants from the Defended Localities, collection and disposal of casualties, and many other details so that everything should work as smoothly as possible.

This was the general lay-out of the Battalion on July 5th, 1942, and I have given it in detail so that it may be seen how the organisation had been built up by this time and the amount of thought and work that had been put in so that the Battalion would function well if necessity arose.

It would take too long to describe the " battle " in all its various phases and therefore I have included the narrative of events as compiled at Battalion H.Q. by the Intelligence Officer, Lieutenant Arnold Payne, which gives a summary of the attack as received by us at H.Q.

NARRATIVE OF EVENTS BY INTELLIGENCE OFFICER

0730 hours Weather fine, visibility good.

0910 „ Reported by C Coy. Stinker (Gas) Mustard, Abington Avenue. — N.S.D. and all Coys., etc., informed.

0933 „ D Coy. report 1,000 lb. bomb on West Bridge destructor. Road closed.

0940 „ No. 1 H.Q. Platoon report enemy advancing up Preston Deanery Lane. Reported to them by 11th N.N. H.G. — B, C and E Coys. informed.

0951 „ C Coy. report enemy advancing on St. Peter's Bridge along railway line from Great Houghton. — 1207 hours we phoned for position. Lieut. Barton reported situation well in hand. Enemy 2 fields away.

0958 „ D Coy. report large enemy force approaching from Nobottle and New Duston.

1005 „ All Posts manned; 1635 reported. — N.S.D. informed.

1005 „ From 11th Bn. 40 enemy approaching Kislingbury Mill, south bank of river. 20 approaching Rothersthorpe.

1013 „ A Coy. 9th N.N. H.G. report enemy approaching Harlestone.

1013 „ D Coy. 9th N.N. H.G. report enemy approaching Moulton from Pitsford.

1026 „ 11th Bn. report enemy attacking Great Billing and Kislingbury. H.Q. destroyed by bomb.

1035 „ C Coy. report Little Houghton captured by enemy.

1044 „ 9th Bn. report Moulton D.L. taken.

1046 „ 11th Bn. report Rothersthorpe captured by enemy, who had 50 per cent. casualties.

1048	„	11th Bn. report enemy entering Delapre Park.	
1055	„	A Coy. say Brampton report enemy forming up to attack level-crossing.	
1056	„	11th Bn. report enemy debussing at Eleanor Hotel 1032.	
1100	„	C Coy. report Great Houghton captured.	
1103	„	Situation Report.	Sent to N.S.D.
1110	„	No. 1 H.Q. Pln. report Generating Station being bombed.	
1119	„	E Coy. report air attack on Castle Station 1110.	
1125	„	B Coy. report Hardingstone H.Q. being attacked.	
1127	„	11th Bn. H.G. report Hardingstone surrounded.	
1134	„	D Coy. report enemy passed through New Duston.	
1138	„	11th Bn. report enemy massing west of Nobottle Wood.	
1138	„	A Coy. report 1 officer and 20 enemy at Boothville Crossroads, working south.	
1150	„	D Coy. report No. 12 Pln. bombed; 25 per cent. casualties. Reinforcements requested.	No action taken.
1208	„	A Coy. report enemy advancing in strength towards Welford Road 3 blocks.	
1215	„	E Coy. report enemy reported at Grange Farm.	
1216	„	A Coy. report enemy on Golf Course by Lack's Farm.	
1223	„	11th Bn. report Duston being attacked.	
1230	„	B Coy. report Phipps' Brewery on fire. Coy. H.Q. moved to Rice's.	
1238	„	11th N.N. H.G. report enemy approaching Rothersthorpe Crossing.	
1242	„	C Coy. report 9 casualties at St. Peter's Bridge. Help required.	No action at time. Later No. 3 H.Q. Platoon sent.
1252	„	Bn. H.Q. bombed out and Stinker attack.	Bn. H.Q. opened at Police Station at 1258. All informed.
1310	„	F Coy. report enemy approaching town, crossing railway rear of Semilong.	
1315	„	A Coy. report 100 enemy approaching Mill Lane Bridge.	
1320	„	A Coy. report fighting in houses in East Park Parade.	
1320	„	No. 1 H.Q. Pln. report 40 enemy south of Gantry Station, moving west near Delapre Wood. Engaged by Smith gun.	
1320	„	11th Bn. report attack on Duston. Road block at Upton surrounded.	D Coy. informed.

1323	„	No. 2 H.Q. Pln. report works surrounded. Some enemy in works. Reinforcements requested.	No action.
1325	„	D Coy. report enemy in St. Andrew's Road.	No. 11 Pln. sent out.
1325	„	A Coy. report enemy on Golf Links, heading for town.	No. 3 Pln. sent.
1330	„	Termination of Exercise.	

As in all good exercises, many lessons were learnt from " Eleanor " which, all told, was the best practice we had during our existence in the testing of our defences. All Company Commanders realised their responsibilities, and there was a general cry for more men to fulfil their requirements. 1,635 Home Guards, together with Regular detachments, seem a lot when they march past on the County Ground, but spread over Northampton they appear very thin on the ground. For example, 70 men were not enough to hold St. Peter's Bridge against a really determined attack, and the Mobile Reserve Platoon had to be sent to thicken them up and make the Bridge safe. Messages were sent and received well, but at times there was congestion on the Battalion line and it was found quicker, as I had always maintained, to send a cyclist messenger with a written message. If officers had not realised it before, it was certainly brought to their attention that all dispositions must be made beforehand and the defence properly planned; there is no time to do this when once the battle begins. Therefore each Company found the need for a reserve Platoon that could go out and deal with the enemy, who would naturally often by-passed the Defended Localities and were able to infiltrate into the town. There was a lack of liaison between the Home Guard and the Civil Defence. Home Guard officers complained that they were not informed of " incidents " that occurred in their areas, and I suppose the Civil Defence groused that they received little information from the Home Guard. Battalion Headquarters worked much better and more smoothly than on previous occasions. 104 messages were received during the six hours of the battle. It was found impossible to send out messages continually to Companies giving the progress of the battle, and it was suggested that the Intelligence Officers of each Company paid periodic visits to Battalion Headquarters, where they could obtain a clear picture of the way the operations were proceeding. Arrangements had been made with the A.R.P. Authorities for the evacuation of our wounded by their ambulances. This did not work satisfactorily, and in my opinion never would, as they would be busy dealing with the civilian casualties caused by bombing. Although this system continued to the end of our days, I always had in mind the use of the Battalion cars and lorries to get our wounded to hospital quickly.

So ended the Eleanor Exercise. Great keenness and enthusiasm was shown by all concerned and the general opinion of the Umpires appears to have been that, if due allowances had been given to weapons, the defence of the town would have held out. Which was a matter of satisfaction to the 12th Battalion.

On August 9th, 1942, an Exercise Mercury was held to test out the communications in the Sub-Area. There is no need to go into detail on this as only the Battalion Headquarters was engaged. It was really a scheme to try out the communications of the outlying Battalions of the Sub-Area. As we were living practically on top of their Headquarters communication by despatch riders was easy. It only remains to state that the Despatch Riders, six of whom were attached to the Sub-Area, functioned in their usual efficient manner.

Early in 1944 there took place the Buzz Exercises, which were laid on by East Central District. It was always a matter of regret that throughout our career, on all these large exercises nothing of importance seemed to happen in the town; in fact, we appeared to have been by-passed on several occasions. And so it was with Buzz, for although the Mobile Companies, D and G, took part, the rest of the Battalion was not called upon. But what a time these two Companies had. One could not imagine a worse night; when it was not snowing it was sleeting, and when doing neither of these it was raining hard. Added to this it was pitch black, so that one had the greatest difficulty in finding one's way. There is an old saying in Army circles that " the worse the weather, the better the exercise." Judged by this standard it was a wonderful show. G Company, who had assembled at their head-quarters at the Barracks and Regent Square Chapel, were almost at full strength late on the Saturday evening for, as would have happened on a real attack, men dribbled in when they had finished their civilian work. The Smith Guns, gallantly towed behind private cars by their owners, were all present on parade, and the Company made a brave show. When I looked in at them with Captain Barton, about 9.30 p.m., one was reminded of the old days of the last war. Some men were eating, some sleeping on the floor or on forms, while in the corners one saw the inevitable " brag " and " pontoon " schools. In the early hours of Sunday morning they were ordered out to proceed to Daventry as an attack on the B.B.C. Station was deemed probable.

In the meantime D Company had assembled at the Rosery and Chestnut Road, and at 7.15 p.m. were told to report to Spratton, as it was evident by then that the Reservoir at Teeton would be one of the objectives of the enemy. This Company had not long been formed, less than two months, and it was their first test. Their task was different from that of G Company for, whereas while the latter were lorried, D Company had to proceed on foot, no light undertaking for a Home Guard Company consisting of men of all ages on a rough winter's night. It is to their lasting credit that they arrived at Spratton without a man falling out. Not only this, but finding the local Platoon very low in numbers they patrolled the roads around the village all night, and then before daybreak proceeded to the Reservoir, where they took part in the defence of the Power Station. They had indeed done a good night's work, and showed that the Home Guard was capable of a much more active role than had been thought possible. During the night the Adjutant and I visited the Company once or twice and found Company Headquarters established at the Schoolrooms and everything proceeding smoothly and satisfactorily. The only drawback was that the School had no phone. However, arrangements were made with the farmer of a nearby farmhouse to establish a phone headquarters there. This meant a journey through the dark and rain of some hundreds of yards, but there was never any lack of volunteers for the job, which I thought showed great devotion to duty on the part of the Intelligence Section. It was not until afterwards I learned that the good lady at the farm, evidently thinking that nothing was too good for the Home Guard, regaled the messengers with a copious supply of sandwiches and hot coffee. A word of praise should also be given to those ladies of the village W.V.S. who worked so magnificently all through the night to provide hot tea and refreshments. Only those who have been on patrol on a cold, wet winter's night know the blessing of a cup of hot " char " after the completion of their duty. D Company were particularly grateful to these ladies of the village for their all-night effort.

With the battle over between eight and nine on the Sunday morning, a return was made to the Schoolroom at Spratton, where a hot breakfast had been prepared by Sergeant Day. Never was a meal more enjoyed; I know, for I was there to partake of it.

The Exercise, like all good exercises should, taught several lessons. First, that D Company had indeed organised itself well since the short time of its inception. The second, that the enemy, even on a wild winter's night, were not confined to the roads, but could make their way with certainty across open country to their objective. Full marks must be given to the enemy Home Guard Platoon from a neighbouring county for their cross-country approach over unknown terrain from Hanging Houghton to Ravensthorpe Reservoir. The third lesson learnt was that in a mobile company such as this, transport was needed for the conveyance of blankets, cooking utensils, reserve ammunition, etc. On this occasion Jordan's lorries were used, but it is not every Company Commander who can provide lorries, and without these a mobile company cannot function efficiently. The last lesson has already been pointed out, that the Home Guard was capable of a much more mobile role than that of Defended Localities.

Other Buzz Exercises were held in the adjacent counties and on these we assisted by the provision of umpires, signallers and despatch riders. For the E.C.D. these were the last tuning-up exercises before D Day, and had the Germans attempted any action in this country at that time, we fell sure that the lessons learnt on " Buzz " would have been of the greatest value to us all.

Before D Day we in Northamptonshire had the privilege of taking part in one more exercise, in its way more real and valuable than any during our lifetime. This was the Megrim Exercise, which was held at the end of April, 1944, with a two-fold object. The enemy on this occasion were paratroops, whose mission on and before D Day was to be dropped behind the German lines in France to sabotage communications, etc. This was their final try-out and was the main object of the Exercise. The secondary one was to practise the Home Guard in the rounding-up of saboteurs. The intention of the paratroops was to lie up by day, and at night emerge from their hiding places, " do their stuff," and regain their lair before dawn. And so the exercise started by the " planting " of these troops in suitable places in Northamptonshire. The Home Guard functioned during the hours of darkness, and here lay the one weakness of the scheme, a weakness that could not have been very well avoided. Had this been the real thing, then these saboteurs would have been hunted by day as well as by night, and it is probable that the Home Guard, with their local knowledge, would have discovered some of their hide-outs. As it was, the Home Guard patrolled roads, bridges and railway lines during the nights and guarded vulnerable points. Under these circumstances the advantages were with the attackers, and therefore the results were hardly a true criterion. Very few of these paratroops were rounded up, although some were captured.

Our job in the 12th Battalion was to patrol the railway line, Northampton —Rugby, from the Borough boundary near Kingsthorpe Moors to the Castle Station, where the 15th took over. In addition the Northampton—Wellingborough Road had to be watched, our section being from Abington Park to Weston Favell, where we joined up with the 11th Battalion. As usual and as was to be expected, for these saboteurs on communications would naturally avoid towns, no incidents happened in the Battalion area. However, on the Saturday night of April 30th a Platoon of G Company, who were the Sector Reserve for the night, had more success. Here is the report of Lieutenant C. M. Edwards, who was in charge of No. 25 Platoon:—

" No. 25 Platoon on the memorable evening of April 30th at 1930 hours were standing-by at Battalion Headquarters, quite prepared to have a more or less comfortable evening of cards and guard duty, interspersed with a modicum of Phipps', with the exception, of course, of the poor Platoon Commander, who as usual would have to be out and about best part of the night.

" On this particular Stand-to there was perhaps an air of expectancy pervading the atmosphere. Our Sector Commander, who had been somewhat restless and energetic of late, had decided that it was bad for discipline to allow stand-by platoons to rusticate, and so night exercises became the vogue in order to keep the men on their toes.

" The county was infested with a large number of highly-trained paratroops of various nationalities and no uncertain toughness, whose job it was to destroy important installations and rail and road junctions, etc. Up to this date they had managed by subversive and underhand means to avoid capture.

" At approximately 2200 hours the Platoon Commander received a message from Sector Headquarters to proceed forthwith to that H.Q. for the purpose of receiving his orders, which were as follows:—

" 'Enemy paratroops had been observed in the vicinity of Chapel Brampton and Spratton and No. 25 Platoon would proceed by transport to a point some 200 yards short of Merry Tom Lane and there debus and proceed with all care, but as speedily as possible, to the railway crossing at Chapel Brampton and thence up the track to three bridges on the line to Spratton. It was thought by the Sector Command that an attempt would be made to blow up the three bridges in question.'

" The Platoon set out from Battalion Headquarters with a feeling that at last something was ' doing,' and en route every man blackened his face and prepared himself for the night's adventure. The debussing point was reached without incident and the Platoon proceeded to Merry Tom Lane in battle order, and with all their senses very much on the alert. Every shadow seemed to shelter a member of the opposition and every likely bit of cover was inspected right down the length of line to the railway crossing. The leading section inspected the underside of the small bridge over the brook adjacent to the crossing with great care, and all dare scarcely breathe in case they gave themselves away. The result was Nil, and the hour by this time was 2345. Presently, however, one of the leading scouts reported back news of the enemy near one of the bridges. One section proceeded on the left of the railway and the other on the right, with instructions to cover the whole area of the bridge, whilst the remaining section followed at short distance, prepared to jump in wherever they were most needed. At this point a catastrophe was narrowly averted between the two leading platoons and a squad of country Home Guards who suddenly appeared on the scene from the opposite direction. After everyone had settled down and had a breather, a ' confab.' was held, and eventually someone brought along a message from Major Jackson requiring our presence at Spratton and requesting us to place ourselves under his command, taking up our H.Q. at Spratton Station. Eventually, after an unsuccessful night, we received orders to return to Battalion Headquarters—time approximately 0200 hours —everyone feeling tired and a little ' browned-off.'

" However, the men had rosy visions of a little 'shut-eye' until the morning, but it was not to be. Our Sector Commander just allowed the Platoon time to get to sleep when once again the Platoon Commander was called for. This time the enemy had definitely been spotted near Cank Wood, Hardingstone, and we were ordered to proceed there with all speed, while the local lads kept the enemy under observation. The Platoon were told that they had to bring someone back, even if it was only the Umpire. It is not difficult to imagine the little ' pleasantries ' which some members passed upon being awakened from a sound sleep and told to get cracking for a second time that night. A Regular Army sergeant-major could not have bettered the language.

" A guide duly arrived to take out the Platoon, and we proceeded on what was to prove, this time, a real adventure. The local Company Commander, a Captain Jones, was contacted and with the Platoon Commander made an inspection of the outside of the wood. The time was now 0300 hours, the night fine, but hellishly cold. The Umpire, a Polish Officer, was discovered comfortably asleep in his flea-bag in an adjoining field, with his kit all around him. This included a very nice .45 automatic, which the Platoon Commander later tried to ' knock off,' but without success. Captain Jones then bade us farewell and moved off with such of his men who were out on duty. It appears there was a spot of milking to be done at 5 a.m. that morning.

" It was decided by the Platoon Commander that Cank Wood was no sort of place to try and clear in the dark. This entailed waiting for dawn, and in the meantime all possible exits were covered. In order to ' anchor ' the Umpire, one enthusiast removed his boots and all his kit to a hedgerow some 200 yards away, with the remark that ' the blighter won't get far without his boots on this ground.' Dawn broke, as it invariably does, about 0600 hours and the wood-clearing commenced. After some twenty minutes came the cry from one of the beaters, ' Here the so-and-so's are! ' and three Polish paratroopers were seen to be struggling out of their flea-bags. The line of beaters swung round in a circle and closed in, everybody no doubt thinking ' Let's be sure of these blokes, anyway.' After a short mix-up in which Corporal Goff was hurled into an adjacent thorn bush, and Sergeant Chambers was heard to state in no uncertain terms what he would do to them if they didn't pack up, the short encounter ended. Our four charges, the three paratroopers and the Umpire, were conveyed proudly to Battalion Headquarters and from thence to Talavera Camp, there to be interrogated and placed in the P.O.W. cage.

" The time was now 0800 hours, the men cheerful but tired, making their way for home, thinking of the tale they had to tell to their long-suffering wives. The Platoon Commander betook himself to Battalion Headquarters to write a short report and to receive from the Adjutant, Captain Barton, positively the best cup of tea he has tasted, before or since.

" It is interesting to note that this Platoon again mustered the same evening, Sunday, May 1st, at 1800 hours, and be it said to their everlasting credit that with one exception, a sick man, the muster was complete."

I can only add to this report of Lieutenant Edwards that I was present at the Drill Hall when the party returned, worn out but elated. As it was understood as part of the Exercise that captured prisoners would make every effort to escape, great was the zeal displayed by the Platoon to prevent this happening. Never have prisoners been so closely guarded. G Company had secured the only success in the Sector Area.

On the last night of the Megrim Exercise a successful attack was made on the Northampton Electric Light Works which, although not in the Battalion Area, was the nearest action we had. As I thought that things might move on the nights of the Saturday and Sunday, I was on duty myself at Battalion Headquarters. On the Sunday night I had on duty with me a supreme optimist in the person of Lieutenant George Beer, of A Company. About midnight he got out his blankets and camp bed with the hope of securing an hour or two's sleep, like a good soldier. Hardly had his head touched the pillow, or what was taking its place, than the telephone bell rang, with a message to be taken. In the first hour this occurred some ten times, so that George, now disillusioned and realising that the ways of Battalion H.Q. are hard, packed up his bed and resigned himself to the inevitable.

From the point of view of the Home Guard the Exercise was of the greatest help, as it gave us practice in what might have occurred around D Day. We only hope that the exercise was equally valuable to those brave fellows, "our enemy," who shortly afterwards played their part in the landings in Normandy. What happened to them we know not, but we sincerely trust that they came safely through their hazardous mission.

Almost the last of our exercises was arranged in July, 1944. With all ideas of a full-scale invasion now at an end, the only likely enemy action in this country was the landing of small bodies of paratroops dropped for the purpose of creating a nuisance and disturbances in the land while our troops were fighting in Normandy, with the hope of keeping British troops back in England. We at Battalion Headquarters therefore arranged an exercise on these lines; a picture of six or seven enemy driven off from their objective, taking refuge in the old Kingsthorpe Lodge on the Kettering Road Golf Links, a derelict building well suited for the scheme. Here was a situation that might have occurred. Each Company delegated a Platoon to represent them, and it was interesting to see how the different Platoons tackled the job of mopping up the enemy.

It was a very useful preliminary to the Battalion Competition which was held at Wootton in the following month. Here on successive evenings on a knock-out basis, Platoons strove for the Jeffery Cup. The last three Platoons left in were those from G, D and B Companies. On a very wet Sunday morning near Boughton Green the final was decided. We had been fortunate in obtaining officers from the I.T.C. to act as umpires for the final, and after a most interesting contest they declared No. 5 Platoon of B Company, under Lieutenant Shelton, the winners. This Platoon went on to the Sector Platoon Competition where, led by Lieutenant John Fitzhugh, they put up quite a good show, being the leaders in the firing, but unfortunately were not successful in winning the competition.

These last exercises showed the great advance in training that had been made since the early L.D.V. days, and had the Germans attempted action in this country in 1944 they would have been up against a very different proposition to the one that would have met them in 1940.

For over four years exercises had taken place in all parts of the town and the surrounding countryside. I have outlined those arranged by Battalion and the Higher Authorities. Besides these there were innumerable Company and Platoon schemes, which by themselves would fill a book. The names of Hackett's Spinney, Delapre Park, Moulton Park, St. Peter's Bridge, etc., will not readily be forgotten by members of the 12th. I believe that all enjoyed these "battles," and if properly planned beforehand and entered into in the right spirit, they provided extremely valuable training, which might have been the means of many lives being saved if the worst had happened.

CHAPTER FIVE

BATTALION PARADES AND SPECIAL OCCASIONS

S UNDAY, OCTOBER 6th, 1940. The first full Parade of the 12th was held on this date on the Market Square, when a short address was given by the Mayor of the Borough, Alderman H. Glenn, who afterwards took the salute in front of the Guildhall. It is typical of the time that in the Orders it was stated that only volunteers in uniform would parade; evidently all the members had not been equipped by then.

SUNDAY, AUGUST 17th, 1941. MILITARY PAGEANT AT FRANKLIN'S GARDENS, organised by E (Railway) Company. This was repeated on Saturday, September 20th, for the Red Cross.

SUNDAY, SEPTEMBER 14th, 1941. The assembly took place in the vicinity of the Drapery and the Battalion marched via Sheep Street, the Mounts, York Road, Cheyne Walk, Victoria Promenade, Bridge Street to the Guildhall, where the Mayor, Councillor A. Chown, took the salute. 1,382 were on parade. It was evident that we had progressed by this time for battle-dress and steel helmets were worn, while the leading files carried rifles. Lewis guns and Thompson sub-M.G.'s were also " on parade."

CHURCH PARADE, SEPTEMBER 6th, 1942. The Battalion paraded on the Racecourse, where they were inspected by Colonel J. L. Short, C.B.E., who had lately arrived as Sub-District Commander. The line of march was Kettering Road, York Road, St. Giles' Street to the Guildhall, where the salute was taken by the Mayor, Alderman J. E. Bugby. The service, conducted by the Rev. Canon Trevor Lewis, was held at 12 o'clock at All Saints' Church. The number on parade was 1,649.

SUNDAY, NOVEMBER 15th, 1942. 100 men from C Company represented the Battalion on Civil Defence Day.

MARCH 20th, 1943. OPENING OF ARMY WEEK. A contingent of 50 members, under Lieutenants W. A. Evans and H. L. Jennings, were on parade from the Battalion.

THIRD ANNIVERSARY OF THE HOME GUARD, MAY 14th, 1943. Extract from a letter from Eastern Command:—

" The Third Anniversary of the formation of the Home Guard falls on Friday, May 14th, and on that evening the Prime Minister proposes to broadcast a message expressing appreciation of their work.

" By direction of the Prime Minister, ceremonial parades will be held to celebrate this anniversary, and will be made the subject of special publicity arrangements. In crder not to interfere with production, the parades will be held on Sunday, May 16th. This is one of the rare occasions which justifies time taken from the normal battle training of the Home Guard.

" Weapons will be carried on these parades in order that the fighting strength of the Home Guard may be demonstrated."

In conformity with this instruction the 12th Battalion arranged to hold its Third Anniversary on the County Ground. The time was short and it was necessary to get cracking at once. We were determined to put on a real good show in this, our first demonstration to the public of Northampton of the various aspects of our training. Each Company was allotted some part of the display, and immediately started rehearsing at their quarters all over the town. Great keenness was shown by all, and the only thing we were really worried about was what the weather would be like on " The Day."

The County Ground on the evenings during the week previous to the Anniversary was the scene of feverish activity. The front of the now familiar house was going up, F Company were practising their wall climbing, C Company were marching and counter-marching, the Despatch Riders were doing their evolutions, and No. 3 Platoon of A Company, who were doing the " battle," were all over the place. The Adjutant and the Quartermaster and the P.S.I.'s had been busy collecting the various properties and effects, including a dummy tank, German uniforms, and " bags " of thunderflashes, etc.

The Day brought forth real Home Guard weather and was ideal. A large crowd of the inhabitants had assembled and filled the stands and terraces. I don't think that any of us who paraded on that afternoon will ever forget the scene as we emerged from the rear of the Cricket Pavilion. I feel that I cannot do better than give the account of the proceedings as described in the " Northampton Independent " of May 21st, 1943:—

" Whatever the thousands of members of a generous public may have given to the collections, on behalf of war charities, taken at last week-end's demonstrations of the Home Guard's Third Birthday, they must have felt amply rewarded by all they saw. Not only that, they must also have felt a renewal of confidence as to the outcome of any attempt by the enemy to violate the British fortress, while wives of the Home Guards must have found abundant consolation for the long and patient sacrifice of their husbands' time and company.

" The demonstration by the 12th Battalion Northamptonshires at the County Ground can hardly have been excelled by any single Battalion anywhere.

" Perfectly organised in every detail, enlivened by an accurately informative, but appropriately racy broadcast commentary, and accompanied by the lively music of the Battalion Band, the whole show succeeded in dramatising the Home Guard in such a way that its work was illustrated in a vivid and quite thrilling style, which completely captured the imagination of a crowd some 5,000—6,000 strong.

" The turn-out at the 12th Battalion demonstration was excellent, quite 90 per cent., and their marching was as impressive as their obvious mastery of their weapons and other training.

" They well deserved the compliments paid them by the Northamptonshire Zone Advisor, Colonel P. Lester Reid, in a spirited address after he had taken the salute.

" Without disparaging any of the fine displays given by other Sections, all ranks of the 12th will agree that the wall climbing, house clearing and the platoon in attack events were quite the high-spots of the afternoon, and none will deny a special word of commendation to Lieutenant Frank Jordan, who not only organised and supervised the building of a most realistic wall and house and a most convincing landscape of hedgerows and folds of cover, etc., across the ground, but also led his Platoon in a battle attack which kept all the rules and wiped out an enemy strong point in determined fashion.

" Another notable show was that by E Company (13th Leicesters), the Post Office Unit, in communications. Not only did they run out and demonstrate in double quick time a field telephone exchange, connect with an adjacent pole telephone wire, and put on visual signalling to show comparison, but they also released a pigeon carrying a message to an adjacent H.Q. in the county, which didn't waste a second in getting on its way.

" Where all the ' fireworks ' were ' scrounged ' from for the 12th show one can only imagine, but they seemed to have got everything that was necessary to heighten realism. The cracking and the thudding went on as if they had ' thousands of everything ' in the store, and this was accompanied by clouds of smoke-screens and the recurrent reverberations of thunder-flashes galore.

"As for the Bosche uniforms of the annihilated enemy, the N.F.S. coats, U.S. helmets and gumboots of the majority of the post matched remarkably well the two genuine outfits which the Battalion had managed to 'chisel out' of the very limited supply available in the Area.

"Finally they had 'secured' a 'pukka' dummy tank, which appropriately received a direct hit at the first shot in the grenade event. The commentary in this show was particularly good. The announcer even got the crowd to count with him the 'One, two, three, four of the seconds between the throw and the detonation, and they were all delighted when the bang duly rewarded their efforts, as all good 36's should.

"Particularly funny among the many funny incidents was the 'how not to do it' part of the gas attack demonstration. There were roars of laughter when, before the awkward squad could get at their respirators, they fished anything from a bottle of beer to an item of lingerie out of their respirator holders.

"A nice touch of inspiring solemnity was lent to the occasion by the address of congratulation by the Mayor (Alderman W. Lees). 'May God bless you all,' he said in conclusion by the singing of two verses of the special Home Guard hymn, composed by Corporal H. Banks (A Company), and by the united singing of the National Anthem.

"With the warmest congratulations to Lieut.-Colonel Barnes, his second-in-command, Major H. St. J. Browne, and all participants, may well be added special commendation of the work of Captain H. D. Barton and Captain A. W. Gardner (Battalion Q.M.) in the matter of 'pin-point' work in the organisation, which was little less than faultless."

The following telegram had been despatched on the previous day:—

"To His Majesty The King,
Buckingham Palace.

The Officers and Men of the 12th Northamptonshire Battalion, Home Guard, assembling to-morrow on the occasion of the Third Anniversary, respectfully offer to your Majesty, their Colonel-in-Chief, this expression of their loyalty and devotion.

L. E. Barnes, Lieut.-Colonel Commanding.

Drill Hall, Northampton.'

The following reply was received and read on the County Ground:—

"Windsor Castle.
15th May, 1943.

Colonel Barnes,
Drill Hall, Northampton.

I sincerely thank all ranks 12th Northamptonshire Battalion for their kind and loyal message.

(Signed) George R.I. (Colonel-in-Chief)."

The number on parade was 2,032, the largest attendance on any parade held during the time of our existence. A collection on the ground realised the fine sum of £50, which was allotted as under:—

Red Cross and St. Dunstan's £7 10s. 0d. each; "Chronicle and Echo" Comforts Fund, Northampton General Hospital, Manfield Hospital, Northampton British Legion, Jugo-Slav Troops' Comfort Fund, A.T.S. Comforts Fund, Police Fund, Widows and Orphans, £5 each.

And so ended our Anniversary Parade. I find that in my training instructions of June, 1943, I said, and I think that the words still hold good: "The extremely fine display given by the Battalion on the occasion of the Third Anniversary Celebrations was as much a revelation to ourselves as it was to the Regulars, the C.D. Services, and the general public of the high standard of efficiency of the men; I think we all feel that the public, as the result of this display, are much more appreciative of the work of the Home Guard."

JULY 1st, 1943. On this date we arranged a Band Concert and Community Singing in Abington Park, in connection with the Hospital Week. As a result the sum of £39 1s. 8d. was handed to the Hospital Week Committee.

SUNDAY, SEPTEMBER 5th, 1943. DRUMHEAD SERVICE, COUNTY GROUND. The Battalion fell in on the Racecourse and marched to the County Ground, where the salute was taken by the Mayor, Alderman W. Lees. The British Legion, by invitation, were with us on this occasion and we were pleased to see so many of them present. The service was conducted by the Rev. L. Hills, S.C.F., and the Rev. H. W. Janisch, O.C.F.

SATURDAY, SEPTEMBER 11th, 1943. COMPANY FETE AT SPINNEY HILL, promoted by the members of A Company. This, the first effort in arranging a Fete, proved an outstanding success, due to the enthusiasm and hard work of the Company, particularly of " Jordan's Lot." A sum of £400 was handed to the Red Cross for the Prisoners-of-War Fund.

FOURTH ANNIVERSARY OF THE HOME GUARD, JUNE 18th, 1944. In accordance with instructions from the Higher Authorities the holding of the Anniversary Parade took place to coincide with " Salute the Soldier " Week, and therefore was held a month later than in 1943. The parade followed what were now familiar lines, an assembly on the Racecourse and a march to the County Ground, headed by the Despatch Riders and the Battalion Band. Lieut.-General Sir John Brown, K.C.B., C.B.E., took the salute and afterwards gave an address on the objects of the Salute the Soldier Week. Demonstrations on the same lines as 1943 followed, an innovation being the march-past of a Platoon of C Company dressed as in old L.D.V. days in civilian clothes, with sticks and armlets, and with one shotgun among thirty men. A collection taken by a party of A Company realised over £90 towards the 12th Battalion bed at the Northampton General Hospital.

SATURDAY, JULY 22nd, 1944. D COMPANY FETE AT SPINNEY HILL. By this time " Jordan's Lot " had become part of D Company and, continuing their efforts on behalf of good causes, promoted another Fete, this time for the Home Guard Hospital Bed and for the Roadmender Club. They achieved even greater success than on the previous occasion, for the net result was £600, which was equally divided between the two causes.

DRUMHEAD SERVICE, SEPTEMBER 3rd, 1944. On this occasion we were honoured by the presence of the District Commander, Major-General E. C. Hayes, who was paying his first visit to the Battalion. Personally I had met him several times before, and always had the greatest admiration for him. He knew his job from top to bottom and as he stood on the County Ground taking the salute he looked every inch a soldier, as indeed he was. Not long after his visit to us he left for a post in the East. The assembly was as usual on the Racecourse, and considering the state of the weather there was a good turn-out of 993. There was also a good attendance of the public, including the Zone Advisor, Colonel P. Lester Reid, who was present at all our Battalion Parades, the Mayor of Northampton, Councillor A. Weston, and members of the Corporation. The service was conducted by the Rev. L. Hills and the Rev. E. E. White, the latter a member of the

Battalion who had just joined us from a Hampshire Unit, where he had been serving since L.D.V. days. We were again pleased to have the British Legion and the Old Contemptibles on parade with us.

This was the last occasion on which we paraded at the County Ground, which had been during the war years the Battalion Parade Ground. One cannot leave the County Ground without expressing our very deep appreciation to the Northamptonshire Cricket Club and the directors of the Northampton Town Football Club for their public spirit in loaning us the ground and stands whenever we asked for them. There was no other spot in the town so available and so suitable, and their action assisted in a large measure to the success of our Anniversaries and Parades. Our best thanks are also due to Mr. Ron Johnson, of the Cricket Club, and Mr. Tom Smith, the manager of the Football Club, for their great help in the ground and gate arrangements.

BATTALION FETE, SEPTEMBER 9th, 1944. During the Summer of 1944 I had felt that the days of the Home Guard were drawing to a close, and I was anxious to leave behind some permanent record of the 12th Battalion which would be a reminder that during the Second World War there was such a band of men in Northampton who gave up so much of their spare time and served with such devotion in order to defend the town should the necessity arise. Monuments and statues are out of date, and we were not content to wait for someone to do something for us, but we determined to make our own memorial. We could think of nothing better or of greater help than to attempt to raise the sum of £1,000 for the endowment of a 12th Battalion Bed at the Northampton General Hospital. There were some among us who thought that this was a little optimistic and perhaps too ambitious, but I felt that with the loyal support of all members this was well within our capabilities. And so the project of a Battalion Fete came into being. At the initial meeting at the Drill Hall of representatives of all Companies the idea was taken up with enthusiasm. The date was a little later than we would have wished, but we were anxious to avoid any clashing with D Company's Fete in July. Let me say at once that, without this enthusiasm which lasted right to the end, success could not have been achieved. So loyally and well did the Fete Committee work that it is only right that their names should be recorded in this history:—

Hon. Treasurer: Captain V. J. H. Harris.
Hon. Secretary: Lieutenant A. Holland.
Committee:
Lieutenant W. T. Whitehouse and Corporal R. Atkins (A Company).
Corporal E. W. Harris and Private G. T. Warwick (B Company).
Corporal E. Frisby and Private H. J. Rickard (C Company).
Lieutenant S. R. Griffin (D Company).
Lieutenant A. E. Harrold and Lieutenant H. F. Lawrence (F Company).
C.S.M. H. A. Savage and Sergeant M. McCullan (G Company).
C.Q.M.S. A. Jeffery and Sergeant K. G. Bayes (H Company).
Lieutenant A. C. Payne and Lieutenant F. Wood (H.Q.).

Each Company agreed to take its share of the work, and there was plenty of it, and it was portioned out as under:—

A Company: Sports Programme.
B Company: Sideshows.
C Company: Entertainments.
D Company: Sideshows.
F Company: Competitions.
G Company: Teas and Refreshments.
H Company: Flower, Vegetable and Fruit Show.
Despatch Riders: Gate Arrangements.

WEAPON TRAINING. THE LEWIS GUN. near Bushland Road School.

(Photo: J. Wright)

Each Company set to work with a will, and after a month's intensive effort, things were all set for the day. Never had fellows worked so hard for a fete as the members of the Home Guard. We had been fortunate in obtaining the True Form Sports Ground, Spinney Hill, kindly loaned to us by their Sports Committee, and we were greatly indebted to them and to their Secretary, Mr. L. Perrin, for their kindness. Without their kind help in granting us the use of the ground, after we had been turned down where we had expected sympathetic treatment, our object would not have been achieved and the Hospitals would have suffered. In the days before the Fete, barrel-organs had been taken out into the streets of the town by the various Companies, B Company, with C.S.M. Martin, being much to the fore in this respect, and a good sum had been collected. An appeal by the Commanding Officer to the citizens of Northampton for donations to cover expenses had met with a very generous response, for which we were very grateful. From the replies from those who were kind enough to help us, one felt that among a large section of the community the work of the Home Guard had been appreciated. I have culled the following extracts from letters received as typical of the expressions of goodwill:—

" It is a pleasure to assist the Home Guard. One gets so few opportunities of showing appreciation for all that they have done since the dark days of Dunkirk."

" Enclosed with our united good wishes and gratitude to the Home Guard." (From three ladies).

" May I congratulate you, and all concerned in the Home Guard, not only on this method of recording the work which you have done, but on the work itself, which has meant many strenuous hours of service."

It was especially necessary to raise this fund so as to guarantee all expenses, in order that exemption from Entertainment Tax could be obtained.

On the morning of September 9th anxious eyes were cast at the skies, for the success of the Fete depended to a large extent on the weather. Although the previous days had been anything but good, on the Saturday there was a change and Home Guard weather prevailed, for the afternoon was ideal and the Fete was a glorious success, far exceeding our anticipations. No less a sum of £1,512 was raised, and this, together with the money raised by previous efforts, brought the total sum to £1,952. At a Final Meeting of the Committee it was decided to endow a Bed at the Northampton General Hospital for £1,000, one at the Manfield Hospital for £500, and to give the balance of £452 to the Special Appeal Fund of the General Hospital.

So ended a remarkable effort. Never had so much money been raised by a fete in Northampton in so short a time, and this result was only achieved by the hard work and enthusiasm of those who toiled so hard to make the Fete such an outstanding success. As a result, there is to-day a permanent record in our Hospitals of the service of the 12th Battalion Northamptonshire Home Guard. Over each of our beds in the Hospitals is the plaque:—

> THIS BED WAS PRESENTED BY THE
> 12th BATTALION NORTHAMPTONSHIRE HOME GUARD
> TO COMMEMORATE THEIR YEARS OF SERVICE
> 1940 — 1944

November 10th, 1945, saw the final episode of the effort, for in the presence of members of the Fete Committee and the Old Comrades' Committee the plaques were unveiled at both the Hospitals. " Memorials to the 12th Battalion by the 12th Battalion."

STATEMENTS OF ACCOUNT OF THE FETE

Receipts	£	s.	d.	Payments	£	s.	d.
To Donations	397	11	0	By Expenses:			
„ Sale of Programmes.	80	18	5	Hire of Marquee	15	0	0
„ Takings at Gate ...	68	14	3	Hire of Boilers	1	11	6
„ Barrel Organ Collec-				Hire of Lorries	1	16	8
tions	146	0	5½	Hire of Stalls	16	17	6
„ Battalion Competition	296	1	9	Printing and Advertis-			
„ Company Compe-				ing	26	2	10
titions	126	5	0	Purchase of Goods for			
„ Refreshments, etc. ...	73	17	1	Prizes, Stalls, etc. ...	86	2	7
„ Flower Show, Sale of				Punch and Judy	1	5	0
Exhibits, etc. ...	148	2	3	Groundsman	2	0	0
„ Dog Show	8	0	3	Cheque Book		4	0
„ Stalls and Sideshows	317	13	11½	Postage and Receipt			
„ Collection on Anniver-				Stamps		14	8
sary Parade	92	3	6	Endowment of Bed at			
„ Collection at Drum-				Northampton			
head Service	45	18	3	General Hospital ...1000	1000	0	0
„ Share of D Company				Endowment of Bed at			
Fete	300	0	0	Manfield Hospital ...	500	0	0
„ Special Donations ...	2	12	0	Northampton General			
				Hospital Appeal			
				Fund	452	8	5
	£2,104	**3**	**2**		**£2,104**	**3**	**2**

STAND DOWN PARADE. And now, with the work of the Home Guard finished, we come to December 3rd, 1944, when, in common with the rest of the country, we held our Stand Down Parade. We fell in, as on that eventful day of May 26th, 1940, at the rear of the Drill Hall, and memories of the old L.D.V. members went back to that first parade. Led by the Despatch Riders and the Battalion Band, as was customary on all our parades, we marched to the Market Square for the final dismissal. Despite the inclemency of the weather, in keeping with the occasion, there was an extremely good turn-out, over 900 being on parade. The salute was taken by Colonel Lester Reid, in the presence of the Mayor, members of the Corporation, and leading citizens of the town. After short addresses by Colonel Reid and myself the final dismiss was given, and for all practical purposes the 12th Battalion had ended. We were very pleased to have with us on this parade a contingent from the Open Cadet Company, the future Home Guard, who lined the Market Square.

While our own Stand Down was being held in Northampton, the final Stand Down Parade of the National Home Guard was being held in London, at which representatives from every Battalion in the British Isles were present. The 12th Battalion was represented by

Lance-Corporal A. G. Tew (B Company).

Corporal H. H. Barrett (C Company).

Corporal G. Marshall (H Company).

In the evening, by kind invitation of the Northampton Brewery Company, a farewell concert was given by the N.B.C. artistes to the members and wives of the 12th and 15th Battalions at the New Theatre. At the conclusion the Mayor, Councillor S. Strickland, on behalf of the citizens of the Borough, thanked the Home Guard for their work during the four and a half years. The broadcast of H.M. The King to the Home Guard, relayed in the theatre, brought a memorable if sad day to its close.

Only once more did the Home Guard appear in uniform. On Sunday, May 13th, 1945, almost five years to the day from the date of its inception, the 12th Battalion took its place in the Victory Parade and Service in Abington Park, along with other Service units and the Civil Defence Services.

Although the 12th Battalion is no more, I am hopeful that the spirit of the Home Guard will still go on by means of the Old Comrades' Associations, and that once a year for some years to come we shall all meet together again at a Drumhead Service which we hope to arrange each year in the month of May, which month in 1940 saw the birth of the L.D.V.

CHAPTER SIX

WEAPON TRAINING

" In present-day warfare you do not see your enemy until some 30 seconds before you deal with him, and he never sees you at all if you have been properly trained."

A LL training can be boiled down into two categories:—
    (1)   Weapon Training.
    (2)   Tactical Training.
The first thing is to know your weapon and to be able to use it effectively, and the second is to be able to manoeuvre so that you can take up a position where you can use it to the best effect.

In the early L.D.V. days we were especially indebted to Lieut.-Colonel A. St. G. Coldwell and his staff at the I.T.C. for the great assistance they gave us in the matter of training. Most of us were extremely " rusty," having forgotten most of our military training from the days of 1914-18. Courses for officers and N.C.O.'s were arranged at the Barracks and were greatly appreciated by all who attended. After the Summer and Autumn months of 1940, when by some happy chance no invasion had taken place, we were allowed a breathing space from the duties of observational patrols. The Winter was employed in intensive training, and in the forefront was weapon training so that every man had a knowledge of his weapon. Those who had the misfortune to listen to my lectures in those days will remember how I always stressed the importance of this. It was no good having weapons—and by this time we had a considerable number—and it was no good getting into an excellent firing position if, when you had got there, you could not be certain of hitting the enemy at a range up to 200 yards. And therefore, in that first Winter we concentrated on the weapons, chiefly the rifle and the Lewis Gun, and later as new weapons were issued we still kept the importance of " knowing your weapon " in the foreground.

THE RIFLE

This was our basic weapon. and the one most familiar to the old soldier of the Great War. There was no lack of instructors on the rifle, for many in the Battalion had been instructors in the last War and with a little rubbing up and a little consulting of the official handbooks they soon became proficient again and were acting as mentors to the younger members.

In those early days we had a few rifles, mainly the Ross, for in Battalion Orders of June 24th, 1940, appears the following: " Two of each patrol, who should be trained men and not cyclists, should carry rifles with ten rounds to each. Rifles should not be loaded unless the enemy is actually in sight. On an alarm, the remaining rifles and ammunition will be issued to the trained men of the Company. Those to carry arms will be detailed previously." It was important in those days when arms were short that the rifles should be in the hands of men who could use them effectively. Shortly after, on the arrival of the Springfield rifles from the U.S.A. with their different ammunition, the Ross rifles were withdrawn. The American rifles with their familiar red bands we retained until the Stand Down. Unfortunately, most of these rifles arrived without slings and pull-throughs. All were eager to fire these rifles on the range, and the first record I can find is that the first range practice took place at Sywell on October 6th, 1940. Later on, this range was allotted to other Battalions of the Home Guard and most of our firing was carried on at Brington. Every available opportunity was taken to use the range, but owing to various circumstances we could not carry out as much practice as we should have liked. There was sometimes the difficulty of sufficient ammunition—a sufficient quantity had always to be kept in case of it being needed for operations; while the greatest trouble was the small allotment for the use of the range we received, for it had to be shared with several other Home Guard Battalions. However, good work was put in, and towards the finish of our career I venture to say very modestly that there were few Home Guard Battalions who had reached a standard of efficiency such as we had attained. By this I am not taking into account the result of competitions, for generally speaking I am opposed to these, especially in an organisation like the Home Guard, for the range is then used by the dozen or so good shots to the detriment of the rest of the Battalion who, when all is said and done, have to use their rifles in an emergency as well as the marksmen. Towards the end of our existence, marksmen's badges were instituted, and in the short time available a good number of the Battalion qualified.

Since the Stand Down, interest has been maintained in shooting by the formation of the 12th Battalion Rifle Club. This owes its inception and its success chiefly to the enthusiasm of Mr. A. J. Smart, who has put in much hard work to get it on a firm working basis. It has 150 members, who regularly use the miniature range at the Drill Hall, and on occasions journey out to Brington to keep their eye in on the open range.

THE STEN

In May, 1941, the Thomson machine-gun made its appearance and on the 31st of this month we were in possession of two of these weapons. One was kept at Battalion H.Q. for instructional purposes and the other was issued to A Company, which in those days was the largest Company. By the end of this year we had been issued with 45 of these weapons, and these had been allotted to the Companies in proportion to their strength. In September, 1942, these were withdrawn and replaced by the Sten. This was not so finished a weapon as the Thomson, but it had the advantage that it was cheap, costing round about 25/-, and the greater advantage that it could be produced in large numbers. Our first allotment was 521, and this, together with the other weapons, gave us what we had always wanted, a weapon per man. Other issues were made until in June, 1943, before the split in the Battalion, we had 1,059 Stens on our charge. For street fighting this was an ideal weapon as it gave a high and accurate rate of fire over short distances, and was easily carried over walls and debris. With a large amount of captured Italian ammunition, which fitted the Sten, range practices were soon started, first at Wootton and then at the R.E.M.E. range at Far Cotton. This latter was extremely convenient for us as in the Summer months much good practice could be carried out in the evenings. We were extremely indebted to Major Parsons, O.C. of the R.E.M.E. workshops, for his kindness in loaning us the range, and for his great assistance on all occasions when we approached him to render us some little service. It would perhaps not be out of place here to thank most cordially all those of the Regular Services with whom we came into contact. Nothing they could do to help us in any way was too much trouble for them, and the liaison in this town, at any rate, between the Regulars and the Home Guard was complete and always most cordial. Reverting back to the R.E.M.E. range, we were extremely fortunate that we were able to keep this more or less

" secret," so that other Battalions did not want an allotment and therefore we were able to use it on every occasion on which we required it.

We were fortunate in the Battalion to have such an excellent band of weapon training officers, men who knew their job and were full of enthusiasm, and to them is due most of the credit for the high state of weapon training efficiency in the Battalion.

Battalion W.T.O.:   Captain V. J. H. Harris.
A Company: Lieutenant F. S. Britten.
B Company: Lieutenant B. S. Woolnough (transferred later to 2001 M.T. Company).
                    Lieutenant F. A. Allen.
C Company: Lieutenant W. Andrews.
D Company: Lieutenant H. H. Howard.

THE SMITH GUN

In 1942, with the formation of G Company, the Sub-District Mobile Reserve, we saw the first of the Smith guns, a sub-artillery weapon, which had the added advantage, so it was said, of being mobile. How it was mobile, except by man-handling, was never stated by the Higher Authorities. The towing of these guns over long distances was only solved by the enthusiasm and goodwill of the members of the Company possessing cars. We pressed repeatedly for the provision of 15-cwt. trucks to tow the guns and to carry the crew and the spare ammunition, but nothing transpired. In the meantime, Lieutenant V. B. Allinson, the Transport Officer of the Company, had many a headache as to how he was to get these guns out into the county, perhaps a distance of 20 or 30 miles. However, we always achieved the impossible in the Home Guard, and by fitting tow-bars on the back of private cars the difficulty was to some extent overcome. Cars, nevertheless, were not designed for the towing of these heavy guns for some 50 miles on a return journey, and there was much damage to clutch and the tyres of the cars, for which the owners received no compensation. It was just one of those things suffered and endured by the Home Guard. When later the 2-pounder anti-tank gun was issued, the problem of its towing was never solved. In 1944, with the issue of more Smith guns, a Battery was formed in H Company by the Engineering Cadets at the Technical College. As the officers of H Company were not so fortunate in the possession of cars as their colleagues in G, this Battery would have had to have been man-handled round the town. With the alteration of the role of the Home Guard in the later stages of the War to that of a more mobile character, one could not help thinking that the towing of these weapons about the countryside had not been given sufficient thought by the Higher Authorities, but that they relied as usual on improvisation by the Home Guard.

THE SPIGOT MORTAR

This was the sub-artillery weapon that found most favour with the Home Guard, and there is no doubt that had enemy action occurred in this country that it would have been most effective and wrought much havoc among both enemy tanks and personnel. All those who witnessed the first demonstration with live ammunition of the Spigot mortar in this district, at Yeldon Range on April 6th, 1942, were much impressed with the possibilities of this weapon. They were first issued to us in May, 1942, and at once became a popular weapon. Our old friend S.M. Collier started the ball rolling by attending a Course and then holding classes at the Drill Hall, and very soon we had a body of N.C.O.'s proficient on the gun. The first practices with inert ammunition were carried out on the Brington Range and later in a field near Clifford Hill, on August 13th, 1942. Afterwards, with the construction of the concrete bases, the main range was the field near St. Peter's Bridge, and here most of the Spigot teams fired the inert. In the meantime, positions had been sited for all the Defended Localities and bases constructed, so that at these sites there was an all-round fire on all the approaches to the positions. In connection with the Spigot there was one incident that might have led to a serious accident, but fortunately the luck of the 12th held and no serious result occurred. On June 10th, 1943, a Spigot team were practising on the grounds of the Town and County School when by some mischance an inert bomb found its way into the dummies. When the gun was fired, to the dismay of the firer, and probably more to the corporal in charge, the inert sped on its way in the direction of Cranmere Avenue. The Battalion I.O., who resides in this select neighbourhood, had the shock of his life when he saw the bomb pass by his front bedroom. Missing the houses, it crashed into a fence and came to rest farther down the Avenue, which luckily was deserted at the time so that the only casualty was the fence, which was considerably damaged. By a whip-round among the members of the Platoon this was repaired, and nothing more was heard of the incident, which might have had serious consequences had it occurred some time earlier when several children were at play in the Avenue.

In June, 1944, with the Home Guard assuming a more mobile role, Spigots were " trooped " to render assistance to infantry with enemy brought to bay.

It was not easy to arrange for live ammunition to be fired from this gun as the danger area of the burst was 400 yards, and there were no places round Northampton that gave this margin of safety. However, one firing practice was arranged, and this took place on August 27th, 1944, at the Harlington Range, near Dunstable. At the same time the opportunity was taken to practice the Smith gun teams of D, G and H Companies, both in direct and indirect fire. Altogether 28 Spigot and 22 Smith gun teams had their first and only firing with live ammunition. It was a most interesting day and was thoroughly enjoyed by all those who participated.

BOMBING

In the very early days it was a case of improvisation, for there was no time to wait until the official issues came along. Molotoff Cocktails were the order of the day. Our particular brand was made of beer bottles filled with benzine, etc., from the local Gas Works, with a piece of oily flannelette screwed in the stopper. These we threw with great gusto at various places on the outskirts of the town, Hunsbury Hill, the tip on the Weedon Road, and how we dreamt of the firing of the first enemy tank that appeared round Northampton! Later on, the self-igniting phosphorus bottles were issued and were a great improvement on our early efforts of improvisation. No lighters or matches were now necessary, for with the cracking of the glass the phosphorus did the necessary ignition. The Molotov Cocktail, later the A.W. bomb, received an increased prestige by the news that at least three of the enemy tanks which had penetrated into the perimeter of the Tobruk defence were destroyed by these missiles. The chief difficulty with these S.I.P.'s was the storage. Nobody cared for this part of the business, for anywhere near private dwellings they were a menace, especially in the case of aerial bombing. Consequently many of them were buried in the fields adjacent to the road blocks, while some were stored in the lake at Franklin's Gardens. It was not until the building of elephant shelters in isolated positions round the town that the wrinkles disappeared from the brows of worried Company and Platoon Commanders. Incidentally, after the Stand Down, their disposal presented a problem. At this time we had over 5,000 of these bottles distributed round the town, and Battalions were ordered to destroy these, preferably in some sandy place: where this was to be found near the town the instructions did not say. Naturally, I had to decline responsibility for their destruction, and they were finally put an end to by Regular R.E.'s in an old quarry near Towcester.

In 1941 Major Northover had invented his projector, which enabled the bottles to be fired up to a distance of 200 yards. Although a weapon of the Heath Robinson character it certainly did its job, and gave added interest to Home Guard training, and before long Northover teams were in full training. On August 20th, 1941, we arranged the first demonstration for officers and N.C.O.'s at the old quarry at Buttocks Booth, and the weapon met with the approval of the great majority of the spectators. When later it was found that the Northover was also able to fire the Mills grenade and the 68 anti-tank grenade, its value was greatly enhanced. By December, 1941, we had 35 Northovers, which gave us two or three per road block.

Reverting back to the early days of improvisation, many of us returned from Courses at Osterley Park and Denbies with various "recipes" for home-made bombs in our notebooks, given us by Major Vernon, who I learn at the General Election was returned as M.P. for one of the London boroughs. Inspired with enthusiasm, some of us set to work, first by procuring the necessary ingredients by sundry ways and means, and then in our sculleries endeavouring to mix and mould these into the familiar jam-tin bomb, reminiscent of 1914 days. Sergeant E. Martin, of D Company, who had also been to Osterley, and myself experimented at the Cedos Works, of which he was the proprietor, and evolved several weird-looking objects that we hoped would achieve their purpose. If the Town Authorities ever found some unaccountable holes in the roadway at the rear of Mill Lane, we now plead guilty that they were made by our experiments with our 1940 improvised grenades. Although these improvisations would no doubt have been better than nothing, the manufacture of any quantity was far beyond our capabilities, and it was not until some time later that we had an issue of grenades capable of dealing with enemy tanks.

However, in 1941, despite the needs of the Regular Army, that excellent stand-by of the infantryman of the last War started to arrive, the Mills or 36 grenade. Although many other types of bombs have been made since, most bombers still swear by the Mills as the best and safest of all bombs. In February we had enough for twelve per road block, but none to spare for practice throwing. In July, 1941, courses in bombing were conducted by the I.T.C. and eight officers and N.C.O.'s qualified and received certificates of efficiency with authority to conduct range practices. More Mills' appeared and it was possible to commence a little live bombing at Hunsbury Hill.

New types of grenades began to make their appearance, grenades containing lyddite, gelignite, nitro-glycerine and other powerful explosives; these aroused the interest of the Home Guard, especially when the success of the Australians with the Sticky bomb in Libya became known. Major Baxter, Lieutenant Sheldon, Sergeant Cox and myself went off one week-end to Kempston Barracks on a bombing course to master all the intricacies of the new types, the 68, the 73, the Sticky, the Bakelite. etc. On our return, lectures and courses were arranged, when the working of the new bombs was explained, and later demonstrations were held at Hunsbury Hill, where the effectiveness of the various kinds were shown. Unfortunately the supply of these bombs, particularly the Sticky, was never liberal enough to allow of many using them, and therefore demonstrations were the only alternative, which was perhaps just as well for with many of these grenades it was almost as dangerous to give as to receive. One of the troubles in those days before the new bombs had been perfected was the number of "blinds" that we had. All these had to be destroyed before we left the range, to avoid any accidents to children from Far Cotton who, directly we had finished bombing, used to swarm over the cutting for " souvenirs." We should never have forgiven ourselves had one of these youngsters been killed or maimed by an unexploded bomb. This was not always easy, for in those days we had no demolition sets, and often " blinds " had to be destroyed by rifle or revolver fire. In only one case was an unexploded bomb left on the range. This was a Mills fired from a cup-discharger. Sergeant White and myself spent a most miserable Sunday afternoon in the rain endeavouring to find this, but our efforts were unavailing. We therefore flagged the area with red flags, indicating danger, but on our visit the next morning all the flags had disappeared. R.E.'s with a mine-detector were procured and in a few minutes the bomb, buried in some six inches of earth, was discovered and destroyed.

In looking through old Orders I find constant reference to, and warnings of, the care with which these grenades should be handled, and naming accidents, many of them fatal, that had occurred to Home Guards in different parts of the country who had neglected safety precautions. Fortunately, apart from one or two very minor incidents, we had no casualties in the 12th Battalion, despite the fact that thousands of bombs of all types were thrown, although on one occasion only the presence of mind of Major Barton averted what might have been a serious accident. There is always a certain amount of risk with bombing, however careful one may be, and here I should like to pay a tribute to my friend, Sergeant Harry White, who was my right-hand man on all the occasions on which we gave demonstrations. To his watchful eye and his vigilance most of the freedom from accidents was due. It is rather interesting how we became acquainted. In 1941 when visiting the O.P.'s on my cycle I came to the conclusion that if anything happened I was not much use on my own, and therefore I asked No. 11 Platoon, who were stationed nearest to my house, to provide me with a cyclist runner, and Harry White volunteered. From that day to the Stand Down he was my constant companion on Home Guard duties, accompanying me on all my visits to the posts during the nights and at dawn, and he probably got to know me better than anyone else in the Battalion. As time went on I managed to instil into him some of my enthusiasm for bombing, and before long he was the keenest bomber. He was the most faithful companion that anyone could desire, and our comradeship will always be to me a lasting memory of Home Guard days.

With all the types of grenades, with the exception of one, we felt perfectly safe. This exception was the 68, fired from the cup-discharger. Throughout the country there were many fatal accidents with these, not always, I am sure, due to the official explanation that the firer had placed the grenade in the discharger the wrong way round. In any case, many prematures occurred, and as the firer was not alive to tell the tale the reason for them was never found. Although White and I fired some hundreds of these 68's we always sighed a sigh of relief when the grenade left the discharger successfully.

I must relate one amusing incident that occurred in those days of 1941 soon after the issue of the E.Y. rifle and the cup-discharger. I was on the County Ground with C Company to demonstrate the new weapon, using dummy grenades for the purpose. We took up our position near the Ladies' Stand and fired first with the gas-regulator fully open. The grenade travelled some 80 yards; then with the regulator half-closed we reached a distance of some 150 yards. At this point some inquisitive member of the Company inquired how far the grenade would go if the regulator was fully closed. Always willing to oblige, we proceeded to demonstrate. The bomb was placed in the discharger, and a ballistite cartridge in the chamber, and the trigger pressed. To our surprise the grenade sailed through the air at a tremendous height, clearing the Football Stand at the other end of the ground and finally came to rest in a garden of a house in Abington Avenue; the biggest hit ever made on the County Ground. Fortunately no damage was done, and the efficiency of the weapon was certainly proved to all the onlookers. Incidentally, to settle all arguments as to the meaning of E.Y., it stands for the initials of Edgar Yule, the inventor of the cup-discharger in the last War.

Sergeant Banks in his most interesting book, " Jordan's Lot," relates another amusing incident that occurred with A Company at Cedar Road School. I quote from the book:—

" This story concerns one evening in Cedar Road School when Major (as he then was) Barnes was giving a lecture on explosives. Picking up a cylindrical packet of dynamite the lecturer mentioned, en passant, that this horribly dangerous and powerful explosive became doubly lethal in frosty weather, under which conditions it became liable to be set off by mere friction. It was at this point that it dawned upon the horrified mind of at least one of the listeners to this able discourse that there was deep snow outside, accompanied by at least ten degrees of frost. Home in these circumstances had never seemed so sweet."

Most of this is quite correct. Dynamite is peculiarly susceptible to frost. What he did not notice was that on my arrival I had carefully placed the explosives on the hot-water radiator in order to avoid any mishap. I always knew that if anything did happen, I should be the first to go through the roof!

On August 4th and 5th, 1942, I was able to repay the I.T.C. in some small measure for their many kindnesses to us. On these days I conducted a short bombing course for the Regular Instructors at the Barracks with a demonstration on Hunsbury Hill of all the latest types of grenades. On this occasion the bombs behaved themselves very nicely, and if I remember correctly we had a 100 per cent. detonation. Later on, bombing demonstrations were also given to the Army Cadets, both the Technical College and the Open Companies.

In 1944 a new type of grenade arrived, the 75 or anti-tank bomb. This had been used with great effect both in North Africa and Italy. When G and F Companies were in Camp at Overstone Park we carried out experiments to ascertain the effectiveness of this newcomer. Various logs and dead trees were " operated " upon with great success.

In addition, the 69 or bakelite bomb had also been issued, and these were thrown in the park, all of which went to the making of a very pleasant Sunday afternoon.

In the Summer of 1944, with the advent of a new Commander of the I.T.C., we received Standing Orders for the Bombing Range at Hunsbury Hill. These specifically stated that it was only to be used for the throwing of the Mills, and no other bomb was to be used on the range. This struck me as rather amusing, after we had used it for every type of grenade for four years. Still, in those days we did not do things by the book or the Home Guard would never have got anywhere. The Home Guard, being unpaid soldiers, were a law unto themselves!

The bombs at Overstone Park were the last thrown in the Battalion. We had derived much pleasure during the War year from our practices with the various types of grenades and we feel certain that the Battalion was as " bomb conscious " as most others in the Home Guard.

OTHER WEAPONS

In the early days, in the absence of a really effective weapon to stop the enemy tanks, many and varied were the suggestions offered, and many the contrivances to be used. One of these Heath Robinson contraptions was the Harvey flame-thrower, and in 1941 we were given twelve of these weapons, one per road block. Various of our officers attended demonstrations of this weapon and all came away with the same conclusion, that they were better than nothing. They were difficult to move and to conceal, their range was limited, the area of their effectiveness small, and the period of the flame was only some 25 seconds. In addition they were certainly a " one shot " weapon, and the manipulators would most decidedly have been a suicide squad. So altogether we were not enamoured with the Harvey. Our twelve were stored in the Goods Yard of the L.M.S. Station, and here they peacefully reposed until their withdrawal in 1943. Whatever may have been their value in the early days, with the advent of the Spigot they became completely out of date.

THE PIKE

No history of the Home Guard would be complete without a reference to this prehistoric weapon. In 1941 a bundle of these arms arrived at the Drill Hall. They were really bayonets fixed on the end of steel tubing, and would no doubt have been effective in the 'dark and at close quarters. We did not desire the 12th Battalion to be an object of ridicule, and we felt that the morale and prestige of the Home Guard would be lowered by their issue to the men, and so while they were with us they remained in a corner of the Drill Hall and only saw the light of day when they were carried on the Fourth Anniversary, and then only to show the progress that had been made. in the arming of the Home Guard.

UNARMED COMBAT

Although strictly speaking this branch of our activities cannot be called weapon training, yet I felt that this Chapter could not be closed without some reference to this most delightful pastime. I am reminded of a drawing that appeared in " Punch " of a Home Guard sergeant instructing his platoon, saying: " In 1940 when we had no weapons we taught you weapon training. Now in 1943 when we have the weapons we are going to teach you unarmed combat." Anyway, it was a most popular form of training and the vacancies allotted to us at the Week-end School at Dunstable were always readily taken up and there was usually a waiting list. Members of the Battalion who attended these Courses used to come back " black and blue," but all agreed that they had had a real good time.

The Unarmed Combat Display at our Anniversaries were always one of the " star items," and as a result of the demonstration in 1943 we were asked by Lieut.-Colonel J. P. Jeffery, C.R.E., No. 13 G.H.Q. Troops,' if we would organise a week-end course for the instruction of selected R.E. officers and other ranks in Unarmed Combat at Whittlebury. I felt that this was a signal honour for the 12th Battalion and we readily accepted.

The following were those selected for this honour:—

Second-Lieutenant G. T. Whitsey (C Company).
Sergeant R. Freeman (A Company).
Sergeant R. N. Saunders (A Company).
Corporal N. J. R. Martin (B Company).
Lance-Corporal H. W. Crask (B Company).
Corporal J B. Richards (E Company).
Lance-Corporal J. J. Marlow (E Company).

This letter was afterwards received from Lieut.-Colonel Jeffery: "I was extremely sorry that my visit to the Home Forces prevented me seeing the Course you so kindly arranged for us in Unarmed Combat. I have heard the highest appreciation, however, of what your people did. May I thank you most sincerely for what you have done in the matter, and will you please convey to all concerned my appreciation of their excellent work."

COURSES

From the L.D.V. days there was always the greatest keenness among the members of the 12th to improve their military knowledge by attending Courses whenever and wherever they might be held. In the first few months many members at their own expense attended the Course at Osterley Park, which was the forerunner of all Home Guard Courses. Others unable to get away availed themselves of the Instruction at the I.T.C. Upwards of 400 officers, N.C.O.'s and men attended Courses of Instruction during our existence, and considering the difficulties this involved, especially in the arrangement of time off from their civilian occupations, it reflects the greatest credit upon them for their enthusiasm. Among the many Courses attended by members of the Battalion were the following:—

Osterley Park.	I.T.C., Northampton.
Denbies H.G. School.	Army School of Chemical Warfare.
H.G. Gas School, Chorley Wood.	E.C.D. School, Welwyn.
W.T. School, Dorking.	Bomb Disposal School, Ripon.
Sub-District Camouflage School.	Sub-District Signal School.
A.O., Saffron Walden.	Fieldcraft School, Burwash.
W.T. School, Amwell.	School of Signals, Catterick.
E.C.D. Intelligence School.	Unarmed Combat Courses, Dunstable.
Bombing Course, Kempston.	Travelling Wings from Denbies.

G.H.Q. Town Fighting Wings at West Ham and Birmingham.

TRAINING FILMS

One valuable means of instruction in the Winter months was by means of films supplied by the War Office. These began to be shown to Companies in 1941. Most of them were of pre-war vintage and out of date. Such films as " Fighting Patrols," " Concealment from the Air," etc., often showed the horse-drawn company limber, with Company Commanders dashing about on horseback. As time went on, however, there was a great improvement and the films issued were right up to date. In 1942 a Security film, " Next of Kin," was in much demand and was shown to practically all Platoons.

By 1943 and 1944 there was a wide range of films from which choice could be made, dealing with Battle Drill, Gas, Camouflage, Street Fighting, Locating the Enemy, etc. A common fault in the Battalion was to attempt too much in one night. This was understandable as the operators and the machines were in great demand, and Platoons naturally desired to see as many films as possible while they had the opportunity. However, there was no doubt that better value could have been obtained by tackling one film at a time, first showing it, then discussing the points raised, and finally running it through again.

The films created much interest and there was always a full attendance on the evenings when these were shown. They were admittedly of the greatest value in the training; in fact, they were the manuals brought to life, and we were much indebted to the Army Kinema Section, and particularly to Lance-Corporal O'Sullivan, of the A.T.S., for their ready co-operation in showing the films to the various Companies and Platoons throughout the Battalion.

CHAPTER SEVEN

THE HOME GUARD AND THE CIVIL DEFENCE

A S stated in a previous Chapter, on the inception of the L.D.V. it was very desirable that the existing A.R.P. organisation, which had been so carefully built up since 1938, should not be dislocated by the enrolment in the new force of members of the Civil Defence. The latter had a big advantage over the L.D.V. in the fact that it was formed in peace time, with plenty of time to think out the best organisation and to find the best man for each particular job. The organisation was there before members joined up. With the L.D.V. formed as it was in almost a panic, things were entirely different. The movement had to get going at once, there was no time to think out elaborate plans; speed was essential. In addition, the members were then enrolled at the Police Station, over 2,000 of them, before there was any organisation at all. In fact, when we joined up, no one had the slightest idea who was to be in charge and how we were to function. Although I had often as a lad seen Major T. E. Manning lead the County side on the cricket field, I had not the pleasure of his acquaintance. It was, therefore, something of a surprise when he appeared at the Bective School one sunny afternoon and desired me to act as his Second-in-Command. This was the first inkling we had of organisation. However, officers were soon appointed, and considering the haste with which these appointments were made it was surprising the very few misfits, there were. Full marks must be awarded to T.E.M. for his judgment in what had necessarily to be a very hurried selection.

But to return to the Civil Defence. Throughout our existence we were always anxious not to enrol any of their personnel, and this was strictly adhered to.

At the end of 1940, after the attack on Coventry, the following was issued to all Home Guard Battalions:—

" Recent technique of German night attack on towns has been to begin by dropping a very large number of incendiary bombs. Subsequent H.E. bombs frequently break water mains. Fires are then difficult to extinguish and, in addition to damage caused, the lighting up of the target area facilitates later attack. It is consequently of the greatest importance that incendiary bombs should be extinguished at the earliest possible moment after falling.

" The A.R.P. Services have, in certain places, found difficulty in coping with large numbers of incendiary bombs sufficiently quickly, and the Ministry of Home Security has asked for assistance from the Home Guard where local conditions make it desirable and practicable. The Commander-in-Chief, Home Forces, has decided that the Home Guard may be used for this purpose. The intention is that such employment would be temporary, to meet any emergency lasting for a matter of hours only. In the event of invasion they must assume their proper duties, which take priority over all others."

Other points mentioned in the Circular were that the early or incendiary phase of the attack occurred in the hours very soon after dark, that the central districts of large towns appear to be selected for the brunt of the attack, and that the aid given, to be effective, must be immediate before the incendiary bombs had time to set alight the building on or in which they had fallen.

In common with other large towns the Northampton Home Guard was asked to provide 300 men nightly for patrol duty in the centre of the town. The Commanding Officer felt that this number was far larger than it was reasonable to expect as, if this had been carried out, all other training would have had to be suspended. A compromise was effected and patrols totalling 100 men commenced duty on Monday, January 20th, 1941, from 7 to 9.30 p.m. each evening, in order to assist the Civil Defence until the latter could make adequate arrangements for the safety of the town. The following details were therefore carried out:—

Company	Area Patrolled	Assembly Places
A Company	Area from All Saints' Church and bounded by Kettering and Harborough Roads.	(1) Premises of B B. Vos and Son, corner of Newland and Campbell Square. (2) Nelson Hall. (3) Drill Hall, Clare St.
B Company	Area from All Saints' Church and bounded by Derngate and Bedford—St. James' Road.	(Late) Warwick Arms, Bridge Street.
C Company	Area from All Saints' Church and bounded by Kettering and Bedford Roads.	(Late) Lord Raglan Inn, Raglan Street.
D Company	Area from All Saints' Church and bounded by St. James' Road and Harborough Road.	A.R.P. Shelter in Silver Street, by Covered Market.

The Home Guard started on these extra duties with enthusiasm, being only too willing to help the Civil Defence until they had put their house in order. In twos and threes every night in the black-out, one hundred Home Guards patrolled the centre of the town. It was a monotonous job and took us away from our real work, which was training in order to meet any enemy ground action. What this patrolling cost the Home Guard in liquid refreshment during this period cannot be calculated, but only estimated. As the nights went by, with apparently little happening to relieve them of this extra duty, there arose a spirit of restlessness among our members. It was all very well to give temporary assistance, but this looked like being permanent. At the outset we had promised the men that this duty would only last a short time, and here it was going on and on, without any prospect of finishing. Lieut.-Colonel T. E. Manning, with his finger on the pulse of the Battalion, sensed this restlessness and several times endeavoured to get relief. As is well known, Government Departments are not noted for the rapidity with which they move, and on February 10th, nearly three weeks after we had started the patrols, the only satisfaction we could get from the Civil Authorities was " that satisfactory progress was being made, and we are doing everything possible to complete the arrangements with all speed." We were informed that the Home Guard patrols could not be discontinued until the assurance of the Chief Constable was received that such patrols were no longer necessary. On this date the Chief Constable could not give this assurance, and so the Home Guard, " browned off," continued on its nightly weary way through the central streets of the town to help out the Civil Defence. No one knows better than myself, who was in close touch with him all the time, the very strenuous efforts made by Lieut.-Colonel Manning to get relief from what had become a most unpopular job and one which was rapidly spoiling the discipline in the Battalion. There was also our promise to the men to be considered, and we were extremely loath to let them down, despite the fact that all along we had acted in good faith, relying on the word of the Civil Authorities. A frequent complaint I received from many members when I visited them on their duties was that " this was not what they joined the Home Guard for, and while they were willing to help the Civil Defence in an emergency, to keep these patrols on for months was a bit too thick." The Colonel and myself had to go round some of the Platoons and almost plead with them to continue.

At the beginning of March, orders were also received for the re-manning of the Observation Posts. It was obviously impossible to carry this out together with the Incendiary Bomb Patrols without putting too big a strain upon the men who, after all, in addition to these duties were doing a full day's work, with some of them on overtime. And so Lieut.-Colonel Manning made a new approach to the Higher Authorities, and on April 14th, 1941, after a period of nearly three months duration, the Incendiary Patrols came to an end. Great was the relief of the Home Guard that once again it could get back to its proper job of training and observational duties.

Looking back, I feel that this was the most difficult period we experienced, and the only one I can remember when the Battalion showed signs of unrest. It was a great pity that this assistance, so wililngly given in the first place to the Civil Defence, should have terminated as it did, and it did not make for the better relations between the Home Guard and the Civil Defence for which we in the 12th were striving.

During our Observational Duties we were granted the use of the Police Boxes on the town boundaries, and each night a guard was placed on these. They enabled all Home Guards to keep in close contact with Headquarters, and had any incidents occurred, would have been the means of saving much valuable time, besides ensuring that no fifth columnists used them for subversive purposes.

In 1941 all Companies attended lectures and demonstrations at the Fire Station on the methods of dealing with incendiary bombs, and we were greatly indebted to Superintendent A. Spence for arranging these, which were of great assistance to the 12th Battalion and would have enabled us to render more skilful assistance had there been an attack on the town.

On July 15th, 1941, there occurred one of the few incidents which befell Northampton during the War, when a Stirling bomber crashed in the centre of the town. The bomber crew consisted of seven men; six baled out and were immediately picked up by the members of the Battalion on duty on their Observation Posts, while the pilot was later found killed in Kingsthorpe Recreation Ground. The bomber had evidently circled the town, for members of the crew were picked up in various place, by the Abington Mill Platoon near their post, by the post on the Northampton Golf Links, and by the post on the Boughton Green Road. The Commanding Officer, Lieut.-Colonel T. E. Manning, was out on his visit on this morning, and while he was at the Electric Light Works the Home Guard observer on the roof reported that he had seen a plane crash in the centre of the town, which had caused an explosion and that fires had started. Let me continue in the words of the report of Colonel Manning:—

" I quickly motored to the Guildhall and found a corner of All Saints' Church on fire and several other fires in the top end of Gold Street. Superintendent Afford was in charge and he agreed that members of the Home Guard would be of great service in assisting the Police to cordon the area affected.

" Within the next 15 minutes about 14 Home Guards arrived in uniform, and these, together with 12 men of the 259 Company, Pioneer Corps, who were billeted on the Market Square, were posted with Police at the various approaches.

"C.S.M. Cannell, of D Company, was early on the scene and was using a stirrup pump before the hoses were in action. He afterwards, with the help of another member of the Home Guard, collected several hundred rounds of S.S.A. which were scattered among the debris.

"About 6.30 hours a platoon of the Northamptonshire Regiment arrived under an officer from the I.T.C. and took over the guard on street approaches from the Home Guard. 1 left the scene at 07.45 hours."

The following is culled from the official report:—

"The engines of the plane were embedded in Gold Street and debris scattered about the streets in the vicinity. A 500 lbs. unexploded bomb was found about 75 yards up George Row. Later, when the Queen's Head public house was opened, another 500 lbs. unexploded bomb was found in the front bedroom. The situation was under complete control at 06.00 hours."

Here is an extract from a subsequent letter from the Chief Constable:—

"I know that you will understand already how much I appreciated the spontaneous services of the officers and men of the Home Guard in connection with the incident of the crashed bomber in Gold Street on July 15th, 1941, but on consideration I have come to the conclusion that it should be recorded that there is perfect understanding between your Headquarters and the Police, and that the services rendered on the arrival of the Home Guard were invaluable.

"The crowds were controlled, the traffic was by-passed without confusion, and with the splendid co-operation amongst the various services concerned the whole situation was in hand within three-quarters of an hour.

"Again thanking you, and with you your officers and men, for the splendid co-operation which I knew would be evident if ever the necessity arose.

Yours sincerely,

J. Williamson, Chief Constable."

This incident, small in itself in relation to the events of the War, only shows the spirit of the Home Guard, who were always willing to render any assistance they could at any time to their fellow citizens. Had more important incidents occurred, I am certain that the Home Guard would have been equally responsive.

On July 5th, 1942, the Eleanor Exercise was held, in which both the Home Guard and the Civil Defence took part. In another Chapter I have dealt with the Home Guard side, so that here I only wish to comment briefly on the co-operation or lack of it between the two organisations. This was the first exercise of this kind that had been held, and many valuable lessons were learnt. The comment of the Chief Umpire was that two battles were taking place in Northampton, the Military fighting one and the Civil Defence another. One cannot deny that this summing-up was quite justified, and led to the conclusion that much greater liaison was necessary between the two.

The difficulty on all exercises is to impart a realistic view to all those taking part. Unless this is done and people get into their heads that this is the real thing, then the exercise is bound to fail, and lessons, which are the object of all such practices, will not be learnt. This lack of realism was particularly noticeable at times. It should have been evident that with the "enemy" in a particular district, it was quite impossible for the Civil Defence to carry on there without the risk of losing all its personnel. That opens up the bigger question of a Civil Defence Home Guard, but of this more anon. Because of this lack of grasp of the real nature of the Exercise, various little incidents occurred which, minor in themselves, led to friction at the time and militated against the smooth working of operations. In this Eleanor scheme a situation had been carefully painted to show that

STEN GUN PRACTICE on the R.E.M.E. Range, Far Cotton.

(Photo: B. Bernstein)

Northampton on this Summer Sunday morning had been literally infested by the " enemy." Bearing this in mind all the time, and realising that speedy decisions would have to be taken and speedy actions carried out, far too much time was wasted on the elaborate inspection and careful scrutiny of identification cards when the person concerned was definitely known to the challenger. Although I was known personally to most of the Home Guard and A.R.P. personnel in the town, I was frequently met with the greeting, " Hallo, Major Barnes; where is your identification card? " This, of course, was quite unnecessary, and after showing it some twenty or thirty times one became a trifle fed-up. It was really fifth columnitis run wild, and in actual battle the constant delays occasioned might have been fatal.

On another occasion the Battalion Reserve Platoon was sent out by lorry to deal with an enemy attack that had been reported in the neighbourhood of the Castle Station. On their way post haste to deal wih this they were hailed by two special constables who, in their exuberance, insisted on examining the identification cards of the men. This was another case of lack of realism, for had these men really been the enemy, one shudders to think what would have happened to these two enthusiastic Specials! Fortunately the Platoon Commander was a man of resolution and drive who had a job to do, and like a good Home Guard he got on with it after a few outspoken words which one imagines were short and to the point.

During the course of the battle we at the Drill Hall were " gassed and bombed out," which necessitated removal to a new Headquarters. This had been foreseen, as in present-day warfare it is always as well to have an alternative headquarters in mind. Arrangements had accordingly been made in the week previous to move to the Police Station. Owing to a misunderstanding, for some twenty minutes we were kept waiting outside, with the result that at an important stage of the battle we were almost out of action.

These little incidents, trivial and amusing perhaps when looked back upon, were the cause at the time of ruffled feelings and showed the need for much closer liaison between all of us in the town. After this exercise we are pleased to record things improved very considerably and there was a much greater spirit of co-operation among the different services. This is the object of all exercises, viz, to test out paper schemes and to find out weaknesses so that they can be remedied. From this point of view the Eleanor Exercise must be written down as a success. Towards the end of 1943 arrangements were made for another Combined Exercise, but unfortunately this did not materialise; had it done so, I feel sure that the lessons of Eleanor would have been carried into effect.

In July, 1942, the assistance of the Home Guard to the Civil Defence was placed upon a clearer footing. In the event of a blitz of the town, the steps taken to deal with this were divided into two phases: Phase 1, immediate work requiring to be done, and Phase 2, the work to be accomplished on the day and days following. It was clear that the assistance of the Home Guard to the Civil Authorities would have to be given in Phase I so that there was no interference with their civil occupations, while the Regulars would have to be responsible for the Military assistance in Phase 2, which would probably last some days, according to the severity of the attack. The 12th Battalion was ordered to provide 150 men for Phase 1, with the stipulation that more could be called out to assist with the sanction of the Sub-District Commander, who, of course, would be in a position to weigh up the Military situation and also to know the number of Regular troops available to relieve the Home Guard. It was always important to bear in mind that the blitz might be accompanied by enemy action on the ground and that the first duty of the Home Guard was to fight. It was therefore unwise to employ large numbers on Civil Defence work if there was any likelihood of them being required for their real role. About this time I was appointed Senior Military Officer to co-ordinate the assistance of the Military to the Civil Defence. There was always the condition that the Home Guard should not be called upon until the resources of the Civil Defence had been exhausted. Regular units in the county, which of course varied from time to time, would have assisted in Phase 2 by order of the Sub-District Commander; Royal Engineers, who are technical troops, to help with broken gas and water mains, etc., infantry to aid in the clearing of roads of debris, etc.

Under these instructions, F Company of the Battalion became the Company responsible for this Home Guard assistance. Their area was in the centre of the town round about the Drill Hall and therefore they could have been mustered very quickly after the worst of the bombing was over. There was also an additional reason for the choice of this Company. Had enemy ground action followed, it would have been much more convenient to withdraw them from their Civil Defence work to the Keep, which was their battle position.

Training in Civil Defence work was arranged for this Company, and we were indebted to the A.R.P. personnel who gave us all possible assistance. The Company rapidly became efficient in its duties, and had it ever been called upon, there is no doubt, would have given a very good account of themselves.

I always felt that it was very desirous that the Home Guard, the A.R.P. and the Police should work together in the closest harmony, and soon after I took over the Battalion, at a Conference with the Chief Constable as A.R.P. Controller the whole matter of liaison between the three services was thrashed out. Since that time, October, 1942, we proceeded along the lines laid down, and there was never the slightest friction afterwards. The following arrangements were made then, and continued up to the time of the Stand Down:—

After severe bombing of the town,

(1) Battalion Headquarters would be opened, the Commanding Officer would proceed to A.R.P. Control and be in close liaison with the A.R.P. Controller.

(2) F Company would assemble.

(3) Company and Platoon Headquarters would be manned by the Commander, 1 N.C.O. and 2 orderlies.

(4) No action would be taken by Home Guards to assist the Civil Defence without permission of Battalion Headquarters.

In January, 1943, a memorandum was issued from the Higher Authorities setting forth concisely the relation of the Home Guard with the Civil Defence Services. The general policy laid down was as follows:—

(1) Under conditions of bombing, where there is no invasion imminent, the Civil Defence Services are of the highest importance and will frequently require help from the Home Guard.

(2) Under condition of invasion the Home Guard becomes of the highest importance and will require such help as can be given by Civil Defence personnel who are able to join the Home Guard and be adequately trained.

This was the policy laid down and we had fulfilled our part of the obligation by rendering all the assistance asked for by the Civil Defence. The strength of the Battalion at this time was round about 2,500, which seems a large number, but when it is spread over an area the size of Northampton it is very thin on the ground, and Company Commanders were very concerned at the duties they had to carry out with the number of men at their disposal. Our strength, too, was going down from week to week as more men were called up for the Regular Services. It was, therefore, with hope that we looked forward to an increase of numbers from the younger and more active members of the A.R.P. With the kind permission of the A.R.P. Controller and his deputy, Inspector Cookson, during the month of February, 1943, I addressed the members of the A.R.P. at five Divisional gatherings—Far Cotton, Kingsthorpe and Central Divisions on separate occasions at the Guildhall, the Abington Division at the Racecourse Pavilion, and St. James' Division at Spencer Schools. I felt very indebted to the Chief, Mr. J. Williamson, who took the chair at one or two of the Guildhall meetings. In my addresses I pointed out the role of the Home Guard, our organisation in the town, and how if there were sufficient volunteers I intended to form Civil Defence Home Guard Platoons in each of the five Divisions, commanded by their own officers. I stressed the fact that their work of Civil Defence must naturally come first, but in the event of their services not being required, or through enemy action they were unable to perform them, then they would be able to give a helping hand to the Home Guard. I felt that this gave an opportunity to those members of the A.R.P. who, through no fault of their own, had been unable to join up with us on our formation. Although at the meetings I felt that there were many who would have liked to have taken an active part in the defence of their homes and not stand idly by while the Home Guard did the fighting, I regret that the effort bore no fruit and the Civil Defence Home Guard did not materialise in Northampton.

Recently there has been published in the Press, Hitler's plans for the administration of this country after its conquest by the Germans. One cannot help feeling that death would have been preferable to the fate so kindly arranged for us. If invasion of this country had taken place, every one capable of bearing arms should have been in a position to play his part. Instead of which, all over the land many thousands of A.R.P. personnel might have had the sad experience of being able to do nothing while the Regulars and the Home Guard were overcome by the enemy.

And that brings us to a point for future consideration, which I am aware was quite impracticable in this War, with the A.R.P. in being before the Home Guard was even thought about. I firmly believe that should necessity arise again, it would be much better for the defence of this country if every able-bodied man was in one force, Home Guard or term it what you will, so that in time of bombing all can turn to and give a hand, while if an invasion occurs, all will be ready trained for the repelling of the invader.

Although we in Northampton were extremely fortunate in the fact that no air attack was made on the town, in other areas which were not so lucky, valuable assistance was rendered by the Home Guard to the Civil Defence. On July 7th, 1944, the following was received from Wing-Commander Sir John Hodsell, Inspector-General of the Civil Defence:—

"Your Home Guard have been giving us magnificent help during the present troubles with the flying bomb, and I should like to express to all of them our very warmest thanks and gratitude for what you are doing."

I am certain that had necessity arisen, the 12th Battalion would not have been behind their comrades in other parts of the country in their assistance to the Civil Defence.

In the early days of the War, when invasion appeared imminent, Invasion Committees were set up in all towns and villages for the purpose of dealing with the many problems which would have arisen had the enemy appeared in this country—food, water supply, billeting of the homeless, feeding centres, evacuation of civilians from dangerous areas, communications, etc. In common with other towns an Invasion Committee was appointed for Northampton with Alderman A. Lyne as Chairman, Councillor S. C. Adnitt and Councillor R. Smith representing the Corporation, the Town

Clerk (Mr. W. R. Kew), and the heads of the Municipal Departments. As the Military member of the Committee to keep liaison between the Civil and Military Services, I can witness to the excellent work done and the intricate preparations made for the welfare of the citizens in case of necessity. Many exercises were held, some of them involving all-night sittings at the A.R.P. Control. Although, fortunately, never called upon to test the measures that had been drawn up, there is no doubt that the Committee would have carried out its duties most efficiently. In September, 1944, the Home Secretary decided that Invasion Committees were no longer necessary, and consequently they were disbanded. In a farewell message he stated that "This has been an entirely new experiment. The organisation of the local Civil resources to meet the needs in invasion conditions of the local community and of the country's defence, and the creation of Committees and the enthusiasm and team spirit of the members, have been a fine example of demoncracy in action."

I cannot close this Chapter without expressing cordial thanks to the Police of Northampton, both Regulars and Specials, particularly to the Chief Constable and to Superintendent W. H. Afford. From the earliest days they have given all possible assistance, especially when we have had Battalion Parades. Their control of the traffic and the management of the crowds were always carried out in their usual efficient manner, which was greatly appreciated by us all. I always had the feeling that had enemy action taken place here, we should have worked side by side in the closest co-operation.

CHAPTER EIGHT

ROAD BLOCKS, VULNERABLE POINTS. ETC.

ROAD BLOCKS

AFTER the experience of France, where the enemy armoured columns were allowed to roam at will on the roads, and where not a single civilian thought of stopping the enemy tanks from obtaining petrol from the various wayside filling stations, the denial of the English highways to the enemy was deemed of paramount importance in 1940. In fact, in those days, apart from observation, the manning of the road blocks was the chief role of the L.D.V. And so there appeared on our roads at selected sites the most marvellous collection of old junk that has ever been seen. In practically the first instruction issued by Sir Hereward Wake, the County Commander, the following were suggested as suitable obstructions:—

> Logs of timber, gates, iron railings;
> Farm carts, wagons, lorries, old cars;
> Wire netting and pig netting;
> Wire to tie materials together.

It was reckoned that some of these which were too old for use could be assembled at once, and others should be located for use if required. One of the primary objects of the road blocks was to impose delay upon the enemy and put his time-table out of gear. A little delay here, a few minutes delay there, and we hoped that his plans would be upset. It was evident that the majority of these blocks would have been of little practical use against enemy tanks, but if they had been ineffective against these, they would certainly have been a hindrance to light cars, despatch riders, etc. Besides, the L.D.V. were doing something which gave them confidence, a confidence that was shared by the general public, and a spirit of confidence was very necessary in those days. Knife-rests were also quickly made and assembled at the blocks. Later on the Ministry of Transport pointed out that a considerable number of accidents had been caused through remnants such as old motor-cars, carts, timber, etc., being left on the road verges and not being lighted at night. As the need for them had gone with the provision of other and better materials, these gradually disappeared from the countryside.

As a matter of fact, in Northamptonshire where the country is generally speaking of an undulating character, there are few defiles and cuttings suitable for road blocks, and most of them could easily have been by-passed by tanks. The only ones of real value were those which denied the passage of bridges to the enemy. Round Northampton we had the following road blocks in 1940:—

> Welford Road on the Borough Boundary.
> Harborough Road near the Cemetery.
> Boughton Green Road near the Reservoir.
> Kettering Road near Manfield Hospital.
> Buttocks Booth.
> Weston Favell near the Trumpet Inn.
> Billing Road near the Borough Boundary.
> St. Peter's Bridge.
> South Bridge.
> London Road by the Hardingstone turn.

Towcester Road near the Cemetery.
Rothersthorpe Road on the railway bridge.
Weedon Road near the Red Lion.
Dallington Road near Hopping Hill.
Dallington Road at Duston—Dallington crossroads.
Dallington Village.
Kingsthorpe railway bridge.

In addition, it was necessary to site railway blocks so that approach to the town could not be made by the railway lines, on the

Rugby and Market Harborough lines.
The London lines.
Blisworth and Wellingborough lines.

Most of these blocks were sited at railway bridges. It was decided also that E Company (the Railway Company) should arrange on emergency to demolish a portion of the bridge over the river in Becket's Park.

In the Summer of 1940 an improved road obstacle came into being in the form of steel rails which were fitted into specially made holes in the road. These, it was hoped, would be strong enough to withstand the enemy tanks. Here is the place, I am sure, to put on record the best thanks of the 12th Battalion to the Borough Engineer, Mr. R. A. Winfield, whose job it was to perform all the engineering jobs that we required doing, including the making of these holes in the road and the erection of the sandbag emplacements and trenches where the defenders would take cover. His cheery willingness to assist us on every occasion, and in every possible way whenever we called upon him, was greatly appreciated and we were much indebted to him for his ready co-operations during the years of our existence. With the appearance of these rails, practices were held on each of these positions, and the Home Guard felt more confident than ever of stopping enemy armoured fighting vehicles.

One suggestion for the further denial of road blocks to the enemy was by hanging two old motor tyres stuffed with sacking or rags and soaked in petrol on the rails. These could then be lit with an A.W. bomb and would burn furiously for some considerable time. The only drawback to this ingenious device was that it also denied the road to our own vehicles and therefore could only be used as a last resource. Still, I have no doubt that had the Hun appeared in our midst, this and other similar contrivances would have been used.

In the Summer of 1941 those familiar objects, the concrete cylinders, made their appearance and were deposited at each road block to supplement the steel rails and to prevent the tanks from having a clear rush at these obstacles. Two hundred and seventy-six had arrived by the beginning of August and on Sunday, August 31st, a practice closing of all the road blocks was held. Much difficulty was experienced in moving these heavy and unwieldy cylinders, which were not easy to get quickly into position, but by experience we found that the provision of long iron bars which fitted through the centre rendered the work less laborious and speeded up the closing. In this first practice closing the average time taken to close the blocks was 40 minutes. The one at Boughton Green Road, a narrow road, was closed in 15 minutes, but the one at Buttocks Booth, which was really four blocks in one, took 90 minutes, while the one at South Bridge was not closed until after 72 minutes, as the cylinders had to be rolled up the slope.

The time to effect the closing caused concern; we should not be allowed anything like the average time taken, and although with practice this time was reduced, yet it was plain that a quicker method of closing must be found. The difficulty was overcome by closing most of the road with the steel rails and cylinders, leaving a sufficient gap for our own vehicles, which gap could speedily be closed on necessity.

There was always the vexed question, and this lasted the whole of our life, as to when the roads should be closed if enemy action occurred. If closed too early, our own vehicles would be handicapped; while if left too long, it might then be too late. We always maintained in this Battalion that the decision must be left to the man on the spot, and full discretionary powers were given to those in charge. It was evident that no general order for closing could be given from Battalion H.Q. beyond a warning that enemy A.F.V.'s were in the vicinity.

When all these road blocks were complete and their closing had been practised on various occasions, a bombshell was dropped in our midst in September, 1941, by the decision that Northampton was to be made into a " Nodal " point and that the existing road blocks were, in the majority of cases, too widely dispersed and presented plenty of opportunity for tanks to " jink " round them and so enter the town. A new plan, therefore, had to be drawn up, making Northampton into a tank-proof town.

As I have said in a previous Chapter, this necessitated the construction of Defended Localities within the town itself. No fewer than 14 of the original blocks had to be given up and only three were retained, the ones on the St. Peter's and South Bridges and the one at Weedon Road, which was still to be manned by the Express Lift Works Platoon.

New blocks had to be reconstructed in the Defended Localities, all cylinders moved to the new positions, while some hundreds more were needed. Altogether, when the work was complete, we had 750 of these around the town. Once again the Borough Engineer was called upon and, despite the shortage of labour, the cylinders were soon moved. As time went on and the threat of a full-scale invasion receded, the road blocks lost their early importance, and although the cylinders were kept near to their positions they only served as a reminder to the population of what might have happened in those days of 1940-41.

VULNERABLE POINTS

It was clear that had invasion of this country taken place, some buildings, factories and works of national importance would have been among the first objectives of the Germans.

In all their invasions of foreign countries the Germans were not chiefly interested in the killing of soldiers, but their technique consisted mainly in destroying the nerves of the man or woman in the street. Among their efforts in this direction was the destruction of the means that affected the life of the inhabitants—water, light, railways, communications, etc. It was therefore essential that these should be denied to the enemy, and these were listed as vulnerable points.

Attacks on vulnerable points could take several different forms:—
(1) Destructive raid carried out by enemy troops landed from the air.
(2) Smash and grab raid carried out by enemy troops landed from the air.
(3) Armed sabotage. Carried out by small organised parties who might already be in the country.
(4) Petty sabotage by individual agents already in the country, who would rely more on cunning and stealth rather than force, and which might take the form of stealing documents or obtaining secret information.

Against all these forms of attack we had to be prepared. On some of these vulnerable points it was necessary to have continuous guards, while on others they were only needed on " Action Stations."

Denial of petrol was of paramount importance, especially as there were two Inland Distributing Depots in the town, one at Cotton End and the other in St. Andrew's Road. On " Action Stations " these had to be manned by personnel who were trained in the disruption and, at the last resort, demolition of these stores of petrol, which totalled some quarter of a million gallons. If the Depots appeared likely to fall into the hands of the enemy they were to be blown up, and this entailed the training of men in the use of explosives, together with the arrangement of the various detonators. A special squad of men from E Company were detailed for this particular job. The Chief Constable and the Police Force undertook the destruction of the petrol pumps situated in the different parts of the town.

In 1940 we had guards on the following Vulnerable Points:—

Northampton Electric Light Works.
Northampton Gas Works.
Post Office.
Express Lift Works.
Northampton Wireless Relay Station.
L.M.S. Railway Bridges, etc.
Northampton Transport Depot.
United Counties Omnibus Station.
Water Department—At Ravensthorpe.
> Main Pumping Station, Stimpson Avenue.
> Boughton Reservoir.
> Pumping Station, Billing Road.
B.B.C. Transmitter Station.
Various works on munitions in the town.

On a number of these it was not necessary to have a continuous night guard, for in some of the works men were working day and night shifts, and while work was being carried on there was no danger of sabotage; guards were only needed when the works and machinery were left unattended. On the railway the vulnerable points were not actually manned, but a nucleus of men were on duty at the Guard Room to proceed to any threatened point. In the case of the Wireless Relay, a guard of 1 N.C.O. and three men were to mount on "Action Stations," and the N.C.O. was empowered to give instructions to the staff to immobilise the station if it was in imminent danger of capture.

In addition a Guard was mounted at the Drill Hall when the Regulars were not in residence there; while there was an armoury guard over Platoon Headquarters each night where more than 30 rifles were kept.

No one who was on duty at the Sub-Ordnance Depot at Martin's Yard will ever forget the experience. The old D Company commenced this guard on November 25th, 1940, and on arrival found their quarters consisted of a hut with a cold concrete floor, very hard to attempt to sleep on, and with holes in the roof through which the wind whistled and the rain descended. Representations were made to the Ordnance Authorities at Weedon that it was unfair to ask men who had to work the next day to spend their nights in such a "guard room," and after a short lapse the roof was repaired, a coke fire was provided, the concrete floor covered with boards, and "beds" fitted. Things were certainly better, but never really became comfortable. Most of the Companies took their turn at Martin's Yard, a guard which was spasmodic, depending on the use of the huts by the Ordnance as an "overflow" from Weedon.

As the danger of invasion became less likely it was not considered necessary to maintain all these guards, and some of them were disbanded for the time being. However, round about D Day, with vigilance again becoming necessary, all vulnerable points were again manned.

Although nothing occurred during our existence, one of the objects of the Home Guard, to relieve the Regular troops from static guard duties, had been achieved.

CHAPTER NINE

THE FEEDING OF THE HOME GUARD, AND WEEK-END CAMPS

THE feeding of the Home Guard on " Action Stations " presented a problem which caused much thought. In the 12th Battalion we had an average strength of over 2,000, and if we had been called out, the feeding and cooking for this large number would have been no easy matter. It was obvious that all plans must be cut and dried beforehand. In the Regular Army, with its various branches, the R.A.S.C. act as the supply column for the Infantry. With the Home Guard this was quite impossible; we had in case of necessity both to fight and feed ourselves. It was clear that however perfect the plans made, it would take some little time after " Action Stations " for things to get into working order. Hence the instruction that each man when called up should bring with him sufficient rations for 24 hours, by which time it was hoped that food would have been drawn and Platoons be self-supporting. Each Platoon had been registered as a Catering Establishment with the Food Office and were entitled to draw food from the various grocers, butchers and bakers in their vicinity, who were required to keep stocks on hand for this emergency.

As cooking would have had to be done in the Defended Localities by the Platoons themselves, it was essential that each had at least one man who could cook. To this end, on November 1st, 1941, a course in cooking was arranged by the I.T.C. at the Talavera Barracks, and 25 members of the Battalion attended the week-end instruction. As time went on, and camps were arranged, the cooks got plenty of practice, and so well did they do their job that I had no misgivings on the score of feeding had we been called out. In some parts of England, particularly in the country districts where the strength of the Home Guard was low and where, consequently, men could not be spared for cooking, the W.V.S. took this upon their shoulders and on various exercises functioned very efficiently. D Company, I am sure, will never forget that night at Spratton on the Buzz Exercise when the ladies of the local W.V.S. toiled all through the night so that there was always a hot cup of tea or soup for those coming off or going on duty.

I am certain that had we called upon them, that the W.V.S. of Northampton, despite their other commitments, would have responded in a like manner. However, we took the view, rightly or wrongly, that, as the cooking for the Home Guard would have had to be done in the Defended Localities, which would probably have been in the centre of the fighting, it would have been unfair to ask the ladies to work in them. And so if enemy action had taken place, the 12th Battalion would have been fed by its own personnel.

In June, 1942, Emergency packs arrived at Headquarters. These contained rations for 10 men for 24 hours and were only to be used if no other food was available. We received sufficient to cover all the members of the Battalion. They were stored at the Drill Hall, and as they were never required, there they remained until after Stand Down. Did I say all? I regret to have to state that some were missing, but with Regular units in residence most of the War, the wonder was that so many remained.

The supply of cooking utensils was never satisfactory, and there is no doubt that the Home Guard would have been left to " improvise " as usual.

With the evacuation of the civilian population from the Defended Localities, this would have presented little difficulty to those ingenious persons, the cooks.

In April, 1943, we were informed that in order to surmount any difficulties that might be experienced on mustering, arrangements had been made for an issue of biscuits on the basis of 3 lbs. per man. These were to be kept at Buffer Depots until such time as required.

Having seen that all the Companies and Platoons had been properly catered for, we thought that it was time that we considered ourselves at Battalion Headquarters. A party of A.T.S., 1 N.C.O. and 7 privates, were allotted to us in case of emergency, to be employed as typists, orderlies and cooks. I feel sure that we should have been in good hands.

The matter of water also received especial attention. It was probable that had enemy action occurred around Northampton it would have been accompanied by a blitz of the town. In such an event there was always the possibility of the destruction of the water mains and the consequent cutting off of the supply. The Guides, under Lieutenant C. S. Catlow, got to work, and it was really surprising the information that they collected. Pumps, wells and springs were located round the outskirts of the town, and even had the water supply failed, each Platoon knew where it could obtain a supply of water pure and fit for drinking. This was only part of the duties of the Guides, and the wealth of material they accumulated was amazing.

Nothing was left to chance, and in February, 1942, we received sterilising powder and detasting tablets, which would have made any emergency water supply fit for use on operations.

By the middle of 1942 we felt that the question of food and water had been properly " tied up " and that had the need arisen the 12th Battalion would have been adequately fed and watered.

WEEK-END CAMPS

In 1942 camps for the Home Guard were sanctioned b ythe War Office. In order not to interfere with the civilian occupations of its members, it was obvious that these could only be of the week-end variety, except for those held at holiday times. The problem of siting camps is always the difficulty of water. There were many spots suitable but, alas, the water supply was not available. Eventually two sites were taken over, one at Overstone Park and the other at Gawburrow Hill, Great Brington. The first was used mainly by A Company, and the second by G Company, while E Company had made arrangements with the L.M.S. for their accommodation at Althorp Park Station. All these camps went very well and there was always a full attendance. Evidently all camps were not run as well as those of the 12th, for in August, 1942, the Sub-District Commander called attention of Battalion Commanders to the fact that at some camps no work was done on the Saturday, and very little on the Sunday, and stressed that some camps seemed to be held more for the enjoyment of being in camp than for doing any worthwhile work. The Commander also that that he was disappointed to find that in a number of camps the cooking was done by outside arrangement, the excuse being that the men should be really well fed, and the Company Commander could not trust the men available to do this. We in the 12th, as regards training, always tried to strike the happy medium by working hard while we were at it and then thoroughly enjoying ourselves afterwards. Training programmes were drawn up and, whatever the state of the weather, were strictly adhered to, always bearing in mind that if the Hun came he would not stop attacking if it rained, and that we had really got to get hardened to all conditions. After the training was over on the Saturday evening, members wended their way to the canteen, where a thoughtful caterer had provided some of the liquid which always seemed so necessary to the Home Guard. Here various games of chance so well-known to the old soldier were indulged in, and the entertainment usually finished with a sing-song. Those in camp with A and D Companies will not readily forget our good friend Alf Campin, whose tuneful voice was heard so often in the shades of the night at Overstone Park in " Moira, My Girl " and other ballads.

At the Brington Camp, G Company usually adjourned to the local hostelry, where the Company cook, Sergeant Reg Billing, entertained all and sundry with his songs and playing at the piano. Happy days, happy nights, which were enjoyed by all. Other duties permitting, there was nothing I enjoyed more than a week-end in camp with one or other of the Companies, despite the fact that I was generally relieved of my surplus cash by those good fellows, the Company officers.

Regarding cooking, we preferred to rely on our own Company cooks rather than seek outside assistance, and never once did they let us down. The meals they served up with the allotted allowance of 4/6 per head had to be seen to be believed. We took the view that as these camps were for the purpose of training, it was just as necessary to train the cooks as the rest of the Company. If they could not cook in camp, they would not have been much good in the case of " Action Stations," when they would have had to cook for much larger numbers. However, as I have said, they always did magnificently and, strange as it may appear, there was never any grousing with regard to the food.

In 1943 and 1944 F Company joined in the camping and ran camps both at Brington and Overstone Park, whilst in 1944 the new D Company held several week-ends, besides that memorable journey to Great Yarmouth. I always felt that it was a pity that other Companies did not run these week-end camps, as I am certain they missed much, particularly that spirit of comradeship that comes from living together if only for a day or so. However, it was never any use trying to force things upon the Home Guard; if you did, you were asking for failure, and so the matter was left.

One of the most successful camps we held was an Officers' Week-end at Overstone on Saturday and Sunday, August 14th and 15th,1943. When we decided to run this, Captain Barton and I made up our minds that we would try to put on a really first-class show. If we were to ask officers to give up their week-end we must give them " value for money." We did our best, and only hope that those who attended thought that their time was not wasted. The main basis of the training was a T.E.W.T. (for the uninitiated, a Tactical Exercise Without Troops) in which we tried to visualise a situation that might have occurred to any platoon commander, with all its different problems. Barton and I spent several days on this, making it as foolproof as possible, and I know from the comments passed afterwards that the officers found this both interesting and instructive. We had the pleasure of a visit from Colonel Short on the Sunday during the course of the T.E.W.T., and as he passed no adverse criticism we were certain that he was satisfied with what he saw.

On the Saturday evening we had a talk from Lieut.-Colonel J. A. Brawn, newly appointed as Training Officer to the Sector, on " The Campaign in Iraq, 1941," in which he took part. We were greatly indebted on the Sunday to Major Hereward Wake, M.C., for his lecture on " With the Eighth Army in North Africa." He had just returned home wounded from that theatre of operations, where he had served from the outset. His lecture was followed with the keenest possible interest and gave us a graphic and informative picture of the fighting in the desert. Those who had the pleasure of being present will always feel grateful to Major Wake for giving up part of his convalescent leave to talk to them.

On this Sunday afternoon we were delighted to have with us several visitors, who afterwards joined up in a " camp tea."

Nearly fifty officers attended this camp, and all, I think, got benefit from it. We were hoping to arrange a similar one in 1944, but the Cadet Camp at the Park, together with various competitions, rendered this impossible, much to our regret.

CHAPTER TEN

BATTALION HEADQUARTERS

FROM July, 1940, when we moved from our temporary abode at the British Legion Office, Battalion Headquarters were at the Drill Hall, Clare Street, and here we had our home for nearly five years, until in May, 1945, it was taken over by the Army Demobilisation Authorities, which necessitated us finishing our career in Overstone Road.

I suppose ever since the Battle of Hastings, if not before, when anything goes wrong in the Army it is the custom to put the blame on Battalion Headquarters, and in the Home Guard the good old Army custom was kept up. There is a French proverb, " To know all is to forgive all," and did the members of the 12th know all that transpired at Battalion Headquarters I am sure that we should be freely forgiven for our alleged shortcomings. Paper warfare went on at a furious rate. Returns in duplicate, triplicate, and sometimes quintriplicate were called for from above; Battalion training programmes had to be compiled, records of hours of attendance at parades kept, houses requisitioned, a record maintained of all expenditure of S.A.A. and grenades, returns made of petrol used, umpires to be found for exercises in the county and sometimes adjoining counties, vacancies on courses to be filled, and often afterwards cancelled; all these were part of the everyday life of the Battalion Staff.

In addition there were all manner of people to be interviewed and conferences attended on various matters. Different Commanding Officers appeared at and disappeared from the I.T.C. To each of these had to be explained our defence system and journeys made to point it out on the ground. Sometimes correspondence of a different nature arrived at Clare Street, of which the following are examples:—

" Dear Sir,—Hurrying to work yesterday morning in the black-out, I broke my nose on the road block near the Cemetery on the Harborough Road. I understand that you are responsible for the erection of this. If and unless, etc."

" Dear Sir,—Last evening a shell from one of your guns sailed down the Avenue where I live, and did considerable damage to my fence. I shall be glad, therefore, etc."

" Dear Sir,—Owing to the erection of barbed wire in one of my fields, I have lost mowing grass to the value of 3/-. Can you tell me how to recover this? "

" Dear Sir,—On their way to the Drumhead Service on Sunday last, one of your companies urinated against the wall at the back of my house. Major ——— was in charge, etc."

All these correspondents had to be appeased and at times the way of the Home Guard was hard.

For the first few months of our existence the Staff consisted of one lady clerk. Things got better in February, 1941, when Quartermasters were allotted to the Home Guard and Captain A. W. Gardner, who had done such valuable voluntary work since the previous May, was appointed to this post. Later on, Permanent Staff Instructors were permitted and Sergeant-Major R. Collier came along. Here I should like to pay a tribute to Collier for the work done by him in those early days. As old soldiers he and I had much in common, chiefly our obsession for weapon training as the basis of all our work. Whenever a new weapon appeared on the horizon, off went Collier on a course to learn all there was to know about it, and on his return you could always see him at the Drill Hall with a squad of N.C.O.'s around him while he initiated them into the mysteries of the Northover, the Spigot, the Smith gun, and later the Sten. That the Battalion became so efficient in the use of these weapons was due in the first place to the instruction and coaching of S.-M. Collier. More P.S.I.'s appeared—Sergeants Blunden, Dowding and Richardson—and with these admirable work was done with recruits and with weapon training round the Companies. Unfortunately, when the split came in the Battalion, Collier and Richardson had to leave us for the 15th, but Blunden and Dowding remained with us to the end of 1944, when the former was posted back to the Regular Army. Dowding, however, remained until July, 1945, and had the uneviable task of helping to clear up. I could say much about his " art " in the return of equipment, but perhaps it would not be fair to give away his secrets, and so the less said the better. Anyway, our deficiencies after Stand Down were very much less than we expected.

It was not until the advent of Captain H. D. Barton, of the Warwicks, as Adjutant of the Battalion in July, 1942, that Headquarters became properly staffed. Knowing his job from top to bottom, a hard worker and, what was more important in the Home Guard, a good mixer, he proved himself a tower of strength to the Battalion. No Commanding Officer could have wished for a better Adjutant or a more conscientious worker. In fact, many a time after I had made the round of the Companies at their training, I called in at the Drill Hall about 10 o'clock to find him hard at work. It was the one time that I had to assert my authority and pack him off home. Whatever may have been our faults, and probably they were many, there never was a Commanding Officer and an Adjutant who worked together with such complete accord. It was a great blow to me when he left in the middle of 1944, and also a great loss to the Battalion, but he had earned well-merited promotion, and the best wishes of all the 12th went with him in his new sphere of activity.

With Captain Barton as Adjutant, Captain Gardner as Quartermaster, with four P.S.I.'s and two very capable ladies, Mrs. Boyce and Miss Brown, in the office, Battalion Headquarters ran very smoothly and, we hope, very efficiently. On the departure of Captain Barton he was succeeded by Captain A. W. Machen, who stayed with us until after the Stand Down.

And what of the Home Guard officers on Headquarters? I venture to assert without fear of contradiction, that there was not a better team in any Battalion in the Home Guard, each an expert at his particular job, and applying himself with enthusiasm to his task. On my appointment as Commanding Officer, Major H. St. J. Browne, who had had charge of C Company, became the Battalion Second-in-Command. Of a quiet, unassuming nature, but with sound military knowledge, he proved himself a great acquisition to Headquarters. A solicitor in civil life, he brought the legal mind to bear on all our problems, and his advice was at all times most valuable. Very often he acted as a brake on the impetuosity of the Commanding Officer, always to the benefit of the Battalion. His work on Audit Boards, etc., with all the uninteresting details was great appreciated. I never had the slightest qualms that had occasion arisen for him to take over the 12th, he would have done so most efficiently and that the Battalion would have been in very good hands.

Lieutenant Arnold Payne was a first-class Intelligence Officer, and in the early days before the coming of Captain Barton, acted as unofficial Adjutant. He and I possess the record of being the only two originals of Battalion Headquarters, and I believe that we are the only two who were present at every Home Guard exercise in the town throughout the course of our existence; this has entailed many all-night sittings at the Drill Hall. The cigarettes we smoked together on these affairs must run into many thousands. Very few knew as much about Northampton and its citizens as he did, while a better man on the phone it would be difficult to find. This was a great asset on exercises and operations, when messages often came in thick and heavy over the phone, genuine and fake, and in the drowsy hours from 2 to 3 in the morning it was so easy to accept a fake message, but never once did he fail to detect the real from the false. I am especially glad to pay this tribute to a very loyal comrade, as when vacancies occurred higher up on Sector and Sub-District, much against my wish he was passed over. I think he knows, and if he does not, he knows now, that I always regarded him as the best of Intelligence Officers and one whom I would not have changed with those who got promotion. The Intelligence side of our work was truly in very capable hands.

Then there was Captain V. J. H. Harris (Jack, for short), our Weapon Training Officer. If you visited the range either at Brington, Sywell or the R.E.M.E. range at Far Cotton, and saw a stalwart figure on the firing-point conducting operations, that was Jack. There he was, in all weathers, dressed in a manner all his own, for in the issue of greatcoats he had managed to procure the only one with bone buttons, as distinct from our ordinary brass ones. From early morn till late in the evening there he was coaching and instructing the beginner and giving confidence to those of a nervous temperament. I have always believed that the criterion of musketry in a battalion does not lie in the winning of cups or pots, but in the general standard throughout all its platoons. Judged by this standard there were not many battalions better than the 12th, and a lot of the credit for this was due to the W.T.O. I cannot pass without relating one story of his prowess on the range. As was usual at the end of an afternoon's firing, the last detail is completed by officers. Down they went with the main interest concentrated on the achievements of Captain Jack Harris. His first shot was greeted with the appearance of the "Wash-out" flag, a result that rewarded his other four shots. Great was the discomfiture of the W.T.O. while the onlookers were more than quietly amused. It was not until afterwards did he learn that it was a pre-arranged plan between the Company Commander and the marker. Major Barton, it was really too bad! Actually, I believe the W.T.O. scored 19 out of a possible 20. Incidents such as this were rife in the 12th Battalion and helped to promote the happy spirit which existed among all ranks. As well as range duties there was also instruction round the Companies on Winter evenings on the rifle and Lewis gun. Besides weapon training, Captain Harris was also the financial expert of the Battalion, and if there was any money to treasure he became the Hon. Treasurer, and in this respect his work in connection with the Fete was of outstanding value.

One of the quieter members of Headquarters was Lieutenant Charles Catlow who, as Guide and Transport Officer, had one of the most exacting jobs. He was the only one in the Battalion who really understood the mass of instructions regarding transport and the requisition of civilian lorries on "Action Stations." Had we ever been called out, all our transport arrangements would have depended upon him, and I am confident that all would have gone well. In the early days when the cry was "Know your area," he acted as Guide Officer and trained the Company Guides most efficiently. It is not as easy as some people imagine to find your way on a dark night round the outskirts of the town. Catlow and his Guides knew every path and every track and the shortest cuts and, what is more could find them on the darkest nights. Besides acting as Guides to the Home Guard it would have been their duty to guide any Regulars who might have operated in the district. This was only part of their job; among other things they had to know all the sources of water supply besides the town system, all the wells and springs, the strength and position of all the bridges and crossings of the river, and a mass of other necessary information.

I have never been gas minded, always regarding gas as a most ungentlemanly kind of warfare, but still, training in anti-gas measures were essential, and here again the expert was found in Lieutenant H .Allatt who, after acting as Gas N.C.O. in A Company, became Gas Officer on Battalion Headquarters. He did extremely well on a course at the Army School of Chemical Warfare, and his work in lecturing Companies and putting them through the gas chamber was greatly appreciated, and he was a very worthy member of the team.

When in 1943 W/T sets began to arrive, a Signals Officer became necessary. 'One surprising feature of the Home Guard was that no matter what work there was to do, an expert could always be found. And so it was that Sergeant G. A. White, of B Company, became Lieutenant White and Battalion Signals Officer. A specialist in wireless in civilian life, he set about the training cf signallers with the greatest enthusiasm. Starting with G Company the Signal Section became very popular, especially with the younger members, who delighted in walking around with an aerial and a W/T set on their backs. There was only one drawback to this, these younger members were constantly getting called up for the Regular Services and had to be replaced. However, this was part of our job, and the training these young fellows received in the Home Guard was of great value to them in their Service career. There was never any difficulty in filling the gaps, several recruits coming from ex-Cadets of the County School, and the Signal Section was always over strength. It was a tribute to the work of George White that on all the Buzz Exercises in 1944 it was always the 12th Battalion Signallers who were asked for by Sub-District.

Captain F. E. Courtney was our first Camouflage Officer and on his promotion to Zone his place was taken by Lieutenant F. Wood. Camouflage is a subject on its own, and whereas to the ordinary layman a few twigs in the netting of the steel helmet and a blackened face constitute camouflage, yet to the artist this is only the beginning, and we were fortunate that our friends Courtney and Wood were both artists and experts at their jobs. We were particularly indebted to Lieutenant Wood for the many plans, maps and charts that he so kindly prepared for us on Battalion Headquarters.

I have always stressed the importance of first aid. If a man knows that if he is wounded in battle he will be quickly and efficiently attended to, then his morale is much higher than it otherwise would be. We were fortunate in having as M.O. such a keen enthusiast as Major G. H. Thompson. Having served together in the 4th Territorial Battalion, I already knew his worth, and under his instruction and leadership the stretcher-bearers became a really efficient body of men who, I felt confident, would have done their job excellently in action had they been called upon to do so. In the Final Stretcher-Bearers Competition for Northamptonshire in 1944, we secured the very creditable position of second, being easily the best team in the Sector. But as I said previously, I would rather judge on the general standard of the stretcher-bearers in the Battalion rather than on one competition team. A large number of the stretcher-bearers gained certificates from the St. John Ambulance Association and the high standard reached reflects the greatest credit on Dr. Thompson, who gave so freely of his time when his labours with his civilian practice were so strenuous. In the last year or two of our life he was ably assisted by Captain G. B. Wallace. Sergeant H. W. Summers also did very valuable work and at all our special occasions was in charge of the first aid arrangements.

ANNIVERSARY PARADE, COUNTY GROUND, MAY 16th, 1943

Another very valuable member of Battalion Headquarters was Lieutenant C. G. B. Allinson, who acted as Ammunition Officer, a position that did not bring him much in the limelight but, at the same time, was of great value, for if we ever had had to fight, it was essential that the S.A.A. and grenades should be in the best condition. This was his duty, and so well were his records kept that they earned the special commendation of the Sub-District Commander. Knowing the requirements of Colonel Short, this was high praise indeed.

Almost the last member of the team, though not the least, was the R.S.M., Fred Timms. Starting as C.S.M. to A Company, he rendered very valuable assistance to them in the first years of their life, and it was a well-merited promotion when he was appointed to his higher position. On all Battalion Parades his was the guiding hand that so skilfully steered the Companies into their allotted places, and the fact that on all these occasions things proceeded so smoothly was a tribute to his tact and efficiency. When parades are held in the Regular Army, it is usual to have at least one rehearsal. This was impossible in the Home Guard, and the splendid assembly of the Battalion on these Parades reflects the greatest credit on the R.S.M.

I have purposely left till last one who right from the early Arcade days until long after the Stand Down served the Battalion right loyally and probably knew more of the inner workings of the 12th than any other individual. On Captain A. W. Gardner fell the brunt of the routine work, and very capably did he fulfil his duty. The Quartermaster is always a much-maligned person, and so it was with Gardner, especially in those early days when the supply of things were short. Each Company and Platoon Commander felt that others were getting more favourable treatment, while he was often accused of keeping things " under the counter." I suppose that this has always been the fate of quartermasters, and will be as long as there is an Army. As a matter of fact, in those days we simply had not got the equipment, and in any case the allotment between Companies was made by the Commanding Officer according to their strength. However, with tact and forbearance he overcame all difficulties, and although not succeeding in achieving the impossibility of pleasing everyone, he maintained a just and even distribution among all Companies. After the Stand Down he was primarily responsible for the winding-up of the Battalion, and the fact that the deficiencies were so low was due to his efficiency and skill in the gentle art of quartermastering. A Flying Officer in the last War, with no knowledge of Infantry work, he readily adapted himself, and contributed greatly to the success of the 12th.

The following are taken from the Report of the Sub-District Commander after his Annual Administration Inspection of Battalion Headquarters:—

1943: " Considering the size of the Battalion (over 2,700 all ranks, comprising in all eight Companies) the Battalion Staff has had an enormous amount of work to do, and in my opinion they have done very well indeed to bring the Battalion up to the present state of efficiency."

1944: " The Permanent Staff, Adjutant, Quartermaster, and P.S.I.'s are all happy and contented. They have all carried out their respective duties well and conscientiously. The Commanding Officer expressed himself well satisfied with his Permanent Staff. In my opinion the Administration of this Battalion is now very satisfactory and reflects credit on all concerned."

I am afraid that this Chapter has been very much on the personal side. The keynote of any success we had on Battalion Headquarters lies in the fact that we all worked together as a happy and contented team, all out for the one purpose, the good of the Battalion, which we all had so much at heart. I felt that no record of the 12th Battalion would be complete unless

I expressed my deep gratitude and appreciation of that body of men who worked so hard in their different spheres and who formed such a loyal band of comrades.

THE HEADQUARTERS DESPATCH RIDERS

Not many battalions of the Home Guard had a section of Despatch Riders, and none had one more efficient than the one we possessed.

In May, 1940, directly the L.D.V. was formed in the town, it was decided to make a Despatch Riders Section. About 20 riders, who had machines of their own, were selected and were put under the command of Arnold Payne, himself an old motor-cycle trials rider.

As these were the only despatch riders in the County in the early days, they were soon " requisitioned " by Sir Hereward Wake, the County Commander, to whom they reported on " Action Stations," and their area of operations was the whole county. This entailed journeys to places as far apart as Peterborough in the north-east, to Thorpe Mandeville in the south-west, and all the Divisional and Group Headquarters were visited. In September, 1940, instructions were received that on " Action Stations " the D.R.'s were to report to the I.T.C., and the area of activities was reduced to cover what was then the Wellingborough Town, Wellingborough District, Brixworth and Northampton Divisions. Later still the area was again reduced, but our D.R.'s were always in demand by higher units and other battalions, and never once was assistance denied. The closest co-operation was maintained with Zone Headquarters, E.C.D., at Dunstable, Sub-District at Bedford, and training was undertaken with the 9th Armoured Division when stationed in the locality.

To many, the D.R.'s were only known as the riders who led the Battalion on its parades and who rode while the rest marched, but this was only a small part of their work, and their training for the job that they might have had to perform was both arduous and strenuous.

Arnold Payne, who by this time had become a Lieutenant and Intelligence Officer, decided that the training should be divided into three categories:—

(1) To make them better riders.
(2) To train the Section to defend themselves efficiently.
(3) To train riders to know the town and neighbouring country thoroughly under all conditions.

At the beginning all the members of the Section had their own machines, but many, like the average pre-war rider, were fair weather and main road motorists. They had to be trained to ride in all weathers and on all sorts of roads and tracks. To that end, journeys were frequently made in rain or fog, rides were planned in muddy lanes, through water-splashes, and in the dark with only dimmed lights, and riders who could pass these tests could ride under any conditions.

In the early days the riding equipment issued was nil, but gradually good waterproof riding suits were obtained, together with crash helmets, goggles and gauntlet gloves. All the riders were supplied with one inch and one-quarter inch Ordnance maps of all their districts, besides having road maps of the towns. They were always able to do ordinary running repairs, while some were very experienced mechanics. Precautions were also taken so that in case of necessity, machines could be quickly immobilised.

In 1941 four W.D. motor-cycles arrived. They were side valve 350 c.c. Royal Enfields, but they were in extremely poor condition, and eventually were replaced by three O.H.V. 350 c.c. of the same make, which were much better. When no petrol was available for civilian motor-cyclists, riders were issued with " G " licences for their machines, and although never having too much petrol, we always saw that they had enough for their training, and for this we were chiefly indebted to the Zone Advisor, Colonel Lester Reid, who ever took a keen interest in the D.R.'s.

Many communication tests were held and in all of these the D.R.'s came through with flying colours. The earliest one was for Major Jackson, of Zone, and later ones were for the I.T.C. Signal Officer, Lieutenant Careless, and for the Sub-District Brigade Major, Major R. M. Jeffery. In the last one a test was carried out as to which was the quicker method of sending messages to all the Company Commanders in the 7th, 8th, 9th, 11th and 12th Battalions—D.R.'s v. Telephone. It was found that more Company Commanders were contacted in a given time by the D.R.'s than by phone.

A large part of a D.R.'s work is done alone and therefore calls for quick thinking and initiative, and to that end the Section were trained to think for themselves, and on rides, bridges and sections of roads were put out of action and alternate routes had to be quickly used. Whilst map-reading was important and it was very necessary for all D.R.'s to have a first-rate knowledge of this subject, it was always found that actual knowledge of the route proved much quicker, and therefore riders had to know all the likely places that they might have to visit, and all H.Q., D.L.'s, O.P.'s, railway stations, important bridges and dumps in their area were frequently visited, and the D.R.'s probably had a greater and more up-to-date knowledge of the disposition of troops in the district than any other body. Close touch was also kept with all the Royal Observer Corps and Searchlight Posts. The absence of road signs made route finding more difficult, but at the same time had the advantage of making the D.R.'s more self-reliant.

Later, although still working together, one Section was made into an Intelligence Branch, and with this Lance-Corporal H. J. Smith did very valuable work.

At first the Section had no separate H.Q., but later these were made at 127, Great Russell Street, and when these were required by the Territorial Association, a move was made to larger H.Q. at 10, Hunter Street, and here the D.R.'s remained until after the Stand Down.

Great help was received in the very early days from the I.T.C., especially from Corporal Tristram, who conducted a very full and detailed course on Map Reading, and from Corporal Morley who taught the Section the mechanics and use of the Bren gun. Later on, under Battalion arrangements, all the personnel did Gas training, went through the gas chamber, had bombing instruction, including the throwing of live bombs, whilst all through their career frequent use was made of the miniature and open ranges, where all became adepts with the Sten gun. In fact, I should say that the D.R.'s as individuals had more firing practice than anyone in the Battalion.

The D.R.'s participated in all the big exercises in which the 12th Battalion took part, and besides this they were often loaned to the Sub-District. This is always the fate of having such an efficient body; everyone is always asking for it. Never once did they fail to deliver their messages, and not once, despite the thousands of miles they must have covered, did they have a serious accident. This is a record of which they are justly proud and upon which they are to be congratulated.

Before D Day and for some time after, the D.R.'s were on duty and slept at Battalion H.Q. in case their services were required. By a coincidence I happened to be on duty with them on the morning of D Day.

Altogether 49 served in the D.R.'s, of which number 24 joined the Regular Forces, eight gaining commissions, a very high percentage. We regret to write that two of these, Sub-Lieutenant S. Yarde and Flight-Sergeant I. T. Clarke, lost their lives on operations.

It would not be fitting to conclude this recort of the D.R.'s without a special reference to two who did so much for the Section, Lieutenant Arnold Payne and Sergeant J. F. Stevens. Arnold Payne was their founder and throughout their existence acted as a father. By the nature of the job he was always in close contact with each member, knowing each one personally. Sergeant Stevens always led the D.R.'s on parade and also acted as Intelligence Sergeant. His efficiency, steadiness and help to all the personnel at all times was outstanding and he well merited the award of a Certificate of Merit by the G.O.C., Eastern Command.

In the early days Corporals Coker and Hawtin did very valuable work until their enlistment in the Regular Forces, and afterwards their good work was carried on by Lance-Corporals Smith, Goff and Devonshire.

As Commanding Officer I should like to pay my tribute to the D.R.'s, who rendered such devoted service to Battalion H.Q. No one could have wished for a better body of men, who at all times of the day or night were ready to carry out such duties as were necessary. I hope to have the pleasure and privilege of meeting them at an annual re-union for many years to come.

In conclusion I can only endorse what was said about them by a Senior Regular Officer: " A very keen section, showing the utmost interest in their job."

CHAPTER ELEVEN

A DREAM OF ST. PETER'S BRIDGE, NORTHAMPTON
(with apologies to the author of " The Battle of Duffer's Drift ")

Dedicated to Major A. G. R. Barton and Lieutenant E. G. Turner,
of C Company, who so gallantly held the bridge from 1940—1944.

By special request of many members of C Company I have included this
Dream, which I gave to No. 8 Platoon at the Brook Factory way back in 1942,
before the days of Spigot mortars, Smith guns and the various other weapons
that arrived later in our existence.

INTRODUCTION

FTER visiting No. 8 Platoon at the Brook Factory, I adjourned—I
must say most unwillingly—to the County Hotel by invitation of
Major A. G. R. Barton. However, as he was so pressing I felt that
it would be most unkind to refuse his hospitality. After partaking
of one or two lemonades, I arrived home at the usual Home Guard time to
find my wife in bed, and with bread, cheese and pickles left out for my
consumption. If you are wearied by this dream of St. Peter's Bridge, blame
not me, but the bread, cheese and pickles *and* Major Barton.

FIRST DREAM

It was eight o'clock in an evening in April when I found myself standing
on St. Peter's Bridge. " Action Stations " had been sent out two hours
before. We had assembled at Clarke Road, where arms and ammunition
had been issued, and now here was I, with 82 N.C.O.'s and men, ordered to
hold this important bridge giving communication between Northampton and
Bedford, one which would probably be greatly used by our Mobile Divisions
to get at the enemy, who had made landings in the Eastern Counties. My
orders were to hold the bridge at all costs. I might get some reinforcements
next day, but until then I had to hold on with the men of my Platoon. I
might be attacked before this time, but it was unlikely, as no enemy was
known to be nearer than Bedford. Other information I had received was
that the enemy had managed to land tanks and guns.

It all seemed plain enough, and as this was the first time I had had an
independent command I was determined to carry out my orders to the bitter
end. For some weeks before, I had studied the ground round the bridge and
had a fairly shrewd idea where to position my men and their weapons.

I felt confident, too, for I had studied during the Winter months all the
manuals of military tactics, my men of No. 8 Platoon were a good, willing
lot—the best in the Battalion, I always reckoned—and would, I knew, do
everything I wanted of them. We were also well supplied with ammunition,
grenades, and rations, and had plenty of barbed wire and a number of picks,
shovels, and sandbags. Visions of a bloody and derperate fight crossed my
mind: a fight to the last cartridge and the last bomb, and then getting in
with the bayonet with a glorious victory, when a discreet cough at my side
brought me back from my day-dreams and warned me that my sergeant
was waiting for orders.

I decided that as the enemy were reported no nearer than 21 miles there was no need to put the bridge in a state of defence that night, especially as my men were tired after their day's work and the excitement of mustering. I felt that it would be as much as they could do to arrange nice and ship-shape all the ammunition, grenades and tools that had been dumped down in front of Parker Gray's house, and to get a meal before dark.

Between ourselves, I was rather pleased to be able to put off my defensive measures till to-morrow, for I was a bit puzzled how to set about it. The plans and schemes I had read about in books didn't quite seem to fit my position, but now I had to take up a defensive position with the probability of an attack by the Bosche, it was a different matter. However, in the morning I daresay things would appear in a different light and be quite easy.

Having issued my orders, I decided to have a look at my front. The enemy having been reported at Bedford, obviously the Bedford Road was my front. Quite naturally I knew there must be a front, for on all Company schemes there always was a front, where the enemy comes from. I decided, therefore, that the Bedford Road was my front, the river on either side were my flanks where there might possibly be enemies, and the town was my rear, where naturally there were none.

Standing on the bridge I had just settled these points in my mind when up drove a Staff car and I was hailed by a Staff Colonel who alighted from the vehicle. He turned out to be a very sympathetic fellow for a Staff Officer and quite realised my difficulties in planning my defence of the bridge, and while I was telling him my job and the number of men I had with me, where they were to sleep, etc., he offered several suggestions of which I made a note. He complimented me on what I had done, and I felt sure that I should be mentioned in dispatches. I was pleased that he agreed with me that there was no need to put the bridge in a state of defence that night, but that the chief consideration was to see that my men got a good night's sleep. He left about dusk, saying that he would look round next day to see how I was getting on, as H.Q. looked upon this bridge as a most important point. I went back to my H.Q., which I had made in Parker Gray's house, and wrote out my orders for the next day, the chief of which was wiring in the position, an operation which I knew my men, being good British soldiers, hated like hell, regarding it as a fatigue. I saw the sentries mounted on the bridge, and the other men had dossed down in the Britannia. On going round the posts at midnight I was pleased to find how alert the sentries were and how well they shouted out "Halt!˙ Who goes there?" in a proper military manner. Turning in myself soon after midnight, I was almost immediately fast asleep.

I was awakened just before dawn by a loud cry of "Halt! Who goes——" cut short by rifle shots. As I left the house the air was filled with cries and rifle and machine-gun fire and the groans of men as they lay or stumbled about, trying to get out of the Britannia. There was so wild shooting from my men, but it was all over in a few moments, and as I approached the road the whole place seemed to be swarming with Bosches. At that moment I must have been hit on the head with a rifle butt, for I remembered no more until I found myself seated on the bridge and having my head, which was dripping with blood, tied up by one of my men.

Our losses were 11 killed, including both sentries, and 23 wounded. The Bosches lost one killed and two wounded.

As I sat watching the column of enemy vehicles crossing the bridge I was to have held, I noticed my Staff Colonel of the previous evening, talking animatedly with officers of the Bosches Army, who referred to him as Oberlieutenant Smidt. I gradually gathered from their conversation what I had partly guessed before, that they had been fetched and guided by my sympathetic friend, the Staff Colonel, and got up to my position in the dark and had carefully marked down our two poor sentries. These they had at once shot on the alarm being given and had then rushed the bridge.

As I sat pondering on my failure, the following lessons kept hammering through my head:—

(1) Do not put off your measures of defence till the morrow, as these are more important than your comfort and the ship-shape arrangement of your stores.

(2) Do not have all your men sleeping in one place at night, and see that each one knows his job before he goes to sleep.

(3) Do not give information of your job and your members to any officer you don't know, whether Brass Hat or otherwise, or how sympathetic he may be.

(4) Do not let your sentries advertise their position to the whole world, including the enemy, by standing in full view on the bridge and challenging in a loud voice.

(5) For a strong isolated point there are no flanks and no rear; it is front all round.

SECOND DREAM

I again found myself in charge of St. Peter's Bridge with 80 men, and as before with ample stores, grenades, ammunition and tools. There was this important difference that, running constantly through my head were the five lessons I had learnt in my first dream, and I was determined to see that these points were rectified this time.

As soon as possible I began to make out my plan of defence without wasting any time. In order to prevent any strangers seeing over my dispositions I sent examining posts of four men to the road opposite the Lodge gate, to the Bedford Road near the arches, and to the railway bridge on the road to Hardingstone. We started wiring-in the position, and though, of course, I still thought the enemy would come along the Bedford Road, I thought it best to prepare an all-round defence. Most of the men were busy wiring, grousing as usual, while a few were looking after the stores and one or two were making tea for the others. When midnight came we had wired practically all round, not as thickly as I should have liked, but still we were wired in.

A Staff Major turned up during the evening, but as I did not know him, and as I had been bitten before, I sent him under armed escort to Battalion H.Q.

At midnight I withdrew my examining posts and posted sentries in pairs, one pair near the bridge and the other pair near the lodge gates, in well-concealed positions. They had orders that one was always to remain concealed and cover the other; they were to challenge quietly with the bayonet from a yard's distance, and they were to bayonet or shoot anyone who did not halt.

Tea was drunk, and bread and cheese which the men had brought with them was eaten. This over, instead of having my men all sleeping in the Britannia, I scattered them, some in the pub., some in the cottages, some in the Lodge house, and others with me in Gray's house. Having visited the sentries and the guard, and having seen all my men comfortably settled down, I turned in myself with a sense of having done my duty and neglected no possible precaution for our safety.

Just as dawn broke next morning there was a sound of aeroplanes, and bombs dropped all round the bridge and houses—many of my men were hit while trying to find cover. Some of the buildings had narrow escapes from near misses. Almost simultaneously there was firing from the direction of Rushmere Road, and two German tanks rushed up the road towards the bridge, followed by infantry. I expected to hear my bombers in the cottages and at the Britannia lobbing their 73's and S.T. bombs at these two tanks, but there was an ominous silence from the bombers. Many of my men, hearing the firing, rushed to the road block on the bridge, where they suffered heavy casualties from the machine-guns of the tanks firing straight ahead. At this time, three German tanks were seen approaching along the Bedford Road. Two of these were knocked out at the railway crossing by my Northover firing 68's, but in the confusion the German infantry from Rushmere Road proceeded quickly up to the bridge and rolled away the concrete blocks and removed sufficient rails to allow the passage of a single tank. They sustained some twenty casualties doing this from my Lewis gun in the tannery. By this time I rallied some of my men in the grounds of Rush Mills. The German infantry, however, gained a footing in the grounds and kept up an intermittent fire with their Tommy and machine-guns on the houses we occupied. Nearly every time my men came to the window-sill to fire they were hit through the head, while several were wounded by bullets coming through the brickwork. However, we were putting up a pretty good resistance and the Bosche was making little headway, when we were shelled from a field gun brought up by the Bosche near the Bedford railway line. One of the cottages collapsed, burying my men inside. I felt that the end was near, and it was, for shortly afterwards I was hit by a splinter of shell in the leg, and with my numbers weakened, the Bosche was able to put an end to all resistance.

As I lay on a stretcher near the bridge after the engagement, I thought over my failure and where I had gone wrong. One of my men, who had been near the Lodge gates, told me that one of their number had seen the tanks coming down Rushmere Road and in his excitement had fired his rifle and disclosed their position. A bomber from the cottages informed me that on the alarm being given they had rushed for their bombs, but found that they had forgotten to detonate these overnight, and by the time they had them ready the opportunity had gone.

As I lay thinking, I was surprised to see that the Bosche had rounded up nearly 200 civilians and, under guard, these were made to work, clearing the bridge and road of the destroyed tanks and the debris caused by the action.

Where had I gone wrong? Eventually the following further lessons formed themselves in my head:—

(6) When defending a place like a bridge, it is not necessary to sit on top of it as long as it is kept under fire.

(7) While I had wired in, I had not taken sufficient care with my firing positions. I had made no loopholes and none of my firing positions had been sandbagged.

(8) I had not taught my men to fire when possible from the back of a room instead of exposing themselves at the windows.

(9) I had omitted to make slit trenches as a precaution against aerial bombing.

(10) I had forgotten overnight to see that my bombers had a sufficient number of bombs detonated.

(11) I had taken no precautions against shelling, although I had been told the enemy had guns. I might have shored up some of the houses and seen that sandbag emplacements had been built for my machine-guns inside the rooms.

(12) I ought to have had everyone standing-to an hour before dawn.

(13) To test the concealment of my firing positions I had neglected to look at them from the enemy's standpoint, and had not made any decoy or bluff positions to draw his fire.

(14) Surprise is a great advantage, and I ought to have taken precautions against this.

(15) It is not good warfare to allow civilians to do nothing while tired Home Guards, who have got to do the fighting next day, are breaking their hearts trying to do heavy labour in a short time.

By the time all these lessons had been well burnt into my brain beyond all chance of forgetfulness a strange thing happened. I had another dream.

THIRD DREAM

Once more was I fated to hold St. Peter's Bridge, but by this time I had learnt many lessons.

On arriving, I again put out my examining posts to prevent strangers entering my strong points and seeing my dispositions. My sergeant had been sent to get as many civilians as he could to help with my preparations. I had obtained beforehand the help of several cyclists, mostly youths of 15 and 16, and these were sent to the following points with orders to communicate instantly with me if anything was seen or heard:—

Hill near Little Houghton.
Railway bridge to Hardingstone.
Bridge along Bedford Road.
Crossroads at Rushmere—Billing Road.

They were to stay in position until 1 o'clock, when I would relieve them.

Soon after, my sergeant turned up with over 100 civilians, all volunteers who were eager to help and who included several of the so-called weaker sex. Under the guidance and with the help of my men they were soon at work— wiring-in, filling sandbags, making loopholes, etc.

While this was going on, I had a look at my position from the enemy's standpoint, and decided which windows I would use as firing positions; these were certainly not the most obvious or the most prominent. I then gave instructions to my N.C.O.'s to sandbag well all these firing positions and the loopholes as a precaution against the genetration of bullets, and also to make dummy ones. With the time at my disposal I found it quite impossible to shore up the houses, but in two I had built sand-bagged emplacements, protected by beams across the top to stand the weight of debris. There were for my machine-guns. Meanwhile all the civilians had been evacuted from Rush Mills, the Britannia and the various cottages. My bombing corporal had seen that the 73's, S.T.'s and Mills's had been distributed in the bedrooms of the Britannia and the cottages. Bombers were told off for these rooms, and bombs were detonated and placed in the bedrooms near the windows, all ready for throwing.

During this time, work on all points was proceeding satisfactorily, the point had been well wired in, many loopholes had been made and sand-bagged, and slit trenches dug for all the men who would be in the open. The civilians had been working most enthusiastically, as the novelty appealed to them, and now that the critical time had arrived they were anxious to do what they could. My N.C.O.'s and men had been busy directing and giving a helping hand here, there and everywhere. By 11.30 I considered that the strong point had been well fortified and I was quite satisfied, so I gave the order to knock off, and the examining posts were brought in and sentries posted. The civilians were given words of thanks for their services; I saw some of the men thanking the young females in a different way.

Tea had been made in the Britannia and all my men had a good drink of tea and then went to their positions. Each man had to sleep near his fire position.

Orders had been issued that all men were to be up by 5, when tea would be served. Rifles and L.G.'s were to be cleaned by 5.30 and the whole detachment was to stand to at this hour in their firing positions until they got the order to stand down. They were not to show themselves until the actual fighting commenced, and then not more than necessary. At stand to there was to be no movement whatever. Four cyclists were detailed to relieve the civilians at 5.30, with orders to tear back to H.Q. at the first sign of enemy activity. As it is nearly all downhill they were be at my H.Q. in a few minutes.

It was now near midnight; I inspected the sentries on the bridge and near Lodge Cottage and saw that they were in a well-concealed position, and had a look at my bombers, seeing that the bombs were detonated.

The relief civilian cyclists had arrived and, mounting a cycle, my runner and I saw the reliefs carried out. The new cyclists were told that they would be relieved at 5.30 and that they could then proceed home.

I then turned in myself at 1.30 with the satisfaction that whatever the outcome I had carried out the lessons I had learnt.

I was aroused at 4.45 and went round the position. Many of my men were already up and cleaning their rifles, and everyone seemed in good fettle. Tea was served at 5.15 and breakfast was eaten from the rations brought out by the men. The cyclists were sent off and all the remainder had cleaned their weapons and were in their firing positions.

At 6.30 it was getting light and I again strolled round the position; not a man was to be seen. A minute or two later, a squadron of enemy aircraft dive-bombed my area, dropping bombs and firing their machine-guns. The noise was deafening and it seemed that none of us would survive, but after the attack I was agreeably surprised to find that, thanks to the slit trenches and the sandbags, we had suffered only two casualties from splinters of bombs.

At 6.40 my cyclist from Rushmere Road came in breathless with the news that enemy tanks were coming south through Abington Park. This information was quickly passed round, and the bombers removed the covers from the S.T. bombs and the tops from the 73's. A few minutes later three enemy tanks were seen coming down Rushmere Road. On reaching the triangle they turned towards the bridge. Not until they reached the cottages was there any sign of the defence, and then a fusillade of bombs landed on the tanks from the bedroom windows. Two of the tanks were disabled and set on fire and the crews on emerging received a hail of 36's. Very few of them escaped. The tank which was undamaged proceeded up to the rails, where it was engaged by the Northover. Their first shot missed, but the two following 68's landed on the tank and put it out of action. This tank, however, had done some little damage to my men in the houses; I learnt afterwards that one man had been killed and three wounded. Meanwhile, enemy infantry had followed up the tanks and had managed to get a foothold in the cottages, where they caused some casualties by firing through the ceilings of the downstairs rooms into the bedrooms. After a short and sharp encounter the enemy was driven off towards St. Andrew's Hospital, leaving several dead behind.

While this was happening, enemy infantry, covered by a field gun, made a determined attempt to rush the road block and the river near the lock gates. Several shells fell near the bridge, but as I had none of my men actually there, little damage was done. The enemy who made this rush were effectively dealt with by my Lewis gun in the tannery, which up to this time had remained silent. The platoon who endeavoured to cross the lock gates were engaged by my riflemen posted in the Mill grounds to watch this crossing. A few managed to get across, but these were soon rounded up by my reserve mobile section, which I had kept under cover in the house to deal with any such emergency. The enemy who had managed to survive the attack made off in the direction of Hardingstone.

The enemy dead and wounded numbered over 50, and one " B.F." on our side had taken a prisoner. Our losses were five killed and 19 wounded. But we had held the bridge.

I need not dwell on the far-reaching results of the holding of St. Peter's Bridge. It is history now, how it was the turning point of the invasion.

During the day we received congratulations from Battalion H.Q., and what was more to the point some much-needed reinforcements, with a replacement of ammunition.

At this moment I felt a tap on my shoulder and heard a voice say, "Arise, Sir Sticky Bomb," but my dreams were rudely shattered by the familiar voice of my wife exclaiming, "If you don't get up at once you'll never be in time to see C Company on parade."

CHAPTER TWELVE

ROUND THE COMPANIES

A COMPANY

Company Headquarters: 21, Abington Grove.

Company Commander	- - - - Major P. Hutton
Second-in-Command	- - - - Captain R. E. Corsby
Intelligence Officer	- - - Lieutenant G. A. T. Vials
Weapon Training Officer	- - Lieutenant F. S. Britten
Ammunition Officer	- - Lieutenant A. G. Beer, M.C.
Medical Officer	- - - - Captain G. B. Wallace
Company Sergeant-Major	- - - C.S.M. E. Malpas
Company Q.M.S.	- - - - - C.Q.M.S. E. Osborne

No. 1 Platoon.   Headquarters: 34, The Broadway.

Platoon Commander	- - - Lieutenant C. W. Johnson
Platoon Officer	- - - Lieutenant M. F. Swinstead

No. 2 Platoon.   Headquarters: The Advance Motor Works.

Platoon Commander	- - Lieutenant W. T. Whitehouse
Platoon Officer	- - - Lieutenant C. W. Marriott

In the days of 1940 when Northampton was a L.D.V. Division, the North Group comprised the men of Kingsley, Kingsthorpe and St. George's Wards, under the command of N. P. Andrews, who in 1914—1918 had seen service in the Grenadier Guards. P. Hutton was his second-in-command, while clerical duties were undertaken by A. W. Gardner, H. J. Payne and E. T. Pack, the latter acting as Group Quartermaster. The first Headquarters were at Duncan House, St. George's Avenue, the home of A. W. Gardner.

The Companies were organised as follows:—

Kingsley Company   Commander: R. E. Corsby   Deputy: G. A. T. Vials
Kingsthorpe Company   Commander: J. V. Collier   Deputy: C. W. Marriott
St. George's Company   Commander: G. H. Oates   Deputy: R. B. Armitt

The area of the North Group extended from the Bush Hill Copse (to the rear of Manfield Hospital) on the right, to the River Nene at Kingsthorpe on the left, and this included Buttocks Booth crossroads, Moulton Park, Boughton Green Reservoir, and the main roads and railways to the north of the town. It will thus be seen that the operational area of this Group was both extensive and important.

The Group immediately got to work on May 26th, 1940; Company and Section rolls were compiled and Section Leaders appointed, while a record was made of the number of lorries, cars and bicycles available, and weapons such as sporting guns and revolvers owned by individual volunteers. Patrol orders were issued by Company Commanders, and on May 27th, 1940, the Group, along with the rest of the Division, commenced the manning of the Observation Posts.

When after some three months had passed the designation of the L.D.V. units was changed, the North Group assumed the title of A Company, with Nos. 1, 2 and 3 Platoons, together with works units. At this time, and for some years afterwards until reorganisation of the Battalion lessened its numbers, the Company was the strongest in the 12th. On August 4th, 1940, its strength was 525, made up as under:—

No. 1 Platoon 189   No. 2 Platoon 149   No. 3 Platoon 133
Advance Motor Co. 30   Painton's Works 24

The system of road blocks had by this time been organised thoroughly and on August 16th, 1940, A Company took over the blocks at Kettering Road (near the Manfield Hospital), Boughton Green Road, Harborough Road, and Welford Road. A plan was drawn up for each of these positions, so that they were well covered by fire, and volunteers were allotted their role in the defence plan.

During those Summer months quite a lot of checking-up of traffic was done. This gave a sense of importance to the Home Guard, and very few motorists or pedestrians escaped without the production of their identity cards. Throughout the British Isles several persons were shot before the public realised that the Home Guard was taking their job earnestly, and that when called upon to halt they had to do so, or risk their lives. After August, 1940, it was decided by the Higher Authorities that this duty was no longer necessary.

During the Summer and Autumn months and also during the Winter, training in the Company proceeded intensively, and Squad Commanders C. Davis, G. H. Sharman, C. R. Bruley, G. H. York, F. Penn and W. G. Whiting, D.C.M., all qualified musketry instructors of the last war, rendered great service to the Company.

As an instance of the great enthusiasm of the volunteers of those early days, the effort of Squad Commander C. Davis is worthy of special mention. Davis was a qualified instructor on the Lewis gun, and as no official manual on the subject was obtainable at the time he resourcefully met the deficiency by compiling his own book of instruction. It comprised drawings of mechanism and details of the working of the gun, and the action to be taken for all possible stoppages. He printed the book himself and distributed it to Section instructors. Improvisation was an art peculiar to the Home Guard.

Tactical schemes, both by day and by night, were carried out, and on August 18th, 1940, the defence of the road block on the Kettering road was keenly tested and was the subject of many interesting discussions.

American rifles had arrived by this time, and on October 18th an armourer's inspection proved that much care and attention had been given to these weapons, which had arrived covered with thick grease. These had been most assiduously cleaned by those fortunate men to whom they had been allocated.

Many volunteers from A Company had eagerly attended the courses of instruction arranged by the I.T.C. at the Barracks, and as a result these instructors were enabled to train their comrades with confidence and with excellent results.

During the Winter of 1940-41 lectures were given, not only on military subjects but instruction was received from specialists in other spheres— district officers of the A.R.P. gave valuable information on the methods of dealing with incendiary bombs and in anti-gas measures; Mr. B. A. Swinden, M.A., gave a lecture on " Gas as a Chemical Agent," Scout Commissioner A. Cann lectured on " Scouting," while Dr. James Orr rendered valuable assistance to No. 1 Platoon by his talks on First Aid, which were followed by a course of demonstration lectures by Officer H. Cooley, of the St. John Ambulance. Cedar Road and Kingsthorpe Grove Schools were regularly used for these lectures every Wednesday evening during the Winter training period, and there was always a full attendance.

1941 opened with the strength of A Company at 496, with a rifle strength of 230, from which it will be seen that there had been a great improvement and that there was now almost one rifle to every two men.

On January 10th, 1941, A Company were suddenly called to arms by a Mobilisation Test Alarm. The result was extremely good; about 90 per cent. of the men were on parade in full equipment in 25 minutes. In this month the Company took their share in the patrolling of the centre of the town to help out the Civil Defence Services, details of which have been given in the Chapter on "The Home Guard and the Civil Defence," with their Headquarters at the Hare and Hounds Hotel in Newland.

During the Summer months of 1941 many field exercises were carried out, often with the hearty co-operation of the 9th Battalion, notably when, on May 22nd, that Battalion provided the enemy for a determined attack on the position held by A Company. Perhaps the most interesting feature of this scheme was the success of the inter-communication of the Company. Telephone lines had been laid and the instruments made by Private T. H. Valentine were found to be thoroughly reliable in the capable hands of the Company Signallers, who included Lance-Corporal A. Holland and Private P. J. Delamere.

Another interesting field exercise was carried out on July 20th in co-operation with No. 4 Overstone Platoon, when an attack was made through Overstone Park with the object of testing the defences of Sywell Aerodrome. It is satisfactory to note that despite the excellence of A Company's plan of attack the defences proved successful.

By this time inter-communication had been strengthened by the formation of a Company Signalling Section, organised by Captain P. Hutton. The instructors of this Section were Sergeant R. W. Halliwell and Corporal C. W. Shrewsbury, both experienced signallers of the last war. Headquarters were established in the Supporters' Room of the Cobblers' Football Club, and the County Ground was used for visual signalling practice.

Sunday, October 19th, 1941, was a memorable day for A Company. The Lewis Gun teams had been detailed to fire a practice at Brington Range, and to make the most of the opportunity it was decided also to fire a rifle practice in the afternoon. The Company paraded at nearly full strength on Campbell Square and marched the six miles to the range. They fired 10 rounds each with good results, and after a cup of tea marched back to Northampton, not a bad Sunday's training for a Home Guard Company with a fairly high age average.

The Winter training programme for 1941-42 was very comprehensive and the school halls were again frequently used for lectures, while very many night operations were carried out in an enthusiastic manner.

In December, 1942, the Company took their share in the "Scorch" Exercise, one benefit of which was the experience it gave to the younger Home Guards in service conditions and routine in action.

During this year the Defence Scheme for Northampton was changed and instead of the perimeter defence, certain important crossroads were made into Defended Localities. The road blocks on the Borough boundary at Welford Road and Harborough Road were given up, and a Defended Locality made at the junction of these two roads at Kingsthorpe; this was held by No. 2 Platoon, under Lieutenant E. Beeston. On No. 1 Platoon front the blocks at Buttocks Booth and Manfield Hospital were relinquished and a Defended Locality made at the Kingsley Park Hotel corner of the Racecourse. Here much hard work was done to put the position in a state of defence. Positions for the Spigot mortars were sited, while barbed wire obstacles were erected on the Racecourse.

In this year, 1942, A Company were the pioneers of the Week-end Camp, and many enjoyable week-ends were spent at Overstone Park by all the Platoons and Sections in turn. Camp routine and discipline were excellent and the programmes of work were always carefully thought out and made interesting.

In July, 1942, the Sub-District Company was formed, and in common with most other Companies A Company lost several of its members to the new unit, including Lieutenant F. C. Whiting, Sergeant C. M. Edwards, Corporal J. Cooch, etc., while shortly afterwards C.S.M. F. Timms, who had rendered such excellent service to the Company, was promoted to Battalion Headquarters as R.S.M. He was succeeded by C.S.M. E. Malpas, who worthily maintained the high example set by his predecessor.

During September and October, 1942, with the direction of men into the Home Guard, the Company reached its peak strength of 583: No. 1 Platoon 226, No. 2 199, No. 3 71, and H.Q. Works Section 87.

Soon after, we decided at Battalion Headquarters that a Reserve Company was an essential for the proper tactical disposition of the Battalion, and so H Company came into being by the amalgamation of the Mobile Platoon and No. 3 Platoon of A Company. I always disliked disturbing Companies, but when new units had to be formed it was only natural that we should look to the largest company, and so I am afraid that A Company suffered considerably during its lifetime in this respect. However, a new No. 3 Platoon was formed under Lieutenant Frank Jordan and Lieutenant A. Holland, with its headquarters at Chestnut Road, and functioned very successfully.

As I have stated in another Chapter, we hoped that this reorganisation of the Battalion would be the last that was necessary, and that the 12th could now settle down to a calm and placid existence, uninterrupted by any further changes. But, alas, plans of a Battalion Commander are often upset by the Higher Authorities, and before the end of the Home Guard further changes affecting A Company had to be made.

In July, 1943, A Company suffered a severe blow in the loss of its Commander, Major N. P. Andrews, who was promoted to the command of the new 15th Battalion. Commander since the L.D.V. days of 1940, " Nobby," as he is affectionately known to the members of A Company, had rendered invaluable service to this, the largest Company of the Battalion, and his work in welding it into such an efficient unit will always be remembered by those who had the good fortune to serve under him. This necessitated several changes. Major P. Hutton, who had acted as second-in-command since 1940, took over command of the Company, with Captain R. E. Corsby as his right-hand man. Lieutenants A. G. Beer and C. W. Johnson filled the vacancies as Commanders of No. 1 Platoon, while Lieutenant F. Britten was appointed Weapon Training Officer of the Company. Soon after, Lieutenant A. G. Beer became Company Ammunition Officer, Lieutenant C. W. Johnson taking over command of No. 1 Platoon with Lieutenant F. M. Swinstead as his Platoon Officer.

In September, 1943, a Fete was organised by the Company on the True Form Sports Ground, in aid of the Red Cross, and the splendid sum of £400 was realised. Although this result was afterwards passed at subsequent fetes, great credit is due to A Company as the initiators of this very profitable form of money-raising for worthy causes.

In December, 1943, the strength of the Company was further depleted by the formation of the new Coastal Reinforcement Company. We hope that A Company looked upon it as an honour that they should have been chosen to form the personnel of this important new unit. Nos. 2 and 3 Platoons were transferred to form the new D Company, under Major Frank Jordan. This necessitated some alterations in the defence system of the Company, particularly of the Defended Locality at Kingsthorpe, but by this time, with the menace of a full-scale invasion past, road blocks and defended localities had lost much of their initial importance.

During 1944 the training of the Company proceeded smoothly and in its usual efficient manner, with frequent camps at Overstone Park. In conjunction with the other parts of the Battalion, A Company played its part in the Exercise " Megrim " and also in the operations before and during the D Day landings, and right up to the Stand Down continued to be a valuable part of the Battalion.

During its career of four and a half years, no fewer than 1,227 had passed through the ranks of the Company. Of these, 271, practically all of whom received their first military training in the Home Guard, had been transferred to the Regular Forces, as follows:—

Army	175
Royal Navy	41
Royal Marines ...	5
R.A.F.	46
Fleet Air Arm ...	4

Many of these achieved promotion in the Armed Forces, and alas, some made the supreme sacrifice.

The Company also played a worthy part in the career of the 12th Battalion, for besides carrying on its duties in a most efficient manner, 35 of its members were promoted to commissioned rank, not only in their own Company but in D, F and G Companies and also on Battalion Headquarters.

An Old Comrades' Association has been formed and still continues to promote the old sense of comradeship and esprit de corps of the War years, and is awaiting the time when it will be possible to have a real reunion of all associated with the Company's war-time activities.

No. 1 PLATOON, A COMPANY

Formed in 1940 on the inception of the L.D.V. as the Kingsley Company, this Platoon had the distinction of being the only Platoon in the Battalion that kept its original designation throughout, for whereas all other Platoons had to be re-numbered owing to re-organisation, No. 1 always remained No. 1.

The first Commanders of the Kingsley Company were R. E. Corsby and and his second-in-command, G A. T. Vials, with their area of operations the ground adjacent to the Kettering Road

The Platoon was divided into four Sections, as under:—

No. 1	Leader: George Scott, D.C.M.	Deputy: W. G. Bowden
No. 2	Leader: C. A. Holmes	Deputy: N. Marshall
No. 3	Leader: F. Jordan	Deputy: S. Brittain
No. 4	Leader: F. C. Whiting	Deputy: A. S. Alibone

The duties of Company Quartermaster were discharged by C. F. Bament. J. F. Jones was appointed Musketry Instructor, assisted by H. Watkinson. The Headquarters of the Platoon were at Chestnut Road, where offices and workshops had been placed at their disposal by Frank Jordan.

On July 30th, 1940, with the new designation of L.D.V. units the Kingsley Company became the No. 1 Platoon of A Company.

The Platoon in this year manned two Observation Posts, one at the Police box at the Borough boundary on the Kettering Road, and the other in Buttocks Booth Lane. Section Leader F. Jordan provided two huts for the use of patrols off duty, and erected a camouflaged platform at each point for observation by daylight. F. E. Courtney drew a panorama sketch from the highest O.P. and marked each landmark with its name and range.

During the Winter of 1940-41 much valuable indoor training was done. A course of bayonet fighting was given by Sergeants Golden and Redley, of the Northamptonshire Regiment, and was keenly attended by the members of the Platoon in the workshop at Chestnut Road, while Section Leader F. C. Whiting conducted a course of instruction on the Mills bomb, which had been issued to the Platoon on February 7th.

On February 1st, 1941, commissions were granted to Home Guard officers, and the officers of No. 1 Platoon were Lieutenant R. E. Corsby, Commander,

THE END OF THE " BATTLE " (County Ground).

(Photo: B. Bernstein)

(Photo: B. Bernstein).

THE NORTHOVER (B Company).

with Second-Lieutenants G. A. T. Vials and F. C. Whiting as his deputies. By the end of March some changes had been made in the Section Leaders. Sergeant C. E. Burton now led No. 2 Section, with Sergeant G. H. Sharman as his deputy, while No. 2 Section was commanded by Sergeant E. Malpas.

The Platoon, besides carrying out its observational duties, participated in all the Company and Battalion schemes that were arranged, particularly in the Exercise "Scorch," in which they found very suitable and comfortable headquarters at the Pavilion at Spinney Hill. Of all the Platoons I visited that week-end, none had made themselves so comfortable as No. 1.

In 1942 the defence plan of the town having been altered, the Platoon very reluctantly gave up its road blocks at Buttocks Booth and the Manfield Hospital and established themselves at the Defended Locality at the corner of the Racecourse. On Summer evenings of that year, members of the Platoon wrestled with pickets and coils of barbed wire, in order to put their Racecourse position in an adequate state of defence. Platoon Headquarters were fixed, on paper, at the Kingsley Park Hotel, but fortunately, or unfortunately, the occasion did not arise for them to be occupied.

Lieutenant G. A. T. Vials had now been promoted Company Intelligence Officer, and Lieutenant F. C. Whiting had departed to G Company, Lieutenant A. G. Beer filling the vacancy as Platoon Officer. Further changes had to be made on the promotion of Major N. P. Andrews to the Command of the 15th Battalion. Lieutenant R. E. Corsby, who had commanded the Platoon since early L.D.V. days, received well-earned advancement to the position of Company Second in Command, Lieutenant Beer taking his place as No. 1 Platoon Commander, with Lieutenant C. W. Johnson as his right-hand man.

By this time the numbers of the Platoon had been depleted by the formation of a new No. 3 Platoon, which had been formed from "Jordan's Lot" at Chestnut Road. Still, the Platoon carried on efficiently, their work being interrupted now and again for Social Evenings at the Kingsley Working Men's Club, where the esprit de corps was further cemented by song, beer and mineral waters.

Various changes had been made in the Platoon, necessitated by promotions or by retirements. Sergeant B. Parkinson was now Platoon Sergeant, while Sergeant C. Bament continued to look after the stores and equipment in his usual efficient manner. The latter was a fine example to all the young fellows of Northampton for, although severely wounded in the 1914-18 War, when the call came in 1940 he was one of the first to come forward, and continued up to the Stand Down. Sections were commanded by Sergeant G. Scott, Sergeant H. E. Hemmings, Sergeant J. E. Dolby, Sergeant M. F. Swinstead, Sergeant F. A. Barratt, Sergeant W. Miles and Sergeant O. E. Howkins, while Sergeant C. Shrewsbury had charge of the Signal Section and Sergeant R. S. Inglis the First Aid and Stretcher Bearer Section.

An interesting member of the Platoon was Private G. F. Grigs. By profession a barrister in the Channel Islands, he left when they were evacuated in 1940 and came to England. He was one of our most enthusiastic members, and although well over the age limit of 65, always participated in all field exercises. Since the Stand Down I have ascertained from him in private conversation that he was then, in 1945, 71 years of age. During 1944 he was temporarily lost to the Battalion as he was on important duty at the War Office in connection with the invasion of Normandy.

No. 2: THE KINGSTHORPE PLATOON

Originally the Kingsthorpe Company of the North Group, on the re-designation of the Battalion this became No. 2 Platoon of A Company. The strength at its inception was 98, all old soldiers of the last war, but there were many with no previous military experience clamouring for admission.

These were absorbed as soon as possible, so that the strength of the unit steadily increased until it reached its peak of 210. Losses to the Regular Forces reduced it a little, but there were always plenty of volunteers, and it maintained a steady strength, so that in December, 1943, after three and a half years of existence, when it was absorbed into the Coastal Reinforcement Company, it still had a muster of 185. I shall always remember this Platoon for the large number of "young" soldiers in its ranks. Some of them had already served over three years in the Home Guard when, at the age of 18¼, they were called up for the Regular Army. As most of these lads had been through my hands at school I was quite aware of the fact that they had grown old very suddenly, but it is sometimes useful to have a blind eye, and one could only admire the spirit of these lads who were so eager to join with their elders in the defence of their country.

Th first Commander of the Platoon was J. V. Collier, who in those early days of May, 1940, organised this, one of the strongest Platoons in the Battalion, into a really efficient unit. He laid the foundations of this most successful body and it was a matter of much regret when, owing to ill-health, he had reluctantly to relinquish the command. He still remained a member of the Battalion, and no one was more delighted than myself when later on, with an improvement in his health, he resumed active work and rendered valuable assistance to H Company.

The Platoon was fortunate that they had in their ranks one who proved himself a very able successor in the person of Eric Beeston, who commanded the Platoon so energetically and so efficiently until the formation of D Company, when he earned well-merited promotion to the position of Second-in-Command of the new Company.

Although throughout the four and a half years of its service, zeal and enthusiasm remained at a remarkably high level, never were they more marked than in those early days when, ill-equipped and untrained, long hours of vigil were undertaken by men who had already put in a full day's work. The only complaint during those glorious Summer nights of 1940 came from one patrol which, on being informed that it need only watch during the dusk and dawn periods, said that they had "—— well come out to do an all-night patrol and they were —— well going to do it, and to hell with what anyone said."

Work they wanted and work they got. All-night patrols, dusk and dawn patrols, guards on the Boughton Green Reservoir, guards on their ill-furnished armoury, and all the time training, training, training. Men were lost to the Regular Forces, recruits were taken in to replace them, establishing a strong Defended Locality when these came into being, and being able to say, "We will deny the enemy entrance to Northampton from the north." Then learning to fight as a mobile force. Weapon training, fieldcraft, anti-gas training, battle drill, tactical exercises, learning every detail of their area, first aid, signalling, bayonet fighting, unarmed combat, street and house fighting, cooking, etc. All these came and had to be learned. Yes, work they wanted and work they had, and despite all, they learned to like it.

In common with all other units in the Battalion, great difficulty arose from the many changes in personnel which inevitably came. Apart from the constant drift into the Regular Forces, many were compelled to terminate their Home Guard service because their physical condition failed to match their zeal. A notable exception to this latter class was Lance-Corporal H. Gale, who, despite having suffered from loss of memory when declaring his age, stood the course until within a few months of the end, and frequently displayed powers of endurance which put younger men to shame, and could always be relied upon to do his full duty in the foulest weather and to produce a quip and a smile at its completion; he was an inspiration to all the members of the Platoon and can truly be called "Kingsthorpe's Grand Old Man."

In those early days excellent work was done by Volunteers W. C. Perkins, E. Tomlinson, H. Baucutt and G. Burnell. Besides his ordinary duties, Volunteer Tomlinson also performed yeoman service as Quartermaster. Unfortunately, in addition to losing their Commander, J. V. Collier, the Platoon were soon deprived of the services of two Section Leaders, W. G. Perkins and Tomlinson, and two Deputy Section Leaders, H. Downs and H. Negus, but their places were adequately filled by Volunteers A. Keene, E. A. Cox, S. Bonnett and W. Bland.

By the Spring of 1941 the Platoon had a strength of 150, and with the institution of ordinary military ranks and titles by the War Office, further appointments were made in order to ensure efficient administration. In April, 1941, the organisation was as follows: Platoon Commander, Lieutenant E. Beeston; Second-in-Command, Second-Lieutenant C. W. Marriott; Platoon Sergeant, Sergeant H. H. Howard; Platoon A. and Q. duties, Corporal A. Wheatcroft; No. 1 Section Commander, Sergeant A. Keene; No. 2 Section, Sergeant E. A. R. Cox; No. 3 Section, Sergeant H. Baucutt; No. 4 Section, Sergeant W. Burnell.

It was in the early hours of July 15th, 1941, that Kingsthorpe had what was to prove its only first-hand knowledge of parachutists. A patrol on duty on the Boughton Green Road, under Corporal Mead, saw a number of parachutes descending from the dawn sky. This, they thought, was the moment for which they had trained and waited. Corporal Mead and his men are to be highly commended on the prompt and efficient action they took. The occurrence was immediately reported through the pre-arranged channels and the parachutists who landed in Kingsthorpe territory picked themselves up to find that they were menaced by grim and determined Home Guards with loaded rifles. From the language of the paratroops it became immediately clear that they were far from being Bosche, for their English, though hardly to be described as pure, was contaminated by no foreign accent, but enriched by those phrases so beloved of all English fighting men when stirred. All was well, but it was only a year of part-time training and discipline which prevented this patrol from taking precipitate action which might well have resulted in the death of members of the R.A.F. Strangely enough, Corporal Mead, who eventually became Flight-Sergeant Mead, a flight engineer in the R.A.F., had his own aircraft shot down over Germany later in the War, and saved his life by baling out. One wonders as he floated earthwards whether he remembered the occasion when his own coolness and discipline saved others in similar plight from possible tragedy.

By the Summer of 1941 the standard and efficiency of the Platoon had reached a high level and it was no longer possible to absorb successfully raw recruits into the existing Sections. These recruits were pouring in and it was decided to form a special recruits' class into which the newly-enrolled were placed until they could pass a proficiency examination. Private S. Payne was appointed Lance-Corporal Instructor and proved an outstanding success.

The importance of adequate Medical Orderly service within each Platoon was being stressed, and a squad of eight stretcher bearers was formed under the very capable leadership of Lance-Corporal Wesley. All members of this squad secured their St. John Ambulance badges, and eventually won the Battalion Stretcher Bearers Competition, going on to become third in the Sub-District Contest, and before long Wesley had earned his promotion to Medical Corporal.

Following reorganisation at Company level, Second Lieutenant C. W. Marriott was appointed to the Command of the newly-formed No. 3 Platoon. No. 2 regretted having to lose him after having him as their Second-in-Command since L.D.V. days, but the best wishes of all its members went with him in his new and more responsible position, a promotion that he had so well merited. Platoon Sergeant Howard was appointed to the vacancy and proved very popular with the Platoon. Private A. L. Taylor was promoted direct to the rank of Platoon Sergeant. I cannot pass on without expressing my appreciation of the work done, no matter what the rank, by my friend Taylor. By profession he was a civil engineer, had had a distinguished career as a commissioned officer in the last war and as Colonial Territorial officer between the wars. On the formation of the L.D.V. he was appointed to the command of a company, but on being transferred to another district by reason of his profession he had relinquished his command. Next he became a Platoon Commander, and on his removal to Northampton he became a full-blooded private in the Kingsthorpe Platoon. In this rank he was quite content to remain, and he was very reluctant to accept any promotion. However, this reluctance was overcome by the Platoon Commander, Lieutenant Beeston, really a most persuasive fellow, who stressed the point that his obvious qualifications for higher rank could not be wasted at a time when the country needed the best in every citizen. Sergeant Taylor was a typical L.D.V., his only concern being to serve his country in whatever capacity he was needed, and it was a matter of much regret when he was moved from the town.

It was during the Summer of 1942 that a crisis of the first magnitude arose in the Platoon. During the first few weeks of L.D.V. existence the Headquarters had been in the lounge of the Commander's home, but Councillor Cyril Chown came to its aid and generously allowed them free use of the commodious premises at the rear of his home at the Court House, Kingsthorpe. Here they spent a very happy time until in 1942 the Court House became a branch of the Sunshine Home for Blind Babies. No. 2 Platoon now found itself homeless with about 150 men and a considerable quantity of arms, equipment and ammunition to house. Not a single building could be found in Kingsthorpe, but eventually Battalion Headquarters requisitioned a paddock in a convenient position and, with the co-operation of Sergeant Frank Jordan, of No. 1 Platoon, sufficient material was " acquired " for the construction of a very large hut. The work of erection was carried out entirely voluntarily by members of the Platoon in addition to their normal duties, under the capable supervision of Sergeant Jordan and their own Sergeant Taylor. Three months of hard work gave them Headquarters fully adequate to their requirements and as good as any in the district. It is interesting to note that these premises still stand and are being used as a boys' club, perhaps as fitting a memorial of its own Home Guard as Kingsthorpe could possibly have.

It was found that with the increasingly high standards of efficiency required in both training and administration, two officers were insufficient to deal with a force which, although a Platoon, had by these days reached a strength of over 200, and an additional subaltern was granted. Private S. R. Griffin, whose powers of leadership and loyalty had been well known since 1940, but whose business ties had hitherto prevented his acceptance of frequently offered promotion, was elected for this position. About this time Sergeant Wheatcroft having applied to revert to the ranks, Corporal W. Chown was promoted Sergeant (A. and Q. duties), with Lance-Corporal A. L. Wilson as his assistant. Sergeant Taylor having once more been transferred, Sergeant E. A. R. Cox was made Platoon Sergeant. With the majority of the Platoon having a static role in the Defended Locality, the younger and more agile members were assembled in No. 4 Section, under Sergeant H. Freeman, Sergeant J. Horwood and Corporal H. Block. This Section had a definitely mobile role, being a well-trained band of men of suitable physique for a light striking force.

In December, 1943, No. 2 Platoon as such came to an end. I have said elsewhere that there are some things a Battalion Commander has to do for which he feels the greatest reluctance, and so it was with the formation of the Coastal Reinforcement Company. And thus the Kingsthorpe Platoon lost its identity and became part, and a very valued part, of the new D Company. Unfortunately there were some members who were in Category 2 and therefore could not get away to serve on the coast if the necessity arose, and these were separated from their old comrades and were transferred to H Company. The Kingsthorpe Platoon from 1940 had loyally played its part and will always hold an especial place in my memory, composed as it was of members, many of whom I had taught as boys at school and for whom I have the greatest affection.

No. 3 PLATOON OF A COMPANY
(later, on reorganisation, No. 2)

This Platoon, formed of the Works Sections of the Advance Motor Co. and Painton's, was a very valuable part of A Company and was one of the few works units in the Battalion that functioned really successfully. On the outbreak of War an amateur Fire Brigade had been formed at the Advance, and on the formation of the L.D.V. this formed the backbone of the Platoon.

It was on June 25th, 1940, that the managing director of the Advance Motor Co., in conversation with A. W. Gardner (afterwards Battalion Quartermaster), suggested the idea of forming a Works Section of the L.D.V. That same afternoon along went Gardiner with the O.C. North Group, Major N. P. Andrews, complete with enrolment forms, and signed up Mr. Power and Mr. W. T. Whitehouse, and on the next day the Section was officially formed. Notices hurriedly posted in the Works called a meeting of all able-bodied men for 6.30 p.m. The object of the meeting was put to the men and the response was overwhelming. The Fire Brigade volunteered en bloc, and altogether 28 men were enrolled. The fact that the Fire Brigade became L.D.V.'s caused a bit of a headache, for now they had a double duty to perform, but to their credit never once did they falter, and they carried out both duties to the end.

Like most other platoons they were a mixed bag of old soldiers and raw recruits, but all were keen to make a start, and stayed on after the day's work for drill instruction by C. Ambidge, the oldest soldier. The Section drilled and carried out guard duties with commendable zeal. Many and varied are the tales that could be told of incidents which happened in the Guard Room, such as the time they roped-in a gang prowling round the factory in the middle of the night, which gang turned out to be Police Specials, Incident and Gas Officers looking for a " gas bomb." The L.D.V. were even accused of spoiling the exercise.

The Section was now No. 1 H.Q. Section, and equipment was becoming more plentiful, but the Section now felt that they wanted more action in the field. Lieutenant Corsby, then in command of No. 1 Platoon, was approached and he most kindly co-operated by inviting the Section to take part with him in a Company exercise. I now continue in the words of Sergeant W. E. Whitehouse, as he then was:—

" The Exercise was an attack on the Kettering Road block near Manfield Hospital by ' enemy paratroops.' It was here that we nearly came to grief through that human dynamo who was later to become our C.O. One never knew how or where he would turn up. To get on with the story: we were nicely concealed in extended order behind the hedgerow facing the brickfield. Presently along came a sergeant and several cadets in blue, hot-footing it along the ditch on the other side of our position. When they got level I gave the order to fire, represented by a rattle. Did those boys take any notice? Like smoke they did. One of our men broke cover and tried to hold up the stragglers, whereupon the sergeant in the lead turned and shouted, 'Punch his head and come on.' As I was taking the exercise most seriously I was not standing for this, so ordered Sergeant Ambidge with two men to chase them and bring the so-and-so's back, and if the sergeant argued, to punch *his* head, with my compliments. About half an hour later a very dejected Sergeant Ambidge returned alone. As he got near I asked him very impatiently, 'Well, what happened?' My sides still ache as I remember the look on his face as he replied 'Major Barnes.' Anyway, we took a couple of prisoners, so we felt that honour was satisfied."

Those were the days when the Air Force Cadets rendered such good service, and when I had the great enjoyment of leading them in their attacks on the platoons of the L.D.V.

The Section did a considerable amount of field work after that and never failed to get a good parade, for all ranks really enjoyed the training. Many were the amusing incidents and near calamities that befell them in those early days. Space does not permit me to go into details, but all of the Advance will remember one occasion when Sergeant Kilsby stopped an attack on the factory by flattening the leading attackers with a shovel, and the time when Sergeant Pate fell off the high wall. It is said hat he is still sore about it!

In the October of 1942 the Section was joined by No. 2 H.Q. Section (Painton's), then in charge of Sergeant Benham, seconded by Sergeant Cator, and the combined Section were designated No. 4 Platoon of A Company. Lieutenant C. W. Marriott was transferred from No. 2 Platoon to take command, and Sergeant W. E. Whitehouse became the Second-in-Command. Charles Marriott was a scout of the old order, and he and Whitehouse got on very well together, and an arrangement was made whereby he directed operations and was responsible for discipline, whereas Whitehouse undertook the training and administrative side. The arrangement worked well, Sections were re-formed and quickly settled down to work. March discipline was practised, and very largely due to the very able drill instruction of Platoon Sergeant W. James the Platoon became one that could hold its own with the best in the Battalion.

Equipment and weapons had by this time become more plentiful, and Equipment Sergeant Derby, assisted by Corporal Handford and Lance-Corporal Power, did yeoman service at Platoon Headquarters. With a variety of weapons at their disposal the Platoon became keener than ever on outdoor training and N.C.O.'s were encouraged to take courses which were then available. Lieutenant Whitehouse, who had already taken courses at the I.T.C. in bombing and fieldcraft, went down to Burwash and came back with material sufficient for many exercises. Platoon Sergeant James was a bombing fiend and took refresher courses, Sergeant Ambidge took the Sten and bayonet fighting, Sergeant E. Whitehouse took camouflage, Sergeant Pearce unarmed combat, Sergeant Sharpe gas, and Corporal Bailey first aid. All developed into good instructors, so it was not surprising that, with so much material at its disposal, Section training was looked forward to with keenness and pleasure.

In December, 1943, with the formation of the Coastal Reinforcement Company there was a reorganisation of A Company, and the Advance and

Painton's became the No. 2 Platoon, with additional responsibility for the defence of the northern sector of the town. During the days of Megrim and the D Day activities the Platoon carried out patrols on the railway along with the rest of the Battalion.

All this time plenty of open range practice had been carried on both with the rifle and the Sten, and Corporal Walker secured his crossed-guns badge and several N.C.O.'s and men qualified as Service shots.

Many of the younger members of the Platoon, whose names appear on the 1940 Roll, are now serving in various capacities in the Regulars, and no doubt found that their Home Guard training stood them in good stead in H.M. Forces.

Before the finish, Lieutenant Whitehouse had taken over command from Lieutenant Marriott, who found that his business activities did not permit of him devoting the time necessary for the commanding of a platoon; only those who have done the job know how the whole of one's leisure was absorbed by the work.

And so we come to the end of the No. 2 Platoon, which will always go down in Home Guard memory as the Advance Works. Generally speaking, Works Platoons for various reasons had not been a great success, but the Advance was an exception to the rule. This was due in a large extent to two members, J. C. Power and W. Whitehouse. The former, the managing director of the works, had joined up in 1940 as a private in the Platoon and all through set an example of devotion and patriotism to the men, and was always keenly interested in the welfare of the Platoon. From the earliest days Lieutenant Whitehouse was full of enthusiasm and this he maintained to the end. The members of the Advance owe a debt of gratitude to him for his leadership during those trying years of 1940-44.

B COMPANY

Headquarters: The Warwick Arms, Bridge Street.

Company Commander	- -	Major A. C. McFarlane
Second-in-Command	- - -	Captain O. J. Hargrave
Intelligence Officer	- -	Lieutenant F. H. Stephenson
Weapon Training Officer	-	Lieutenant W. C. Pepperell
Ammunition Officer	- -	Lieutenant F. A. Allen
Company Sergeant-Major	- - -	- C.S.M. J. Martin
Company Q.M.S. -	- - -	- C.Q.M.S. H. W. Revell

No. 5 Platoon. Headquarters: 60, Bridge Street.

Platoon Commander	- -	- Lieutenant H. S. Sheldon
Platoon Officer	- - -	- Lieutenant R. J. Fitzhugh

No. 6 Platoon. Headquarters: "Flower in Hand," West Street.

Platoon Commander	- -	Lieutenant F. K. Thornton
Platoon Officer	- -	Lieutenant W. A. Gilkerson

No. 7 Platoon. Headquarters: The Station House, Cotton End.

Platoon Commander	- -	- Lieutenant L. W. Lucas
Platoon Officer	- -	Lieutenant N. J. T. Martin

Originally in L.D.V. days the South Group, B Company was perhaps the most stable of all the Companies in the Battalion, for there were fewer changes, both in its responsibilities and in its personnel. Major A. MacFarlane was the only Company Commander who formed his Company in 1940 and was still commanding at the time of the Stand Down. In addition Captain O. J. Hargrave, after a brief visit to H Company, finished where he had started as Major MacFarlane's right-hand man.

The name of the Warwick Arms will always be remembered in connection with B Company, for in "this well built and commodious edifice" the

Headquarters of the Company had its being throughout the whole of its existence. We should like here to record our very grateful appreciation of the interest that Messrs. P. Phipps and Co. always took in the Home Guard. They readily placed at our disposal premises such as the Warwick Arms, Lord Raglan, etc., which were invaluable as headquarters of Home Guard units. In addition, many a Home Guard social has had greater success by the provision of a little of the commodity for which they are famous, an action which, in those days of shortages, was greatly appreciated by all the members.

Besides the Warwick Arms, Station House, Cotton End, was another well-known landmark in the Company, for here No. 7 Platoon had its Headquarters for four and a half years. Brilliantly captured in 1940 by Lieutenant Lucas, possession was retained of this building, despite numerous and prolonged attacks by the L.M.S. authorities, until the time came for the Platoon to be wound up. As a matter of fact, in view of the pressing demands, every endeavour was made to find alternate accommodation, Captain Barton and myself spending a day searching round Far Cotton, but we found that it was simply impossible, and so No. 7 Platoon continued in its original home. I believe that it would have broken the heart of Sergeant P. L. Chapman had a move been forced upon them, for he was indeed the "Lord of Station House," and no headquarters in the Home Guard could have been kept in a more spick and span manner than his realm. He was one of those methodical and tidy individuals that I so much admire, as my character is quite the reverse. I sincerely trust that Lieut.-Colonel T. E. Manning has forgiven me for my habit of covering Battalion Headquarters with my cigarette ends and ash.

The Manor House, Main Road, will also be long remembeed by members of the Company, for here Lieutenant F. K. Thornton and his merry men practised the gentle art of street fighting and house clearing, and here the first demonstration of this side of our work was given by the members of B Company to the Battalion officers and N.C.O.'s. Towards the end of our career, so well had the Manor House been used that there was very little of it left standing, but it had played its part in the training of the Home Guard and done valuable work. Alas, I believe that it has now been demolished and is now no more, but it will always remain in the memory of the men of B Company.

The Action Station of the Company was the Defended Locality at the South Bridge, undoubtedly one of the most important positions in the town, with its Observation Post on Hunsbury Hill. This was the main, and practically the only means of entrance to the town from the south, and we always had the utmost confidence in the ability of B Company to hold this position if the emergency arose.

In the Autumn of 1942, with a reorganisation taking place in the Battalion, the Company had a great influx of strength for they were joined by the Electric Light and United Counties Bus Platoons, which gave it a most welcome addition to its strength and, from a tactical point of view, put it upon a much sounder basis. Unfortunately, this happy state of affairs did not last very long, for a few months later both these Platoons departed from the Battalion, the former to the new 15th Battalion and the United Counties Bus Platoon to form the 2001 M.T. Company. And so B Company returned to its original character. During those months while Captain Hargrave was away with H Company, Captain F. H. Holder, from the Electric Light Platoon. acted as the Second-in-Command of the Company, but on the transfer of this Platoon to the 15th he naturally preferred to accompany them, to the regret of all in the 12th, for he had been one of the most enthusiastic and loyal officers, and the high state of efficiency in his Platoon was due in a large measure to the keen work that he and Lieutenant Jennings had put in from the early days.

In the Anniversaries on the County Ground in 1943 and 1944 the Company was responsible for the Bombing Demonstrations, and right well were these carried through, both by the demonstrators and by the commentator, Major MacFarlane. Who will forget the counting of the crowd as the Mills bomb burst after the regulation four seconds, and the direct hit scored on the dummy tank by the very first shot from the Northover? The demonstration was a great credit to the Company and especially to Sergeant Emery, who was ever to the fore where bombing was concerned.

All this time the Platoons in the Company had been functioning very well. No. 6 Platoon, under Lieutenant Thornton, was now housed at " The Flower in Hand " in West Street, while the Reserve Platoon, No. 5, under Lieutenant Sheldon, had its home at 60, Bridge Street. Many exercises and schemes were held in Delapre Park and the surrounding country, all of which were keenly carried out.

On March 14th, 1944, there took place an effort at Commercial Street Schools that had not been attempted by anyone else in the Battalion, the staging of a play, " Patrol Orders," dealing with street fighting. This was written and produced by Lieutenant Thornton and J. Rice. So effective was this on its first production to the Company that it was repeated to the officers and N.C.O.'s of the Battalion, when we were honoured by the presence of the Sub-District Commander, Colonel J. L. Short, and the Sector Commander, Colonel G. S. Watson. Incidentally, besides the value of the play from a training point of view, it was also instrumental in raising a considerable sum for the Comforts Fund of the Northampton " Chronicle and Echo."

In August, 1944, No. 5 Platoon, led by Lieutenant Sheldon, was successful in the Battalion Battle Platoon Competition and were the first and only holders of the Jeffery Cup. A month later, under Lieutenant J. Fitzhugh, they put up a very creditable performance in the Sector Competition, gaining the leading place in the firing part, but being beaten in field training.

Besides the officers already mentioned, another most enthusiastic officer and one of the originals was Lieutenant P. C. Williams, who in his spare time from Home Guard duties was mine host of the Angel Hotel. Unfortunately, in 1942 he had to undergo a most severe operation, which necessitated his resignation from the Company, but making a most gratifying recovery he later found himself a niche as Transport Officer in the 15th, and with them continued to the Stand Down. It is especially pleasing to put on record this tribute to Percy Williams for a particular reason. In 1940, with the country in dire peril and with the formation of the L.D.V. in Northampton for the defence of the town, one would have thought and expected that the lead to its citizens would have been given by the " city fathers." However, only two responded to the call of Mr. Anthony Eden, Councillors Percy Williams and J. V. Collier. No doubt the others had sufficiently good reasons for their action, or rather inaction, but credit should be given to these two for their spontaneous and wholehearted enthusiasm in helping to build up the L.D.V.

B Company had in its ranks one whose service must be almost unique. Volunteer Walton, who in 1940 was 83 years of age, knocked twenty years off his age, and in the Summer months of that year carried out his all-night patrol duties and put to shame many young men of the town. Although forced to retire when " officially " he reached the age of 65, he was, I am pleased to say, with us on the Stand Down Parade, and is still going strong.

No record of B Company would be complete without mention of that Home Guard stalwart, C.S.M. J. Martin, whose heart and soul were in the well-being of his Company. He had a particular flair for the training of

N.C.O.'s and the capable body that he turned out were a great tribute both to his work and his personality. Although offered a commission in another Company, his real interest was in his old and loved B Company, and he preferred to remain with them to the end. He was a typical Home Guard, keen and enthusiastic in all he did, and withal imbued with that fighting spirit which makes the good soldier. Had I been a Bosche paratrooper, one of the last men I should have wanted to meet would have been C.S.M. J. Martin.

C COMPANY

Headquarters: 63, King Edward Road.

Company Commander	Major A. G. R. Barton
Second-in-Command	Captain H. Clayson
Intelligence Officer	Lieutenant F. E. Watts
Weapon Training Officer	Lieutenant W. M. Andrews
Ammunition Officer	Lieutenant E. G. Turner
Company Sergeant-Major	C.S.M. T. A. Ball
Company Q.M.S.	C.Q.M.S. W. G. Covington

No. 10 Platoon. Headquarters: Bushland Road School.

Platoon Commander	Lieutenant V. R. Sherwell
Platoon Officers	Lieutenant G. Seago and Lieutenant A. J. Cockerill, M.C.

No. 11 Platoon. Headquarters: Brook Factory, Clarke Road.

Platoon Commander	Lieutenant J. W. Spires

No. 12 Platoon. Headquarters: Town and County School ,Billing Road.

Platoon Commander	Lieutenant F. H. Collins
Platoon Officer	Lieutenant A. L. Bason

No. 13 Platoon. Headquarters: 111, Adnitt Road.

Platoon Commander	Lieutenant P. Lawley
Platoon Officer	Lieutenant C. Hiam

When the name of C Company is mentioned, thoughts at once go back to various places, St. Peter's Bridge, Bushland Road School, the Brook Factory, and Rushmere Road, where so many strenuous and, we hope, happy hours were spent by its members.

One of the original Companies, being formed in L.D.V. days and being responsible for the defences on the east of the town, C Company maintained its character throughout the many changes that occurred in the Battalion, and at the close was still operating on the ground where they commenced.

The old East Group of the L.D.V. days was composed of three Companies: Weston, St. Michael's and St. Crispin's, with F. Freestone, Charles Oakey and Major St. J. Browne as Commanders, and with W. Care as the Group Commander and S. H. Barber as his Second-in-Command. This arrangement did not last very long for the Group Commander departed to Zone as Quartermaster, S. H. Barber retired under the age limit regulation, F. Freestone received a Government appointment, while the worth of Charles Oakey had been spotted by the Brixworth Division, who made him their Adjutant, a position he held until after the Stand Down. These departures necessitated several promotions. By this time the Groups had been renamed Companies and Major H. St. John Browne took over the new C Company with Captain S. B. Patrick as his Second-in-Command, while Lieutenants C. H. Brown, A. G. R. Barton and C. G. Harris became the Platoon Commanders.

These were the days when the skies were watched by C Company from the Observation Posts at Rushmere Road and from the position east of The Headlands, the spot from where the photograph at the beginning of this book was taken. On those August and September nights, from the post at

Rushmere Road there could be seen the barrage over London when the enemy was trying to reduce the Capital, a sight that was always fascinating and one which certainly helped to pass away the long nights. About this time the positions at St. Peter's Bridge and Abington Mill, which had hitherto been included in the B Company area, now passed over to C.

Early in 1941 there took place on the " Eastern Front " one of the most interesting Company exercises that was held, for on this occasion the opposition was provided by the K.R.R.'s, who were billeted in the district. We were particularly indebted to Major Williams, of that Regiment, for his very meticulous planning of the attack, and his very successful effort to stage it on the tactics used by the Bosches. Incidentally, Major Williams had already seen much fighting in France, where he was one of the last of the heroic garrison of Calais who fought until their last cartridge had been expended. Only then, although their casualties had been extremely heavy, did they think of surrender. By their determined action they undoubtedly delayed the enemy long enough for the remains of the British Army to get away from Dunkirk. Taken prisoner when Calais fell, he was being marched away back to Germany when he made his escape and, after some weeks of adventure, managed to reach the coast where, after more delay, he was able to procure and hide a rowing boat. On the first suitable night he rowed out into the Channel and, after a considerable lapse of time, was picked up by a British destroyer and brought to England. Home Guards of C Company will be pleased to know that he came safely through the many actions in which his regiment was afterwards engaged. Such was the man who assisted us so much by this scheme to test out the eastern defences of the town.

This was by far the most realistic exercise in which we had participated up to that time. No one seems to have kept a record, so that this is an account of the evening, written from my recollections as an Umpire. I first contacted the " enemy " at the kicking-off point at Cogenhoe, where they were resting by the side of a hedge with their lorries well concealed under trees. My first impression was the difference in equipment from ours in the 1914—1918 War. Gone were the pack and other paraphernalia with which we were adorned in those far-off days, their kit being cut down to an absolute minimum, while instead of the heavy army boots, all wore plimsolls. Equipment was sacrificed for speed. At the appointed time the attack began and, preceded by motor-cyclists, they moved off in their lorries. The first opposition was met at the crossroads near Little Billing Station, and here a regular battle ensued. Warned by their motor-cyclists the troops were off their lorries in a flash and into the fields adjoining the roads, and in a few minutes had mopped up the defenders. What might have been a nasty situation happened here, for some of the country Home Guard, in their excitement, were charging with naked bayonets. Only by promptly putting them out of action was a probable accident avoided. This position having been dealt with, the troops speedily mounted their lorries and were soon off. The next opposition was encountered at Little Houghton, where the road blocks were quickly overwhelmed from the rear. Here it was that a valuable lesson should have been learned by the local platoon. In all their exercises the grounds of Mrs. Smythe had been treated as sacred and out of bounds. The K.R.R.'s were no respectors of private grounds and in a very short time were through them and on top of the defenders from an unexpected quarter. This lesson, that in warfare no grounds or houses are " private," but that the enemy would have made full use of anything that suited their purpose, would no doubt have been very hard for the people of these islands to learn. As a matter of fact, on this occasion it was considered as hardly playing the game for the attackers to make use of the cover provided by these private grounds. All this time, it was now about 9 p.m., Lieutenant A. G. R. Barton on St.

Peter's Bridge had been pestered with fifth columnists. Major Williams had appreciated the fact that this position at the Bridge was the strongest that he would probably encounter on this front, and had endeavoured to upset the defence by the use of these agents. Some of these were such as would have been probable, but the appearance of a cricket team with tommy guns in their kitbags would hardly have been likely in actual warfare. However, there is no doubt that our friend Barton, had a most gruelling time, so much so that on the appearance of six men who had been sent forward by Lieutenant Mills, of the Bus Company Station, he promptly put them all under arrest as enemy agents. And so the plan of Major Williams had succeeded, for there is no doubt that by the time the attack on the Bridge actually commenced, the defence was considerably rattled. Under cover of a frontal attack, a section of men, led by a young lieutenant whose name I have forgotten, made their way down the river unobserved. This they swam in their kit and took the Bridge from the rear.

As I was not on the other parts of the front I am unable to give an account of the happenings there, but it is certain that the exercise was a most valuable one from the Home Guard point of view, and if it taught no other lessons it certainly opened the eyes of all of us to the speed at which the enemy moved, and also to the disturbing influence of fifth column activities.

And now, having digressed at some length on this most instructive and valuable scheme, let us return to Company matters. In July, 1942, with the formation of G Company and the promotion of Captain S. B. Patrick as its Commander, Lieutenant A. G. R. Barton became the Second-in-Command of C Company, while Lieutenant Turner took over No. 11 Platoon. This situation did not last very long, for on the change in the Battalion command Major H. St. J. Browne moved to Battalion Headquarters as Second-in-Command and Major Barton became O.C. C Company, with Captain H. Clayson as his right-hand man. Hughie Clayson had started in L.D.V. days as C.S.M. of the Company, and latterly had been acting as Platoon Commander of No. 12 Platoon, originally the Stimpson's Mill Platoon. Like most works units this had presented a little difficulty, and in 1942 had been extended to include others than those who actually worked at the Mill. Captain Clayson had worked extremely hard, and with his knowledge and enthusiasm, combined with an endless amount of tact, had welded the Platoon into a most efficient unit. So that it was a well-merited promotion that saw him as Company Second-in-Command.

Major Barton and Captain Clayson retained their positions to the Stand Down, and under their command and guidance C Company was a particularly happy and efficient unit.

The Eleanor Exercise of July, 1942, had shown the need for all Companies to have a reserve platoon, and in the Autumn of this year C Company, in common with all other Companies, formed a new Platoon, No. 13, with Lieutenant Lawley as Platoon Commander and Lieutenant C. Hiam as Platoon Officer. This unit had its Headquarters at 111, Adnitt Road and did most of its indoor training at Stimpson Avenue Schools.

In the meantime Nos. 10 and 11 Platoons had been functioning smoothly. No. 10 throughout its existence had revolved round Bushland Road Schools, and for a long time was commanded by Lieutenant C. H. Brown until in July, 1942, when on account of ill-health he had to retire, and Lieutenant Sherwell took over. It is interesting to note that this Platoon provided the Battalion with no less than fourteen officers, men who in the old L.D.V. days had been N.C.O.'s and privates in the Platoon.

No. 11 Platoon had its Headquarters for four and a half years at the Canteen of the Brook Factory in Clarke Road, thanks to the generosity of the directors of that firm. Although at times the atmosphere got real fuggy the Canteen provided a " real home from home " for the members of No. 11, and here any night of the week one could always find someone either discussing the well-being of the Platoon, stripping a Lewis gun or a Mills grenade, or arranging a social event. It was this Platoon that every Christmas time arranged a Children's Party, which was always eagerly anticipated by the many youngsters of the members. They were most enjoyable affairs and reflected great credit on the wives and lady friends, who, in those difficult days of catering, provided a wonderful spread for the children. Much of the success of these parties was due to Corporal Chaffe, who undertook the duties of organiser.

Lieutenant Turner was the Platoon Commander of No. 11 for a considerable time until he became Company Ammunition Officer. He was succeeded by Lieutenant G. Whitsey, who unfortunately after a brief period had to resign on account of ill-health. His successor, Lieutenant J. Spires, stepped into the breach and continued in that capacity until the Stand Down. Lieutenants Oakey, Barton, Turner, Whitsey and Spires; No. 11 Platoon had indeed been fortunate in its Commanders.

No. 12 Platoon, originally the Stimpson's Mill unit, had a more varied career. In the first place comprised of the personnel at the works, it was later opened up to other members with beneficial results. Another change that militated for the good of the Platoon was its alteration of Headquarters to the Town and County School. As has been stated, Captain Clayson by dint of hard work and enthusiasm had pulled the Platoon into shape, and after his departure to Company Headquarters the good work was continued by Lieutenants Cockerill and Collins. Throughout its career, very valuable work on the administrative side had been performed by Lieutenant A. Bason, who acted as Platoon Officer throughout the whole of the four and a half years. Mention must also be made of Sergeant Malpas, an old friend of mine in Territorial days, who did excellent work in training the Platoon to the state of efficiency that it ultimately reached.

In C Company area there was positioned for most of the War a Search-light Battery on the Billing Road site. Close liaison was kept with this, and in case of necessity the members of the Battery were to assist in the defence of the road block near the Town and County School and, I feel sure, would have provided a much welcomed reinforcement.

On all Battalion Parades C Company could always be relied on for an excellent turnout, and at the Anniversaries on the County Ground one of the highlights was the Drill Display so ably taken by Sergeant W. Noble. At the Battalion Fete in September, 1944, the Company displayed its usual enthusiasm, and no one present will easily forget " Tattenham Corner," where every competition known to mankind was carried on for the benefit of the good cause.

And so with its Headquarters at 63, King Edward Road, C Company carried on to the end, but the record of the Company cannot be closed without a reference to the hard and devoted service rendered by C.Q.M.S. Covington. Quartermaster Sergeants do not often come into the limelight, but they do most valuable work behind the scenes, and a good one is a Godsend to Company Commanders. It is therefore all the more pleasing to pay tribute to these worthy individuals, and in this case to C.Q.M.S. Covington, who so ably and for so long gave valuable service to C Company.

A final word. The Company could not have reached its high state of efficiency without leadership, and in Major Barton they had one who, while maintaining a high standard of discipline, yet was a friend and comrade to all those who served under him. Starting as a private in old L.D.V. days, he filled all ranks and his promotion to the Command of his Company was a well-merited honour. To men such as these the Home Guard owed its success.

THE ORIGINAL D COMPANY

(in July, 1943, transferred to the 15th Battalion)

On the formation of the Northampton Division of the L.D.V. in May, 1940, the West Group consisted of the members residing in the Castle, Spencer and St. James' Wards, with Major R. Manning as the Group Commander and A. S. Baxter as his Second-in-Command. No. 1 Company (Castle Ward) had its Headquarters at the Working Men's Club in St. Andrew's Road and was commanded by J. S. Mennell. Unfortunately the health of the Commander did not permit of him holding the office for many months, and on his retirement S. F. Bennett took over and continued in this capacity until the split in the Battalion, with H. T. Bird as his Second-in-Command.

No. 2 Company (Spencer Ward) was commanded by P. G. Jones, with its Headquarters at "The Warren," Harlestone Road.

No. 3 Company, commanded by C. Phillipson, had its Headquarters at Franklin's Gardens. Unfortunately, here too an early change had to be made, and before long W. H. Pancoust took over command, with G. Thomson as his deputy.

In those early days road blocks were held at Hopping Hill on the Rugby Road, and on the Weedon Road near the "Red House," while many anxious nights were spent on the Observation Posts at Hopping Hill and The Tip on the Weedon Road.

In September, 1941, a change was made in the defence of the town and Defended Localities came into vogue. To the great disgust of the Company, the West Group having by this time altered its designation to D Company, the road blocks at Hopping Hill and Dallington were abandoned on the orders of the Higher Authorities and new ones had to be constructed on the river crossings at the West Bridge and the St. Andrew's Road junction near Spencer Bridge. Although no doubt that this was tactically correct, the members of the Company, particularly those residing in St. James', did not relish the fact that in the event of invasion they were allowing the Hun a free run among their homes. However, orders were orders, and the new Defended Localities came into being. Fortunately the Platoon at the Express Lift Works were able to take over the road block at the "Red House" and would thus have been able to offer resistance to the enemy before he actually got into St. James'.

In 1942 the Company lost its Second-in-Command, Captain A. S. Baxter being deservedly promoted to the command of the new F Company, which was in course of formation, and Captain P. G. Jones filled the vacancy. The Platoons were now officered as under:—

No. 11 Platoon	Commander:	Lieutenant S. F. Bennett
	Platoon Officer:	Lieutenant H. T. Bird
No. 12 Platoon	Commander:	Lieutenant H. E. Lea
	Platoon Officer:	Lieutenant A. V. Hawkins
No. 13 Platoon	Commander:	Lieutenant W. H. Pancoust
	Platoon Officer:	Lieutenant G. Thomson

In the late months of 1942, with a reorganisation in the Battalion the Company was strengthened by the addition of the Express Lift and the Gas Company Platoons, which change, we believe, was to the mutual advantage of both Company and Platoons. Both these Platoons had been in existence since L.D.V. days, primarily for the defence of their works. They had rendered valuable assistance to the Battalion, but had led a somewhat isolated existence, and in such circumstances it is always difficult to keep interest going. The Gas Platoon, commanded by Lieutenant N. C. Batten and Lieutenant F. Cole, particularly had a hard furrow to plough, for their numbers were constantly decreasing by men being called up for the Services and they had a large and important area to guard. By including them in D Company we hoped that an added interest would be given, and should the necessity have arisen they could have been quickly reinforced from the Company. The Express Lift Platoon were in a slightly different position for their numbers maintained a steady strength, due to the fact that they were engaged on important Naval work of national importance. Under Lieutenant V. H. Amberg and Lieutenant F. H. Salter they had proved themselves a most efficient unit and, contrary to most Works Platoons, had displayed the greatest interest in Home Guard activities, due in a large measure to enthusiastic leadership. However, it would have been quite wrong tactically to have left an isolated Platoon on the outskirts of the town in the area of a Company to which they did not belong. And so the Express Lift Platoon became a part of D Company under the reorganisation.

During all this time the Company had gone on working enthusiastically under Major Dick Manning and had proved itself a most efficient unit. They had loyally co-operated in all Battalion Exercises and Schemes and had played their part in the Third Anniversary on the County Ground. It was therefore with feelings of deep regret that we were reluctantly compelled to agree to their parting from the 12th. I have mentioned in another Chapter what I felt about the split, and I am sure that D Company had no desire to part company with us. However, on July 1st, 1943, we said goodbye to them as they passed over to the new 15th Battalion. Since that time we watched with deep interest their career and were pleased to note that, with the other units who left the 12th at the same time, they proved themselves a body of whom the parent Battalion was always proud.

D COMPANY (THE COASTAL REINFORCEMENT COMPANY)
Headquarters: "The Rosery," Kingsthorpe.

Company Commander - - - -	Major F. Jordan
Second-in-Command - - - -	Captain E. Beeston
Intelligence Officer - - -	Lieutenant A. Holland
Weapon Training Officer - -	Lieutenant H. H. Howard
Ammunition Officer - -	Lieutenant G. H. Sharman
Company Sergeant-Major - -	C.S.M. R. W. Saunders
Company Q.M.S. - - - -	C.Q.M.S. W. C. Chown

No. 14 Platoon. Headquarters: Chestnut Road.

Platoon Commander - - -	Lieutenant T. C. Wright
Platoon Officer - - - -	Lieutenant L. M. Bayly

No. 15 Platoon. Headquarters: Welford Road.

Platoon Commander - - -	Lieutenant S. R. Griffin
Platoon Officer - - - -	Lieutenant J. Horwood

No. 16 Platoon. Headquarters: Welford Road.

Platoon Commander - - -	Lieutenant H. Lansman
Platoon Officer - - - -	Lieutenant R. Freeman

No. 17 Platoon. Headquarters: Chestnut Road.

Platoon Commander - - - -	Lieutenant F. Parker
Platoon Officer - - - -	Lieutenant E. A. R. Cox

In November, 1943, when we were considering the strengthening of the Battalion Reserve (H Company), orders came from above which completely put an end to these considerations, for in order to thicken up the Coastal

Defences and to reinforce the Home Guard there, selected inland Battalions were to form Companies to proceed to the coast in the event of enemy landings. Need I say that, as usual, the lot in this area fell upon the 12th Battalion. These Companies were to be self-contained units, complete with weapons, ammunition, cooking equipment, mess tins, water bottles, blankets, ground sheets, etc., and on arrival would come under the command of the local Commander. As I have stated previously, in forming this new Company two things were essential, speed and as little dislocation of the existing Companies as possible. It all sounds so simple now, looking back, but believe me Captain Barton and I spent many hours, often until far after midnight, deciding on the best means of getting this Company going. Many schemes were put down on paper and almost as soon discarded as not giving us what we were after. At length we hit upon one in which we could find no flaws. We decided to combine No. 2 Platoon of A Company from Kingsthorpe, and No. 3 Platoon from Kingsley. This gave us the required numbers and did not cause too much dislocation. Lieutenant Frank Jordan was given the Command, with Lieutenant Eric Beeson as his right-hand man. I know of no one who gets cracking on a new job with as much enthusiasm as Frank Jordan, and in a short time he had evolved the outline of the new Company. I had laid down and had insisted upon with the Sub-District Commander that there should be no demotions because of the transfer of N.C.O.'s from the old Company to the new.

On December 15th, 1943, the new D Company came into being with a strength of 12 officers and 188 other ranks. Lieutenant A. Holland was appointed Intelligence Officer, Lieutenant H. H. Howard Weapon Training Officer, Lieutenant G. H. Sharman Ammunition Officer, while Sergeant Saunders, known to everyone as "Lofty," became Company Sergeant-Major. The organisation needed many days of hard work, but Frank Jordan, now Major, had found the right men for the right jobs, and these were made responsible for their particular side of the Company work. There was only one position we could not fill, that of Interpreter Orderly, for we had no German speaking member in the Company. However, all the other offices were well filled.

Accommodation was found at "The Rosery," Kingsthorpe; how this was acquired I never dare ask, as it was already in the possession of the American Army. The house was in a terribly dilapidated condition, but with the help of various fatigue parties, who got to work with broom, brush and incinerator it was soon made a real home from home. By a stroke of luck or good judgment, it had the added advantage of being in close proximity to two hostelries, who never seemed to run short of the necessary refreshment.

Three Battle Platoons were formed, No. 14 under Lieutenant T. Wright, No. 15 under Lieutenant S. R. Griffen, and No. 16 under Lieutenant H. Lansman, with Second-Lieutenants L. M. Bayly, J. Horwood and R. Freeman as their Platoon Officers. No. 17 Platoon, with Lieutenant F. Parker and Second-Lieutenant E. A. R. Cox, became the Support Platoon with the appropriate Home Guard sub-artillery.

Everybody set to work with a will. The C.Q.M.S. was busy issuing stores, and the additional items of kit needed by a unit that might have to proceed to the coast. The Orderly Room staff had its hands full getting out orders and instructions and making the necessary records of everybody and everything. The Intelligence and Signal Sections were fully occupied in their mysterious callings with maps, routes to the coast, battle and message boards, etc., and what to do with any Germans who wished to give themselves up (by this time, after all my lectures, they ought to have known), with German phrases thrown in, some of which were very rude, but very

THE SMITH GUN (G Company).

(Photo: B. Bernstein).

THE DESPATCH RIDERS, with "The House" in the background.

(Photo: B. Bernstein)

understandable. Sergeant Day, the Company cook, meanwhile with his assistants were collecting all the cooking kit that they could lay their hands on or that the Battalion Quartermaster would give them, and working out the different quantities of rations required, together with how and where the meals would be cooked. The Weapon Training Officer made it his business to see that every man was properly armed and knew how to use his weapon, and the Ammunition Officer was involved in calculations as to the number of rounds of S.A.A., bombs and grenades necessary, and how he was to get them to the coast, while the Company evidently expected to have its share of casualties, for on one of my visits to "The Rosery" the Medical Sergeant seemed to have bandages, splints, blankets and stretchers all over the place.

The first test of the Company took place on the Buzz Exercise on January 22nd-23rd, 1944, when they operated on the Spratton front. I have dealt fully with this in a previous Chapter, but it was a great tribute to D Company that after being in existence only just over a month they should have come through with flying colours and earned the "plaudits" of all the "higher-ups."

The Company being now firmly on its feet, we thought that it was time that we made a reconnaissance of the battle position at Great Yarmouth, part of whose defences we were to form. Accordingly, Major Jordan, Captain Beeston and Lieutenant Hill and, together with Captain Barton and myself, set off one cold Winter's morning early in February for the East Coast. All went well until we reached a particularly bleak spot a few miles past Thetford, when D Company's transport failed us. First a puncture in the back tyre, and then, on taking out the "spare" this also "went," and we were left stranded on a snowy Winter's afternoon miles away from anywhere. I looked at Barton and Barton looked at me, but neither said a word, but at that moment standing on "Windy Corner" I am certain that neither of us had a great opinion of the Company's transport. However, "Intelligence" got to work and hailing a passing lorry proceeded with the two tyres to the next village, some eight miles away, to get the necessary repairs done. However, all good things come to an end and after a delay of some two hours we resumed our journey. Unfortunately, instead of arriving at Yarmouth in the light, dusk only found us at Norwich. The weather by this time had gone all amuck, the night was very dark and cold and stormy, with plenty of snow and sleet. A wrong turn at Acle and we found ourselves wandering in the wilds of Norfolk. At such a time, with the night pitch black and with no signposts and no hedges at the side of the road, one almost felt like cursing the fate that had sent us on this journey. However, the Intelligence Officer, with the aid of a small-scale map and a torch, extricated us from the dilemma and Yarmouth was reached in the late evening.

On the Saturday various conferences were held with those responsible for the defence of Yarmouth, and we were given the plan with our part in it. A reconnaissange was made of the area, which involved much tramping along railway lines. I always consider that walking along railway lines is one of the most fatiguing of exercises. Whoever laid those sleepers at Yarmouth put them down as awkwardly as possible, just to annoy Home Guards, for there was all manner of intervals between them and no uniformity, so that you had to watch your step the whole of the way. As there were some miles of them, we certainly earned our Home Guard pay for that day.

D Company scheme of defence was drawn up to fit in with the main defence plan, and altogether a very profitable if strenuous week-end was spent. In the following month arrangements were made for all the officers and the senior N.C.O.'s to visit Yarmouth for a week-end, and an intensive reconnaissance was carried out. The whole of the area allocated to D Company was very carefully gone over, fire positions sited, Company and Platoon Headquarters fixed, and communications arranged, while contacts were made with the opposite numbers of the local Home Guard. The party was housed in the local Drill Hall, getting what sleep they could on a hard floor with a blanket for warmth, in March on the East Coast, a real hardening-up process. They were self-supporting; the C.Q.M.S. and the Sergeant Cook making all arrangements for feeding, which they did in their usual quiet but efficient manner. The party went down for work and they certainly got it; what with miles of barbed wire, beach obstacles, tank traps, barrage balloons, and thousands of mines laid in all places, Yarmouth was very much in the front line. Those of us who knew the town in peace times were sadly disillusioned, and many rubbed their eyes in amazement and wondered if they had really come to the right town.

In the meantime, training at home had been progressing satisfactorily. Embussing and debussing drill had been practised, specially enlarged maps of the area prepared and all the necessary details of positions discussed with the Platoons.

At last I felt that the time was ripe for the whole of the Company to make the journey to the coast for a full-dress rehearsal, and so this was arranged for the Easter week-end. I was particularly anxious that the Company should have settled down into full working order before this was undertaken, for it is anything but child's play to transport a Company of nearly 200 officers and men, together with their equipment, some 140 miles to the coast, house and feed them while they were there, and bring them back again safe and sound. Six United Counties buses were required to convey them, and here we were indebted to the 2001 M.T. Company for their ready help and co-operation, and they are to be congratulated on the efficient way in which all the transport arrangements were carried out. The feeding problem presented quite a headache, as all food and cooking utnsils had to be taken. It is amazing what 200 men can eat and drink in the course of two days. Security was drummed in the ears of the members of the Company, but it was a difficult job where wives and sweethearts were concerned to keep the matter quite as hush-hush as it should have been.

An Advance Party set out on the Saturday morning, consisting of the I.O., the W.T.O., the C.Q.M.S. and the Company cook, to contact the military authorities, to arrange for a place for the men to eat and sleep, and to deal with the many things that inevitably crop up in spite of the most carefully made plans. Accommodation with cooking facilities was found in a former holiday camp at Hopton, between Gorleston and Lowestoft, right on the cliff edge and in close proximity to the usual barbed wire and mines and several coastal batteries.

On a bright and sunny Easter Sunday morning the Company set off from their Headquarters at " The Rosery " and Chestnut Road, and had a pleasant journey, the tedium being passed with the usual games of skill so well-known to soldiers of the 1914—1918 War, and by the singing of many familiar songs, some of which have appeared in print, while others are not likely to do so. A break was made at Norwich and, strange to say, this coincided with the opening of the local places of refreshment. The Battalion Quartermaster and I had gone on slightly ahead and, besides getting one in first, had made a reconnaissance of these places near the centre of the town so that on the arrival of the Company everyone was able to refresh the inner man. In the early afternoon the Camp at Hopton was reached and sleeping quarters allocated, although the floor was the only place on which to sleep. Later on in the afternoon the whole of the Company went to their allotted positions in the defence area and became thoroughly acquainted with their terrain, which was singularly reminiscent of the type of country over which our men fought in Holland, even down to the windmills. Returning from the afternoon's operations the men had tea and then there were "Liberty" buses to take them into Yarmouth for an evening's recreation. At midnight we sallied forth again, this time to man the positions by night and to enable the patrols to find their way in the dark. Although cold, it was a lovely moonlight night, and in spite of their tiredness excellent work was done by all of the Company. Hot soup had been prepared by the cooks on the return to camp, and after that all slept the sleep of the just. A late breakfast and the promise of a fine day—it was Easter Monday— revived any drooping spirits, and the morning was spent on the cliff edge carrying out Sten and Lewis gun practice by firing into the sea with live ammunition, quite a change from the range at Brington. In the afternoon the Company had a stand easy, most of them sunbathing on the cliffs, whilst a Conference was held with the Garrison Commander and other Senior local Officers by the officers of the 12th. The Garrison Commander expressed great appreciation of the way in which D Company had undertaken and carried out its obligations, all of which reflected the greatest credit on Major Jordan and all his members. An early tea followed, after which was the final packing of kit and equipment and the tidying up of the Camp, which was so well done that it even evoked the approval of the Camp Commandant, who we had found was not an easy man to please. Then came the long journey home, which was reached round about midnight. I am sure that all the members of D Company will never forget their week-end at Great Yarmouth, one which, although strenuous was nevertheless most interesting and enjoyable. Much of this enjoyment was due to the efficient work of Sergeant Day, the Company cook, who, like all cooks, never seemed to sleep, but who saw that the Company was fed, and fed well, during its stay.

With the experience of knowing their battle stations, and what was required of them when they reached them, the Company polished up its training "in patient expectation" for the call which, fortunately or unfortunately, never came. D Company, in common with other Companies of the Battalion, hoped that they would be mustered as the long-awaited D Day approached, and perhaps sent to the coast until any danger of enemy retaliation was past. But it was not to be; the Home Guard was not required.

During the remaining months of its existence the Company steadily went on with its training, and in July arranged a very successful Fete for charitable purposes by which the sum of £600 was raised. Following this they took their share along with other Companies in the Battalion Fete.

When the Stand Down came in December, 1944, D Company was then only a little over a year old, but had rendered excellent service in its short but eventful life.

E (THE RAILWAY) COMPANY

In those perilous days which followed the capitulation of France and the withdrawal of the British Forces from Dunkirk, when the L.D.V. came into being, the peculiar and vital position of the railway systems of the country was fully realised by the Authorities, and in common with all other sections of the community, railway men were among the first to answer the call, and railway platoons, companies and even battalions sprang up throughout the land.

The guarding of railway property, with all the attendant buildings, sidings and vital undertakings on the lineside, called for a definite and well-developed knowledge of the territory, as well as first-hand acquaintance of railway operation and function. Men who daily performed their duties on the lineside and were in close and familiar contact with railway organisation, were the ones who could best be utilised to guard and protect the railways from enemy attack.

There was the further and most important question of the safety of the line and traffic during normal functioning of the railways, which by their very nature and extent offered obvious opportunity for sabotage. For these reasons the War Office decided with the Railway Executive that so far as was possible, railway staffs should be formed into separate railway units, which in turn, for administrative and operational reasons, should be part of the local Home Guard Command.

And so E Company came into existence, and until their transfer to the 15th Battalion in 1943, formed a very important and valued Company of the 12th Battalion. It was comprised of some 500 railway men of all grades, and although the number fluctuated during its life, due to call-up for the Regular Forces and changes of location of their employment, during its connection with the 12th Battalion it maintained a steady strength of some 400 personnel.

Started in May, 1940, mainly through the interest and energy of Major E. W. H. Powell, who had an excellent record of service in the last War and who was himself a railway official, the organisation rapidly began to function smoothly. It was in no sense an easy Company to command, one of the main difficulties being the irregular hours of duty worked by the railway staff throughout the War period, with the result that it was rarely possible to get a good muster of men on parade. There were always men on duty, and others either just going on or coming off. However, it is true to say that these difficulties were offset by the keen interest of all ranks to perfect themselves in the training and duties required of them, and to the work of the Company Commander, Major Powell, who spared no effort to produce and maintain a high standard of discipline and efficiency.

It is an interesting fact that from its inception the Company had within its area and responsibility no less than 50 vulnerable points, including bridges, buildings, stations, and other railway property of the highest importance from the viewpoint of effective railway operation. The operational area comprised the L.M.S. lines and buildings in the County Borough, extending from Kingsthorpe to the south entrance to Hunsbury Hill Tunnel and from Bridge Street Motive Power Depot to Hardingstone Crossing—a very considerable area. In its orbit the Company contacted many of the town Companies and Platoons, particularly the Platoons of the Electric Light Company and the Gaslight Company. The liaison between E Company and these two latter platoons was indeed always most close and extremely cordial, and in its training they were fortunate at frequent intervals to be able to combine in exercises and meetings of a less official character.

E Company was eventually organised into four Platoons, the layout of organisation being as under:—

Company Commander - -	Major E. W. H. Powell
Company Second-in-Command -	Captain R. J. Marfleet
Company Adjutant - - -	Lieutenant R. G. Bayes
Company Sergeant-Major -	G. Quartermain, D.C.M., M.M.
No. 14 Platoon - - - -	- Lieutenant S. Hasler
No. 15 Platoon - - -	- Lieutenant W. E. Wood
No. 16 Platoon - - -	- Lieutenant J. Nightingale
No. 17 Platoon - -	- Lieutenant E. Prentice, D.C.M.
Weapon Training Officer -	- Lieutenant W. Rainbow
Lewis Gun Officer -	- Second-Lieutenant W. H. Best

E Company at this time consisted of 136 Category 1 and 119 Category 2. These Category 2 men were to be retained for railway operations and only released when circumstances were such that railway oprations no longer required them.

In conjunction with Battalion H.Q. the system of defence was formed, weapon pits and other defensive aids were constructed and a patrolling system of the area instituted. The Company, by virtue of the extensive locality it was called upon to defend, was required to perform a great deal of patrol work, and during the years that the Company served in the 12th Battalion in all changes of temperature and weather, men devotedly patrolled the running lines and buildings, in exposed territory and over very difficult terrain. Those Home Guards from other Companies who patrolled the lines round about D Day will, I am sure, very heartily agree with this last point. It is a tribute to E Company that despite the calls of railway duty, heavy and arduous as they were, this work was performed most cheerfully, and in addition all spare time available was devoted to training and capturing or re-capturing the arts of weapon manipulation, fieldcraft, discipline and other essential branches of the military profession.

Stress should indeed be laid upon the arduous and exacting calls of railway duty during the War years, which fell particularly heavy upon the men in the operating grades, train crews, signal men and similar staff, who in addition to working irregular hours of duty were continually called upon to carry a very heavy additional burden of extended hours. It is greatly to the credit of such men, who were indeed the backbone of E Company, that they faced up to their duties in the Home Guard in manful fashion and were a great asset to the Battalion.

From early days the large stores of petrol and oil held by the Pool Petrol Board had caused much concern to Battalion H.Q. in case of invasion. After the experience of France, where petrol was readily available to the invading Germans, it was essential that these stocks should be denied to the enemy. Early in 1942 it was decided to form a Platoon, recruited from employees of the Board, whose primary duties consisted of the demolition of the extensive stores of petrol and oil which were stored on their several premises adjoining or forming part of the Railway property of Northampton; it was therefore decided that this Platoon should be part of E Company. It is an interesting fact that these stocks approximated some 250,000 gallons of petrol and oil, and it can well be imagined what use the enemy would have been able to make of such stores had they ever landed here. As it was, this new Platoon, which came into being on May 6th, 1942, was trained for the specialised and quite intricate duties of disruption and then destruction of the stocks, and at the same time undertook training in arms and fieldcraft to enable them to defend their depots and to join forces with E Company in their defensive plan. The Platoon was commanded by Lieutenant F. Sketchley, with Second-Lieutenant W. H. Eastwood as his Second-in-Command, and was of great assistance to the Company. Lieutenant Sketchley exchanged mutual training in demolition work with certain selected personnel from E Company to ensure that whatever the position, men would be available for this vital duty, and in turn the Company embraced the areas of these Inland Distributing Depots in their defensive schemes to provide covering support to the demolition parties.

One of the most successful activities of the Company was its Summer Camps. By the official permission of the L.M.S. they were given the use of Althorp Park Station at week-ends, and this locality proved most suitable for teaching fieldcraft, wood and house fighting, and also gave opportunity for friendly and keen exercises with the local Platoons of the 9th Battalion who lived in the area. All ranks derived the greatest benefit from the change of air, from the break from their everyday occupation, and from the varied and interesting instruction provided. Another small but very welcome asset was the modest allowance of liquid refreshment thoughtfully supplied by mine host at the Fox and Hounds in Brington village. Here often contact was made with the members of G Company who, from their lair at Gawburrow Hill, had stolen forth on a similar mission. Many members of E Company who were fortunate enough to spend a week-end at Althorp will treasure kindly memories of the comradeship and team spirit created and fostered there.

One of the outstanding characters of the Company was the C.S.M., George Quartermain, D.C.M., M.M., who was a tower of strength and an inspiration to all the members. He will not readily be forgotten, and his application to duty, often in the most difficult circumstances produced by railway duty—for George was and is still an engine driver—was an example to all. When at very short notice the Battalion was asked to find one Home Guardsman to represent the Sub-District on the King's Parade in London in May, 1943, what better representative or more typical Home Guard could be found than C.S.M. George Quartermain. I well remember seeing him off at the Castle Station with a feeling of pride that such a man as this, a perfect example of a good soldier, was to represent the 12th Battalion.

In training and efficiency the Company was always to the fore and was particularly prominent, as one might expect, in first aid, and in this connection two figures were especially prominent, Corporals B. T. Johnson and Broome, both for their accomplishment in training the Company and also for the reason that they have been many times commended by railway and civil authorities for their prompt and skilful treatment of accident cases. Those who were privileged to attend one of their lectures and demonstrations complete with the most horrifying apparatus, gained much knowledge therefrom, and they will not easily forget the staging of various accident scenes which they put over so effectively.

Early in 1943, with various changes taking place, Lieutenant K. G. Bayes took over command of the Company. In those most difficult days he proved himself a man of initiative and leadership, and it was largely due to his enthusiasm and devotion that E Company carried on so successfully in those trying times. No Commanding Officer could have wished for a more loyal helper.

When the division came in the Battalion in July, 1943, it was with the greatest regret that we parted with E Company, Ken Bayes, George Quartermain and all the other good fellows who had helped to make the 12th Battalion, what we all hoped, a credit to the town of Northampton. However, it was not long before Ken Bayes reappeared in the 12th as a private in H Company, having transferred from the 15th. This action was typical of the man, for as long as he was serving in the Home Guard, rank did not count with him. But such a man could not remain a private for long, and as Sergeant K. G. Bayes of H Company he played an enthusiastic part in the organisation of the Flower, Fruit and Vegetable Show so efficiently conducted at the Battalion Fete.

Although they were not present with us at the Stand Down, we shall always have the happiest recollections of the part played by the Railway Company in those strenuous early days of the Home Guard.

F COMPANY (THE KEEP)
Hetdquarters: The Drill Hall, Clare Street.

Company Commander	-	- Major A. S. Baxter, O.B.E.
Second-in-Command	- - -	- Captain C. G. Harris
Intelligence Officer	- -	- Lieutenant T. E. Manning
Ammunition Officer	- -	- Lieutenant J. H. Cooch
Company Sergeant-Major	- - -	C.S.M. F. W. Bailey
Company Q.M.S. -	- -	C.Q.M.S. C. W. Boddington

No. 19 Platoon. Headquarters: 2, Upper Mounts.

Platoon Commander	- -	- Lieutenant A. J. Burton
Platoon Officer	- - -	- Lieutenant S. G. Leach

No. 20 Platoon. Headquarters: 23, Hunter Street.

Platoon Commander	- -	- Lieutenant J. R. Barratt
Platoon Officer	- - -	- Lieutenant A. E. Harrold

No. 21 Platoon. Headquarters: Working Men's Club, Craven Street.

Platoon Commander	- -	- Lieutenant W. A. Evans
Platoon Officer	- - -	- Lieutenant J. H. Lawrence

In the early months of 1942, under the new system of Defended Localities it became necessary to have a Keep in the centre of the town which, in case of need, would be the rallying point and also "the last ditch" of the Battalion. Unfortunately, one central keep was not possible, as the area to be defended would have been too great, so it was divided into three parts, the Drill Hall, the new Police Station and the Barracks. To man the Keep a new Company had to be formed. As has been pointed out in a previous Chapter, the formation at this stage of a new Company presented many difficulties, but with the adaptability of the Home Guard these were speedily overcome. Major A. S. Baxter, O.B.E., who had from the early days acted as the Second-in-Command of D Company, was promoted to the command of the new F Company. The nucleus was formed by No. 9 Platoon of C Company with its Headquarters at the Lord Raglan. With enthusiasm the Company got to work and, commencing with a strength of 86 on June 30th, 1942, was built up by the posting of directed personnel, so that in three months time a total of 205 had been reached. The maximum strength of 218 was attained in the following November. From this date, in common with other Companies, their numbers gradually declined as more and more men were called up for the Forces while the flow of directed personnel dried up.

Major Baxter gathered around him a body of keen officers who had done good work as N.C.O.'s in other Companies. They were early tested, for within a fortnight of their formation they guarded the Keep in the Eleanor Exercise.

Their battle positions being in the centre of the town, the Company had naturally to concentrate on street fighting and house clearing. We managed to loan two derelict houses in Crispin Street, by kind permission of the local Education Authority, and here wall climbing with toggle ropes, house clearing and street fighting were practised. These houses and the adjoining land were almost ideal for our purpose, although it was said that those who used these buildings often came away with more than they entered with! Lieutenant Harrold proved himself a tower of strength in this type of training and reached a high state of efficiency with his men. Those who were present at the Anniversaries on the County Ground will always remember "The House," with the men of F Company scaling the walls and entering the windows, and the final emittance of the "dead Hun." This incident, no matter how often repeated, always amused the onlookers, and roars of laughter greeted the "Hun" as he bit the dust.

On May 23rd, 1943, the Director General of the Home Guard, Lord Bridgeman, on a quick visit to the Battalion, desired to see the training that was being done in street fighting. He witnessed a realistic attack on the Crispin Street houses by the members of F Company, and expressed his appreciation of their efforts. In the following month the Company arranged demonstrations for the officers and N.C.O.'s of the Battalion.

Major Baxter, being like myself a bombing enthusiast, made many excursions to Hunsbury Hill with his men, whenever his efforts to persuade the Quartermaster to let him have " only a few more bombs " were successful.

One of the best days of the Company was on October 18th, 1942, when a day's outing was arranged at Brington Range. It began with a route march to the range in the morning, with a lunch of haversack rations and tea, with beer for those few with whom tea did not agree. In the afternoon firing took place, while the practice in the firing of the Spigot mortar was also held. In the evening the return journey was made to the town by buses after a most enjoyable and instructive day.

In the Summer of 1943 the Company arranged two week-end camps at Gawburrow Hill, Brington. These were much enjoyed and proved very helpful in the training, whilst at the same time promoting that good fellowship that meant so much to the Home Guard. In July, 1944, another week-end camp was held, this time at Overstone Park, and an equally good and valuable time was spent.

Besides the training in street fighting the Company also arranged many field exercises, in which the Electric Light Works loomed largely, for the co-operation with the Home Guard Platoon at the Works was of the most cordial nature, and if the latter at any time wished to test out their defences, F Company were only too willing to oblige.

As I have pointed out in the Chapter on the Home Guard and the Civil Defence, this Company was specially trained in A.R.P. work and became very efficient. This training included the object and method of the incendiary bomb attack, types of incendiary bombs and the method of dealing with them and the resultant fires, light rescue work, etc. I am certain that had the necessity arisen they would have been of great assistance to the Civil Defence Authorities.

F Company also had the distinction of having in their ranks one of the two lady members of the Battalion, for Miss Tench rendered much assistance on the clerical side and her work was greatly appreciated by the male members.

Various Company and Platoon Socials were held, and an Old Comrades' Association is going strongly.

This Company, formed like G, when some of the initial enthusiasm had worn off, and consisting mainly of directed personnel, had many problems to solve and many difficulties to overcome, and the fact that these were surmounted and the Company welded into a really efficient fighting unit is a tribute to Major Baxter, his officers and N.C.O.'s.

G COMPANY (THE SUB-DISTRICT RESERVE)
Headquarters: The Barracks, Northampton.

Company Commander	- - -	Major S. B. Patrick
Second-in-Command	- - -	Captain F. C. Whiting
Intelligence Officer	- - -	Lieutenant V. H. Purdy
Transport Officer	- - -	Lieutenant V. B. Allinson
Signals Officer	- - -	Lieutenant F. W. Barker
Ammunition Officer	- - -	Lieutenant C. C. Pearce

Company Sergeant-Major - - - C.S.M. H. A. Savage
Company Q.M.S. - - - - - C.Q.M.S. T. I. Pepper

No. 22 Platoon. Headquarters: Victoria Road Schools.
Platoon Commander - - Captain A. E. Cleaver, M.M.
Platoon Officers - - - Lieutenant H. L. Simon and
Lieutenant R. L. Wheeler

No. 23 Platoon. Headquarters: 45, Kingsthorpe Road.
Platoon Commander - - - Lieutenant P. H. Rowe

No. 24 Platoon. Headquarters: 45, Kingsthorpe Road.
Platoon Commander - - - - Lieutenant J. Watts

No. 25 Platoon. Headquarters: 45, Kingsthorpe Road.
Platoon Commander - - - Lieutenant C. M. Edwards

When in July, 1942, the Northamptonshire Sub-District was ordered to form a Mobile Reserve Company, the 12th Battalion as usual had " to carry the baby." A new Company, F, had recently been formed, and now to make a completely new unit of Category 1 men to act as a reserve for Sub-District presented a problem not easy of solution. Colonel J. L. Short, a New Zealander and a Regular soldier, was the Sub-District Commander at this time, and if there was one thing he did expect it was efficiency in all who served under his command. It was therefore necessary from the Battalion point of view to see that this new Company became an efficient unit and one that would be a credit to the 12th.

Captain S. B. Patrick, who at the time was acting as Second-in-Command of C Company, was selected as Company Commander. I felt at the time that no better choice could have been made, and time has only confirmed this opinion. He, with Captain Fred Whiting as his right-hand man, formed an ideal combination, which had much to do with the success achieved by the Company. I remember in November, 1943, when the formation of a Coastal Reinforcement Company was under discussion, my arrangements for this did not meet with the unqualified approval of the Sub-District Commander. I pointed out to him that I was the one who had to form this new Company, as I had had to form G Company, and I asked him if he was satisfied with this. His reply that he was more than satisfied was a high tribute, coming from Colonel Short, and reflected the greatest credit on Major Patrick, who had so ably guided the Company through its early and difficult days when it was very much in the position of an " unwanted baby."

In the formation of the Sub-District Reserve the first difficulty we ran up against was the matter of organisation. The strength of the Company was to be 250 men of Category 1. These were to be divided into a complication of sub-units, unheard of in the Home Guard; three battle platoons, a battery of 10 Smith guns, motor transport for the whole Company, an Intelligence section, a Signal section, a Medical section, and all the H.Q. organisation required to maintain a mobile reserve in the field. This seemed at the time an impossible proposition, but in the Home Guard we always achieved the impossible, and slowly but surely the Company got going. The nucleus were the members of the Mobile Reserve Platoon, who were in Category 1. These were joined by some of the younger members of other Companies, and by a Works Platoon from the Armstrong Whitworth Works on the Houghton Road, produced by Lieutenant Patton, an Artillery officer who had just been discharged from the Regular Army. Like most other Works Platoons this presented a problem, and it took approximately 15 months to overcome this works complex. Directed personnel were coming forward at this time in good numbers, and the fitter and younger members were posted to G Company, until gradually the establishment was built up.

As in all organisations, whether in civil or military life, the strength of any concern is the sum total of the staff controlling the endeavours of the men, who do the job. Men born of British blood will always carry out their task, whatever it may be, provided that they have the right leaders, and it was particularly essential that in this new Company that the right leaders should be found. Captain A. E. Cleaver set to work with the Battery and in course of time knocked it into shape, and the Works Platoon became an efficient sub-unit of the Company. Lieutenants Rowe, Watts and Edwards mastered the technique of battle platoon leadership and very soon could, and did, mop up any enemy on exercises by right or left flanking movements or pincer movement. The Intelligence Section trained under Lieutenant Dixon until he was called up, and then under Lieutenant Purdy, and became well practised in the complicated business of "Intelligence," and never failed to supply the Company with the necessary information on all occasions. "Signals" were trained to a high pitch of efficiency by Lieutenant G. A. White, the Battalion Signals Officer, and later by Lieutenant Barker, a very able pupil of "George" in all matters of R/T and signal procedure. This Section was originally composed of seven enthusiasts who spent many hours on a home-made morse tapper and many Sunday mornings doing "flag-wagging." Eventually 16 R/T short-wave sets were received and the Section rapidly obtained new members. Assistance was received from Sergeant Jones, of Sub-District Signals, and also from Lieutenant Dean, of the 13th Leicesters (the Post Office Company). Besides Lieutenant Barker excellent work was done by Sergeant W. B. Morgan and Corporals J. Button and R. Carvell, and the Section became a very competent unit.

In the Home Guard we always tried to fit the square peg into the square hole, and in the case of the transport problem of G Company we certainly succeeded, for in Lieutenant Bertie Allinson, a garage manager in civil life, we had the ideal Transport Officer, who in ear-marked vehicles collected from his private customers, always managed to get the Company to the right spot at the right time. His cheery disposition and his fund of humorous stories at the Company Socials were also a great asset.

The Medical Section, under Sergeant Perry, gradually became a well-working unit and in 1944 finally excelled themselves by finishing second in the Northamptonshire Stretcher Bearers Competition.

Many others did their work in building up the Company, including C.Q.M.S. Tom Pepper, a veteran of Boer War days and still one of the best shots in the Battalion. Like all good Q.M.'s he managed to keep one of everything up his sleeve, an art that takes years to acquire. Sergeant G. Spencer acted as Weapon Training N.C.O. and did very valuable work, producing many successful candidates for the Proficiency Examinations. Although offered a commission, he preferred to remain where he thought that he could do the most valuable work for the benefit of the Company. C.S.M. Savage besides his official duties often indulged in his favourite pastime of bombing, while Sergeant R. Billing, the Company Sergeant cook, not only looked the part but certainly succeeded in a most uncanny manner in feeding the Company on the exercises and at the Gawburrow Hill camps.

As a mark of distinction the Company were granted the privilege of wearing green lanyards by the Sub-District Commander, and were in consequence often known as the "Green Howards."

G' Company being a Sub-District Reserve Company, were naturally in close contact with H.Q., and here they received the greatest help from the Brigade Majors functioning there. It was no easy job that Major Patrick undertook in the formation and training of this unit, but a very understanding Brigade Major R. M. Jefferies in those early days was of the greatest assistance. It is related that the Sub-District Reserve Company was really hatched out in a homely hostelry at Boughton, where over a few pint tankards of ale the Brigade Major and the Company Commander thrashed out the organisation and the role of the Company and its use of the Intelligence Section and the Recce Group. Major Jefferies inevitably succeeded to a higher command, but the good work was carried on by Major S. J. Bartley, a lawyer by profession, who took the greatest interest in the Company and by his quiet advice helped much in the smooth running, especially on the Buzz Exercises in 1944.

Speaking of exercises, G Company was probably among the most disappointed of Home Guard units. The turnouts were always excellent, often over 90 per cent., and the Company always arrived at its operational area in time. But senior commanders were invariably very cautious in the use of their Mobile Reserve, with the result that it was usually very late in the day that they finally made up their minds to risk using it, and then, when all was ready and everyone keyed up, along came the inevitable umpire with the " Exercise finished." Afterwards followed the long trek home, often in the early morning, without a show. On one Buzz Exercise the Company had its rendezvous in Daventry Market Square. From here they watched the " battle " on Borough Hill while the Battalion Commander tried to make up his mind. Of course, when he did so the B.B.C. Station had " gone," and so had the enemy paratroopers.

In the early months of its life the training was done at the old Barracks, but with the approach of Winter with its dark evenings, indoor accommodation had to be found. And here the Company for a time became truly mobile. The Chapel buildings in Lorne Road were secured, and very suitable quarters they were. The place was thoroughly cleaned up and lights fixed in all the rooms, but after a stay of some three weeks the Regulars came along and took over the buildings. St. Lawrence's Hall was the next training centre, but after a brief stay we had to leave at very short notice. The next port of call was the Imperial Hall, which we managed to hold for some months, but finally had to give up for the use of the A.T.S. Why, I never understood, for I did not hear of them using it. A fleeting visit was paid to " The Rosery " at Kingsthorpe until the Company finally settled down at Regent Square Chapel buildings. The difficulties of the Company will readily be understood from the following lists of its Headquarters and storage places: Company H.Q. were at the Barracks; Company Stores at 45, Kingsthorpe Road; Signal Office in Gold Street; training at Regent Square and Victoria Road Chapel buildings; while the Smith guns had their home at St. Andrew's Road Garage.

During 1943 and 1944 week-end camps were frequently held, the favourite venue being Gawburrow Hill, near Brington, while one visit was paid to Overstone Park. These camps, as has been pointed out, served a dual purpose, for while valuable training was done, the social side was of great importance. In a Company such as this, with its members drawn from all over the town, their only chance of meeting was on training nights, and then the time was necessarily limited. Therefore the camps gave the opportunity for all to know their fellows more intimately, which was all to the good. At Gawburrow Hill, after the training was over a move was generally made to the local hostelry, and here, over a glass of ale, friendships were further cemented, many of which I am sure will last a lifetime. Already one reunion has been held at the Fox and Hounds at Brington, and I have no doubt that for many years this will be an annual affair.

The record of the Sub-District Reserve would not be complete without reference to the work undertaken by Mrs. Patrick, the wife of the Company Commander, who was one of the two lady members of the Battalion. As enthusiastic as her husband where Home Guard matters were concerned, she was the " unofficial Q.M.," and it was due to her wise spending of the allowance, combined with the excellent cooking of Sergeant Billing, that enabled the men to be so well fed during their stay in camp. When the Battalion Fete for the Hospital was first suggested, G Company undertook the provision of refreshments for the crowd, a prodigious task in those days of rationing. However, by the efforts of Mrs. Patrick and those of the members and their wives, large quantities of tea and food were assembled, and the feeding of the " five thousand " was accomplished in an astounding manner.

Before leaving the matter of camps I remember that when spending a night in camp with the Company, at Lights Out one member was absent. No one knew of his whereabouts and it was not until the early hours of the morning that he appeared. I heard a rumour that in his time he had done a fair amount of poaching, and while the other members had " dossed down " he had been busy setting his nets and snares. I never found out if this was true, but I should not be surprised, for the Home Guard could do anything, and anybody.

And so G Company continued until the end full of keenness and enthusiasm, its training progressing excellently in each branch, until by D Day they were a most capable unit and a great credit to the 12th. They were unique in the fact that they were the only Home Guard Mobile Reserve Company in the whole of Northamptonshire, and I am certain that had the necessity arisen they would have played their part manfully, wherever and in whatever circumstances they had been called upon.

H COMPANY (THE BATTALION RESERVE)
Headquarters: 15, Kingsthorpe Grove.

Company Commander - - -	Major A. W. Blason
Second-in-Command - - -	Captain R. B. Armitt
Intelligence Officer - -	Lieutenant A. G. Barratt
Ammunition Officer - -	Lieutenant J. V. Collier
Company Sergeant-Major - -	C.S.M. A. A. Butcher
Company Q.M.S. - - - -	C.Q.M.S. A. Jeffery

No. 26 Platoon. Headquarters: 43, Kingsthorpe Road.

Platoon Commander - - -	Lieutenant F. E. Blason
Platoon Officer - - -	Lieutenant C. J. Hollowell

No. 27 Platoon. Headquarters: Oliver Street.

Platoon Commander - - -	Lieutenant H. A. Watts
Platoon Officer - - -	Lieutenant H. F. Webber

No. 28 Platoon. Headquarters: 61, Kingsthorpe Road.

Platoon Commander - - -	Lieutenant H. Cattell
Platoon Officer - - -	Lieutenant W. E. Hancock

This Company had perhaps the most chequered career of all in the Battalion. In the early L.D.V. days a mobile platoon had been formed under Captain Devaliant to act as Battalion Reserve. This officer did not continue for any length of time, and very shortly Lieutenant A. W. Blason took over command and acted as Platoon Commander until, in 1942, it was decided to enlarge the Platoon into a Company. In those young days the Platoon had been trained into a very efficient fighting unit, so much so that in every exercise in which they took part they were never beaten; at least, that was the impression I gathered from the various " inquests " that I attended. However, this was all to the good, and we always felt that this Platoon was a real fighting force. It was with much regret that in 1942, on the formation of G Company, I considered it was necessary to make a re-arrangement. I was hoping that Lieutenant Blason and the Platoon would go over to G Company en bloc, but unfortunately many of the men were in Category 2 and therefore not eligible. However, those in Category 1 transferred and formed the nucleus of the Sub-District Reserve. Lieutenant Blason preferred to remain with the remainder of the old Platoon, and I have always felt sorry for him that the Platoon which he had trained so enthusiastically for over two years should have been split in this manner. However, as I have said, military exigencies have to come before personal feelings, and the good of the Battalion must come before everything else.

In the reorganisation of the Battalion in the Autumn of 1942 it was clear that one platoon, and a depleted one at that, was not a sufficient reserve for a Battalion the size of the 12th. It was therefore decided to make a new Company as a reserve, by amalgamating the Mobile Reserve Platoon and No. 3 Platoon of A Company, which was commanded by Lieutenant Rex Armitt. Since the L.D.V. days this Platoon, to become the 27th, had its Headquarters at the rear of Miss Bradford's house in Kingsley Road. This good lady, without any payment whatever, placed her rooms at our disposal for four and a half years, and this Platoon will always remember her kindly action with gratitude and appreciation.

Captain O. J. Hargrave, who had been Second-in-Command of B Company since its formation, was promoted to the command of the new H Company, which had its Headquarters at 21, Kingsthorpe Grove. Lieutenant Armitt acted as Second-in-Command and the Company was very soon organised into platoons, and got settled down to work.

With the division of the Battalion in July, 1943, and the transfer of Captain Holder to the 15th, B Company was left without a Second-in-Command, and Captain Hargrave, in order to help in the situation that had arisen, returned to his original appointment. Captain Armitt assumed command of H Company, although doubtful whether in the state of his health at that time he would be able to give the time and energy needed by the office of Company Commander. However, he agreed to carry on for the time being, but at the end of some four months he felt that it would be better for the Company if a change was made in the command. The success of the Home Guard was due to a large extent, as I have pointed out elsewhere, to the fitting of square pegs into square holes, and I am sure that I shall be forgiven by Captain Armitt when I say that he was a far better organiser and administrator than a field soldier. He felt that his " hole " was at Company Headquarters rather than in the field training the Company. A more loyal and self-effacing man I have never met; his only thought was the good of the Battalion, and as long as he was doing his bit he was quite content, no matter what the position he occupied might be. It was indeed a privilege to serve with men like this. Captain A. W. Blason became Major and the Commander of the Company, which for the first time really got settled down. Unlike Rex Armitt, Major Blason was a field soldier, who always wanted to be where the action was taking place, and he and Armitt made an ideal combination.

About this time the formation of D, the Coastal Reinforcement Company, took place. Some of the Kingsthorpe Platoon, owing to the nature of their civilian work, were unable to undertake a duty that might have taken them away to Great Yarmouth in case of necessity, and so were transferred to H Company, who received a much needed addition of strength. Included among these were J. V. Collier and H. Cattell, two enthusiastic members from L.D.V. days, and these proved a great asset and soon were promoted to commissioned rank. The Engineering Cadets at the Technical College, who were undergoing an extensive course there, were also posted to the Company and formed a Smith Gun Battery under Lieutenant Hancock.

The record of H Company cannot close without a reference to their transport, the familiar yellow lorries of Messrs. Latimer. From the very earliest days these had been placed at the disposal of the Company by the generous action of the firm. Throughout the whole four and a half years they were freely used, and had the necessity arisen the quick transport of the Mobile Company depended on these lorries. Hugh Latimer, a member of the firm, was himself an enthusiastic Home Guard and performed a very valuable service in the driving and supervision of the transport. The Home Guard had many friends, but none better than the firm of Messrs. Latimer.

And so in the last twelve months of our existence the Company was made into a really efficient unit, under the enthusiastic leadership of Major Blason, who, whatever the circumstance, maintained his keenness to the very end. I should imagine that he was one of those who deeply regretted the passing of the Home Guard.

THE BATTALION BAND

In 1941 Major E. W. Powell, commanding E Company, had formed a band mainly from the remnants of the Northampton Silver Prize Band, which at the outbreak of War had been disbanded. As a Railway Company Band they had rendered good service, especially at the Pageants at Franklin's Gardens. Early in 1943 I was approached by some of the leading members of the Band with a view to them becoming a Battalion Band instead of a Company one. They held the view, and I must say that I agreed with them, that they would have a greater prestige if this was done. Despite the added administration that this involved, I fell in with their proposal, but was extremely careful to point out that a split in the Battalion was imminent and that they were attached to a Company that would probably form part of the new unit. They had therefore the choice of remaining in the prospective new Battalion or transferring en bloc to the Headquarters of the 12th. The decision was left to them entirely, and after much meditation they came to the conclusion that they preferred to become the 12th Battalion Northamptonshire Home Guard Band. Although I had put no pressure upon them whatever, I felt very pleased at their decision, and I hope that now the Home Guard is no more, they do not regret their choice. They certainly provided the 12th with something that other Battalions lacked, and on all our Battalion parades gave invaluable assistance and contributed greatly to the success, especially on the Drumhead Services. Bands are always supposed to be temperamental, but this Band was different if such is the case, for a better and more willing set of fellows I have yet to meet. Nothing was too much trouble for them, and on every occasion that I asked them for their services there was always a willing response. Besides their professional engagements, they gave voluntary service to Regular Army units in the town, to Army Cadets, to the British Legion, to the Girl Guides, and many more organisations, as well as giving concerts for the troops at the Y.M.C.A. By their efforts in these directions they added prestige to the 12th Battalion, for which I thank them most sincerely.

In common with other Home Guard units they had their difficulties, for from time to time members were called up for H.M. Forces and it was not always easy to replace a drum major or a " tenorhorn." In addition, too, when we took over they had a debt of some £100 which hung like a millstone round their necks. However, with Major H. St. J. Browne as Band President, this was gradually wiped off, so that at the Stand Down they were clear and were able to start again as the Northampton Borough Silver Prize Band free from debt. They are still continuing their valuable efforts on behalf of all good causes, and in October, 1945, by a concert at the Fanciers' Club, they raised a sum of £28 10s. for the Manfield Hospital.

Besides their musical duties the Band were trained as stretcher bearers, and if they had been needed in this respect I am sure that they would have performed their duties as ably on the battlefield as they did leading the Battalion on its various parades. One member, however, Private H. W. Gribble, more bloodthirsty than the rest, always stipulated that in case of enemy action he wanted a Sten and not a stretcher. We saw that he would have one.

I cannot close this account without a personal note of thanks to the Bandmaster, Mr. O. Mason, to the Band Sergeant, W. J. Jenkinson, and to Corporal H. Cook, who did so much to make the band such a success.

NORTHAMPTON POST OFFICE COMPANY, HOME GUARD

It was obvious that had invasion of this country taken place, Post Office buildings with their telephone exchanges would have been one of the first objectives for the invader. It was necessary, therefore, that these buildings should be strongly held. When in May, 1940, the L.D.V. was first formed, the staff at the Northampton Headquarters eagerly joined up and formed a Company of the Northampton Division. W. R. Morton was appointed Company Leader, with J. S. Duke as his Second-in-Command, and throughout the whole of the four and a half years these two served in the same capacity, and were still acting at the Stand Down.

In August, 1940, much to the regret of the local Home Guard, the Post Office Company left the Battalion. On War Office instructions, in view of the special problems connected with the Post Office, the employees throughout the country were formed into special Post Office units. And so this Company became E Company of the 47th Warwickshire (24th G.P.O.) Battalion.

Training was on similar lines to the ordinary Home Guard Battalions, but special attention was paid to the protection of Post Office buildings and telephone systems, plant, etc. Particular duties included:—

(a) The guarding of vital points in the main North—South telephone system, such as repeater stations;

(b) The arming of telephone repair workers, when necessary, working in the rural areas;

(c) The provision of armed guards for Post Office vehicles when on rural journeys.

Certain essential workers, who could not be released for Home Guard duties until the last possible moment, wore blue and white flashes on the sleeves of their battledress. The telephone system naturally had to be kept in action as long as possible, and operators might have had to work although the enemy was in the town.

On February 20th, 1941, the War Office requested the P.O. Home Guard to enrol and train members to operate telephone exchanges as their Home Guard duty in an emergency such as might have arisen from attempted invasion. The provision of personnel from the Regular Army for these duties was found by the War Office to be impracticable for a number of reasons. Members were recruited at Northampton, Kettering, Rushden, Cogenhoe, East Haddon, Brixworth, Weedon, Daventry, Towcester and Creaton; these were enrolled in the Company and were trained to operate the telephone exchange in their own particular locality.

A "flying squad" was formed from the members at Northampton to operate in any area in this district should heavy enemy action, e.g., air raids, render such a course necessary.

In November, 1942, the P.O. Home Guard were instructed by the War Office to provide Signal Officers to be responsible for organising alternative means of communication in case the ordinary telephone system was disorganised, and Lieutenant W. J. Dean was appointed to the Northampton-shire Sub-District, and Lieutenant A. J. L. Knights was appointed to No. 2 Sector. We regret to have to record that the latter was killed in a cycle accident on September 29th, 1944. At the same time as these changes occurred, Sergeant C. H. Parsons transferred to the 10th Battalion North-amptonshire Home Guard and was commissioned as Signal Officer in that unit. A Signal Section was organised and trained by Lieutenant Dean to assist Northamptonshire Sub-District Signals in an emergency.

In April, 1943, owing to reorganisation in the 47th Warwicks, the Company was transferred to the 13th Leicestershire (25th G.P.O.) Battalion Home Guard, and with them they remained for the remainder of their existence.

At the Stand Down the Company strength was 9 officers and 223 other ranks, together with two women auxiliaries, while a total of 463 had served at various times in the Company.

The following is the roll of officers serving at that time:—

Officer Commanding	- - -	- Major W. R. Morton
Second-in-Command	- - -	- Captain J. S. Duke
Signals and Intelligence Officer		Lieutenant W. J. Dean
Company Quartermaster	-	- Lieutenant S. C. C. Boyce
Platoon Commander No. 1	-	- Lieutenant F. D. Browett
No. 2	-	- Lieutenant A. B. Cooper
No. 3	-	- Lieutenant J. T. Jeffery
Kettering	-	- Lieutenant O. E. Butcher
Platoon Officer	- - -	- Lieutenant H. Underwood

During the four and a half years of its life the members of the Company showed the keenest interest in all the various duties falling to their lot. Ninety-three courses and camps were attended, the former including Signals and Bomb Disposal. It is interesting to note that the officer who attended the latter worked with a Regular Army Bomb Disposal Unit in London for a week on actual disposal of enemy bombs. Proficiency badges were obtained by 291 members, while four N.C.O.'s and eight men qualified as a first aid party, passing the St. John Ambulance Association Examination. In addition Sergeant S. J. Kirk, of the Wellingborough Section, was awarded a Certificate of Merit by Eastern Command.

Although after the first few months the Post Office Company was not a member of the 12th Battalion, yet the co-operation between us was of the closest possible character. On all our parades and anniversaries we were always pleased to welcome them and they were always represented in strength. For this happy state of affairs we were greatly indebted to the O.C., Major Morton, who worked so amicably with us to the mutual benefit of both units. I am certain that had we ever been called upon to go into action, the same spirit of comradeship would have permeated all ranks and that we should have functioned together in perfect liaison and harmony.

WIRING PARTY (Abington Park).

(Photo: J. Wright).

ST. PETER'S BRIDGE.

(Photo: J. Wright)

MEMBERS OF THE BATTALION SERVING AT THE STAND DOWN

BATTALION HEADQUARTERS

Lieutenant	Allatt, Harry.	Private	Manning, Albert.
Lieutenant	Allinson, Charles Graham Birkett.	Private	Marriott, Walter John.
		Private	Mason, Arthur Osborne.
Lt.-Colonel	Barnes, Leslie Edwin.	Private	Mobb, Kenneth Herbert W.
Private	Brown, Edward.	Private	Mottishaw, Denis.
Corporal	Brown, James Lombard.	Corporal	Norton, Edwin Frank.
Major	Browne, Harold St. John.	Lieutenant	Payne, Arnold Cyril.
Private	Bull, Cyril Charlie Joseph.	Private	Plackett, William George.
Lieutenant	Catlow, Charles Stanley.	Private	Roper, George Victor.
Captain	Courtney, Fred Ernest.	Private	Smith, Frank William.
Private	Coleman, Reginald Walter.	Sergeant	Smith, John Alfred.
Corporal	Cook, Harry.	Private	Smith, Ralph George.
Private	Dunkley, Frederick Arthur.	Private	Spatcher, Bertram Edward
Private	Farmer, Charles Edward.	Private	Stockwin, Alfred Charles.
Private	Goodwin, George Henry.	Sergeant	Summers, Harold Wilfred.
Private	Gribble, Horace William.	Private	Taylor, Frank.
Private	Hall, Brian Gervase Hall.	Major	Thompson, George Herbert
Captain	Harris, Victor John Henry.	Private	Thomson, John Henry.
L/Corporal	Harrison, Archer Owen.	R.S.M.	Timms, Frederick.
Private	Harrold, Percy James.	L/Corporal	Turland, Cyril Montague.
Private	Hatton, Edwin.	Private	Waters, Edwin Henry.
Private	Herbert, William Robert.	Private	White, Edwin Ernest.
Private	James, Alfred Ernest.	Lieutenant	White, George Alexander.
Sergeant	Jenkinson, William John.	Sergeant	White, Henry Ellis.
Private	Lever, Harry.	Sergeant	Wilson, Stuart.
Private	Lewis, John Arthur.	Lieutenant	Wood, Fred.
Private	Liggins, Clyde Glenmore.		

DISPATCH RIDERS

Private	Ambidge, Cecil Charles.	L/Corporal	Goff, Arthur Jordan.
Private	Arnold, James Michael.	Private	Hamp, Reginald.
Private	Britten, Arthur Stanley.	Private	Joyce, Arthur Leslie.
Private	Burden, George William.	Private	Mason, John Clifford.
Private	Burgess, Bevan.	L/Corporal	Smith, Howard James.
Private	Charlton, George.	Sergeant	Stevens, James Frederick.
Private	Denton, Percy Donald.	Private	Thornton, Wm. Thomas J.
L/Corporal	Devonshire, Albert Wm.	Private	Tompkins, Ernest Fred.
Private	Drage, Horace Reginald.		

A COMPANY

Private	Abbey, Archibald Robert.	L/Corporal	Gardner, Frank Stewart.
Private	Abel, Edward.	Private	Gill, Thomas.
Corporal	Ager, Alfred.	Private	Gillies, William Bedford.
Sergeant	Alibone, Arthur Samuel.	L/Corporal	Glover, Eric Harry.
Corporal	Allbright, Ernest William.	Private	Goodger, George Henry.
Sergeant	Ambidge, Benedict C.	Corporal	Greaves, Bert Lawrence.
Private	Ambrose, Lawrence E.	Private	Griffiths, Edward William.
Private	Anderson, Edward Henry.	Corporal	Grundy, Sidney Allexander
Private	Arter, Leonard George.	L/Corporal	Hall, Albert.
Private	Ash, Jack.	Sergeant	Halliwell, Robt. Whittaker.
Corporal	Atkinson, Ronald.	Private	Halsey, John Luther.
Corporal	Bailey, Horace Edward.	Corporal	Handford, Ernest Stanley.
Private	Balfour, George Wilfred.	Private	Harris, Kenneth William.
Sergeant	Bament, Cyril Forder.	Private	Haughton, Frank.
Private	Barford, Albert.	Private	Hedge, Frank Albert.
Sergeant	Barratt, Frank Albert.	Private	Height, Frederick Greville
Lieutenant	Beer, Alfred George.	Sergeant	Hemmings, Hubert Ernest.
Private	Belcher, Henry Gordon.	Corporal	Hobson, James Miles H.
Private	Bell, John Ablitt.	Private	Hodkinson, Edward George
Private	Bell, Norman Mindham.	Private	Holloway, George Sewell.
Private	Bellchambers, John Edgar.	Corporal	Holton, Arthur Ernest.
Private	Billinghurst, John Alfred.	Sergeant	Howkins, Oliver Ernest.
Private	Boswell, Victor Reginald.	Major	Hutton, Philip.
2nd/Lieut.	Britten, Francis Samuel.	Corporal	Inglis, Robert Scott.
Private	Burton, Charles Ernest.	Private	Irons, Frank Derrick.
Private	Calley, Thomas Joseph.	Private	James, Leslie.
Sergeant	Cator, Walter Stanley.	Sergeant	James, Wm. Joseph Arthur.
Private	Child, Albert William.	Private	Jervis, David William.
Private	Clare, Robert Frank.	Lieutenant	Johnson, Clifford Walter
Corporal	Clarke, Howard John F.	Private	Johnson, Frank William.
Private	Clarke, Malcolm Doyel.	Private	Jones, Charles Henry.
Private	Clayton, Reginald.	Private	Jones, Maurice.
Corporal	Clemett, James Richard.	Corporal	Jordan, Donald Frederick.
Private	Coombs, Robert Edward.	Private	Kendall, Francis James.
Private	Cooper, Peter John Fredk.	Sergeant	Kilsby, Thomas Bernard.
Captain	Corsby, Reginald Ernest.	Private	King, John.
Private	Cory, Frederick Payne.	Private	Labrum, Arthur.
Private	Cotching, Frederick Wm.	Private	Labrum, Ernest Walter.
L/Corporal	Curtis, Thomas William.	Private	Levett, Alfred.
Sergeant	Davies, John Christopher.	Private	Lightwood, Ernest George.
Sergeant	Davis, Cyril.	Private	Lineham, Reginald.
Sergeant	Derby, Leslie Stuart.	Private	Loakes, Henry.
Sergeant	Dolby, James Edwin.	Private	Mabbutt, Frank.
Private	Edwards, Bernard L.	Sgt.-Major	Malpas, Edward.
Private	Ellis, Frederick Arthur.	L/Corporal	Manger, Frank Charles.
Private	Eyre, Charles John.	Corporal	Mann, Edwin Victor.
Private	Fall, Thomas Arthur.	Private	Mann, Thomas Sydney.
Private	Farmer, Albert Ernest.	Private	Marriott, Charles Arthur.
Private	Fell, Joseph Percy.	Lieutenant	Marriott, Charles William.
Private	Feltham, Albert Cyrus.	Private	Mattock, Joseph.
Sergeant	Foster, David Charles.	L/Corporal	Metcalf, Harold Joseph.
Private	Francis, Frederick Wm.	Corporal	Miles, William Frederick.
Private	Galt, Alfred Alex Issott.	L/Corporal	Morse, Arthur William.
Private	Gammons, William Arthur.	L/Corporal	Muddiman, Arthur Edward

Private	Murby, Christopher Harold	Private	Spence, Frank Kirby.
C.Q.M.S.	Osborne, Edgar.	Private	Steele, Christopher V. H.
Sergeant	Parkinson, Bertie.	L/Corporal	Steward, Ernest William.
Sergeant	Pate, George Harry.	L/Corporal	Stewart, William Albert.
Private	Payne, Reginald Thomas.	Private	Swallow, Eric.
Private	Pell, Arthur.	2nd/Lieut.	Swinstead, Malcolm Frank
Private	Perkins, Malcolm Stanley.	Corporal	Talbot, William John.
Sergeant	Peirce, Harold.	Private	Thompson, Reginald S.
Private	Pirie, Robin Alexander.	Corporal	Varnsverry, Arthur James.
Private	Porter, George Wm. John.	Lieutenant	Vials, George Arthur T.
Sergeant	Power, Joseph Charles.	Private	Waights, Philip Robertson.
L/Corporal	Rayson, Edward Granville.	Private	Wakes, George.
Corporal	Revitt, William Arthur.	Corporal	Walker, Harry Thomas G.
Private	Roberts, David Harold.	Captain	Wallace, George Burns.
Private	Roberts, Harold.	Private	Waugh, Norman.
Private	Robinson, Cyril Edward.	Private	Wells, Arthur Thomas.
Private	Robinson, Edward L.	Sergeant	Whitehouse, William Eric.
Private	Robinson, Ernest Moore.	Lieutenant	Whitehouse, Wm. Thomas.
Private	Russell, Arthur Leonard.	L/Corporal	Whyte, Charles Henry P.
L/Corporal	Saunders, Sydney Herbert.	Private	Wilcox, Arthur Edwin.
Private	Scotney, Osmond Charles.	Corporal	Wilson, Geoffrey Thomas.
Sergeant	Scott, George.	Private	Winton, David.
Sergeant	Sharpe, Charles Henry.	Private	Wootton, Frederick Arthur.
Private	Sharpe, Henry Vivian.	L/Corporal	Worrall, Ernest George.
Private	Shears, Arthur Edward.	Private	Wright, Ernest Alan.
Sergeant	Shrewsbury, Charles Wm.	Private	Wright, George.
L/Corporal	Smart, Arthur Joseph.	Private	Wright, Hubert.
Private	Smith, Cyril George.	L/Corporal	Wright, William Stanley.
L/Corporal	Smith, Frederick James.	Corporal	York, George Harold.

B COMPANY

Private	Adams, Arthur William G.	Private	Brent, Reginald William.
2nd/Lieut.	Allen, Frederick Arthur.	Corporal	Bridgeman, Charles T. C.
Private	Allinson, Frederick Wm.	Private	Bull, Reginald George H.
Corporal	Armstrong, Samuel Victor.	Private	Burdett, Albert Edward.
Private	Arnold, Jack.	Private	Busby, Frances William.
Private	Ashton, Charles William.	L/Corporal	Bush, Cyril Stanley.
Private	Bailey, Sidney Albert T.	Corporal	Butlin, William George T.
Private	Barden, James Charles.	Private	Cadd, Frederick Joseph.
Private	Barford, Leslie Herbert.	Private	Carr, Gilbert Cecil.
Sergeant	Barker, Frederick William.	Private	Carter, Arthur Raymond.
Private	Barnes, Walter George.	Private	Cattell, Walter Henry.
Private	Beaver, Alfred John.	Sergeant	Chambers, Arthur.
L/Corporal	Beckwith, Edward Henry.	Private	Chapman, Arthur E. S.
Private	Beeby, Harry Major.	Sergeant	Chapman, Paul Leslie.
Private	Beech, Stephen Oliver J.	Private	Chapman, Percy John.
Private	Beerbohm, Harry.	Private	Charlesworth, James.
Private	Beesley, Harry.	Private	Chubb, Kenneth Crews.
Private	Bellas, Hugh Hunter A. D'A.	L/Corporal	Coleman, Robert James.
Private	Black, Samuel.	Private	Coles, Maurice Alfred.
Private	Blick, Charles William H.	Private	Coles, William Alfred.
Private	Booth, Frederick James.	Private	Collier, Ernest John.
Private	Brent, Frederick Ernest.	Private	Collyer, George Henry.

Private	Corkram, William Joseph.	Sergeant	Kirk, Conran Reginald W.
Sergeant	Crask, Henry William.	Private	Kunn, Leonard.
Private	Craxton, Bernard.	Private	Labrum, William James C.
L/Corporal	Cribb, John Albert.	Corporal	Lambourne, Wm. John G.
Private	Cripps, Frank William.	Private	Lane, Frederick Alwyn.
Private	Cross, George Wilfred.	Private	Langley, Cyril.
Private	Cufflin, John Henry	L/Corporal	Langley, Herbert Charles.
Private	Dalton, William Hubert	Private	Lawrence, Albert Oliver.
Private	Day, John George.	Private	Lewis, William Thomas.
L/Corporal	Dickens, Percival Aubrey J.	Private	Lightfoot, Herbert E. O.
Private	Digby, William Ernest.	L/Corporal	Lovell, Joseph Harold.
Private	Dix, Harry.	Lieutenant	Lucas, Leonard Welles.
Private	Douglas, Harry.	Major	McFarlane, Archibald.
Private	Elston, Arthur Walter.	Private	Malpas, George Alfred.
Private	Elston, Thomas.	Private	Marriott, Owen.
Sergeant	Emery, Thomas Arthur.	Sgt.-Major	Martin, J. William Bowers.
Private	Evans, Harry William L.	2nd/Lieut.	Martin, Norman James R.
Sergeant	Eyre, Frank Michael Boyer.	Private	Martin, Percy Neville.
Private	Finch, Frederick Laurence.	Private	Miller, William John.
Sergeant	Fisher, Harry Cansdale.	Private	Mitchell, Ernest Arthur.
2nd/Lieut.	Fitzhugh, Reginald John.	Private	Mumford, Edwin George.
Private	Floyd, John.	Private	Mumford, Herbert Henry.
Private	Ford, Albert Stanley.	Private	Murphy, Michael Joseph.
Private	Gamble, James Reginald D.	Private	Muskin, William Lyford.
Corporal	Garrett, William Alfred.	Corporal	Neal, Ernest John
Private	Gayton, Alfred Gourlay.	Private	Nichols, Edward James.
Private	Gibbins, Arthur James.	Private	Nobbs, Raymond Ernest.
L/Corporal	Giddings, Albert Henry.	Private	Oakenfull, Geo. Ethelbert.
Lieutenant	Gilkerson, William Arthur.	Corporal	Oakley, George.
Private	Gill, Frank Alfred.	Private	Pallett, Donald Archie.
Private	Gill, John Frederick.	L/Corporal	Palmer, Reginald.
Private	Green, Albert William.	Private	Pancoust, Lewis George.
Private	Hall, Alfred John.	Private	Paul, Frederick Edwin.
Private	Hall, Stanley Frederick.	Private	Pearson, Norman Arthur.
Private	Hamp, George.	L/Corporal	Pell, Frederick Alfred.
Private	Hardwick, Archie Jeffrey.	Private	Pell, Kenneth Reginald.
Captain	Hargrave, Oswald John.	Sergeant	Penna, Albert Edward.
Corporal	Harris, Ernest William.	Lieutenant	Pepperell, William Charles.
Private	Harris, James.	Private	Perkins, Arthur Reginald.
Private	Harvey, Frederick James.	Private	Platt, James.
Sergeant	Haynes, Stanley.	Private	Poole, Sydney James.
Private	Herbert, Ernest James.	Private	Pusey, George Thomas.
Private	Heron, Robert.	Private	Race, Thomas Arthur.
Corporal	Hill, William Lewis.	L/Corporal	Redwood, Stanley Ernest.
L/Corporal	Hinds, Kenneth Richard.	C.Q.M.S.	Revell, Herbert William.
Private	Holton, Archibald.	Private	Rice, John Cecil.
Corporal	Holton, Lancelot Ernest G.	Private	Richards, William White.
L/Corporal	Horn, Harry.	L/Corporal	Riseley, Edward Charles.
Private	Howard, Frank.	Private	Robinson, Charles Henry.
Private	Hughes, James.	Private	Romain, Arthur.
Private	Irons, Albert Alfred.	Private	Round, William Edwin.
Private	Jackson, John Charles.	Private	Rush, William Oliver.
Private	Jeyes, Frederick.	L/Corporal	Scrivener, Bernard John.
L/Corporal	Johnson, Charles Edward.	Private	Seabrook, Arthur.
Private	Kinns, Hubert Reginald.	Private	Sharpe, Shirley Herbert F.

Lieutenant	Sheldon, Harold Stephen.
L/Corporal	Siddons, Francis James.
Sergeant	Skinner, George Edmund.
Corporal	Smith, Arthur Gerald.
Private	Smith, Leonard Frank.
Private	Smith, Reginald.
Lieutenant	Stephenson, Francis H.
L/Corporal	Stockwin, Arthur.
Private	Stroulger, Percy.
Private	Sullivan, Richard John.
Private	Summerfield, Arthur D. J.
Private	Summerford, Frank Edw.
Private	Swan, Harold Alfred.
Private	Tarrant, Herbert Arthur.
Sergeant	Tarry, Frederick Ernest.
L/Corporal	Tew, Albert George
Private	Thompson, Albert Charles.
Lieutenant	Thornton, Frank Kennels.
Private	Tinston, Arthur H. J.
Private	Tomlin, Herbert Reginald.
Sergeant	Walmsley, Alfred Ernest.
Private	Warwick, Edward Philip.
Private	Warwick, George Thomas.
Private	Welsh, William Thomas.
Private	White, James Henry.
Private	White, William Henry.
Sergeant	Wigfall, John William
Private	Williams, Jeffery Clements.
Private	Woodward, Robert.
Private	Worley, Harry.
Private	Wright, Alfred Edward.

C COMPANY

Private	Abrahams, Hyman.
Private	Ager, James.
Private	Allen, Kenneth Clifford.
L/Corporal	Allen, Phillip John.
Private	Andrews, Stephen Jack W.
Lieutenant	Andrews, William Mundy.
Private	Ashby, Harry.
Private	Ashton, Walter.
Private	Baker, William Thomas.
C.S.M.	Ball, Thomas Arthur.
Private	Barker, John Barkus.
Corporal	Barker, Walter Herbert.
Corporal	Barrett, Henry Herbert E.
Private	Barnes, Frederick George.
Corporal	Barrows, Reginald Alfred.
Major	Barton, Alfred Gerald R.
Lieutenant	Bason, Arthur Leonard.
Sergeant	Bean, Alf.
Private	Beeby, Alfred Thomas.
Corporal	Benton, Frank Serbert.
Sergeant	Bernstein, Bert.
Private	Billingham, Arthur H. D.
L/Corporal	Blake, Arthur Sidney.
Sergeant	Bland, Leslie William.
Sergeant	Botterill, Kenneth Noel.
Private	Boughton, George Thomas.
Private	Bowers, Ernest Sydney.
Private	Bradbury, Sydney Louis.
L/Corporal	Britten, Frederick Albert.
Sergeant	Brooks, Alfred Frederick.
Private	Broughton, Thomas Giles.
Private	Brown, Frank.
Private	Brown, Howard James.
Private	Bull, George William.
Private	Button, Harry.
Private	Byrne, William Frederick.
Private	Carroll, Reginald.
Private	Caulcutt, Ronald Herbert.
Private	Cave, Arthur Urban.
Corporal	Chaffe, Clarence John
Private	Chapman, Bertram Chas.
Private	Charlton, Roland Victor.
Private	Chown, Cyril Edgar.
Private	Chown, William.
Private	Clarke, Alfred George.
L/Corporal	Clarke, George Harry.
L/Corporal	Clayson, Bert.
Captain	Clayson, Hugh.
Lieutenant	Cockrill, Arthur John.
Private	Coe, William.
Private	Coles, Frank Noble.
Lieutenant	Collins, Frank Henry.
Private	Cooper, Henry.
L/Corporal	Cotton, William Noel.
C.Q.M.S.	Covington, William George
Corporal	Crake, George Henry.
Private	Crane, Herbert Henry.
Sergeant	Craxton, Stanley Alfred.
Private	Dakin, Leslie Charles.
Private	Davis, Ernest Frank Geo.
Private	Dawkins, Edward John.
Corporal	Dawkins, George Charles.
Private	Day, Arthur Charles.
Private	Denton, Albert Owen.
Private	Dolby, George Richmond.
L/Corporal	Donald, Ben Wainman.
L/Corporal	Donald, Charles George.
Corporal	Draper, Alfred Frank.
Private	Driver, John Thomas.
L/Corporal	Dunmore, Norman Frank.
Corporal	Dunn, Herbert Ross.
L/Corporal	Dyer, Percy Trevor.

L/Corporal	Edwards, Albert Clifford.	Private	Leathersich, Enos Robt. C.
Private	Edwards, Ralph Herbert.	Private	Leeson, Albert Edward.
Sergeant	Elson, William Arthur F.	L/Corporal	Lepper, Harold Murray.
Private	Etheridge, Albert Thomas.	Private	Linnitt, Horace.
Private	Fletcher, Gordon Stewart.	Private	Lyman, Sidney George.
Private	Fletcher, Stephenson.	Corporal	Lyon, George.
Sergeant	Fletcher, Stephenson.	Sergeant	Malpas, Horace Joshua.
Sergeant	Forsyth, William James.	Private	Mann, Edward Sydney.
Private	Frankland, Arthur.	Private	Maris, Bernard Frederick.
Corporal	Frisby, Edgar Morris.	Private	Martyn, Philip Henry.
Private	Ganderton, Geo. Lancelot.	Corporal	Mayes, Philip.
Corporal	Garrett, Charles.	Private	Meadows, Alfred.
Private	Gibson, Alec Leonard.	Private	Mee, Frederick A.
Sergeant	Goodman, Alfred William.	Private	Meredith, John Merrick.
Private	Goodrich, George.	Sergeant	Middleton, Herbert M.
Private	Goodson, Herbert Edw. W.	L/Corporal	Mills, Donald William.
Private	Gratton, Francis Wilson.	Private	Molcher, Claude Morris.
L/Corporal	Green, Frederick George.	Private	Mortimer, Leonard John T.
Private	Grooms, Gordon Sidney.	Sergeant	Moss, Ernest William.
Private	Groome, Ralph Eric.	Private	Mott, William Lascelle.
Private	Hall, John Geoffrey.	Private	Muddiman, Thomas Frank.
Sergeant	Hambleton, John.	Private	Mumford, Robert Charles.
Private	Hancock, Horace.	Private	Muntzer, Antony.
Private	Harman, Walter Arthur.	Private	Murfitt, Rex Harold.
Private	Harrison, Albert Edward.	Corporal	Neale, Reginald George.
Private	Harte, Kenneth	Sergeant	Noble, William Dickens.
Private	Havart, Norman Alfred.	Sergeant	Owen, Henry Wm. Morris.
Private	Haygarth, Frank Binns.	L/Corporal	Panter, Albert.
L/Corporal	Hewitt, Clarence Charles.	Sergeant	Parker, Frederick Thomas.
Lieutenant	Hiam, Charles.	Private	Partridge, Cyril George.
Corporal	Hickman, Paul Francis H.	L/Corporal	Pay, Frederick Alfred E.
Sergeant	Hickman, James Lawson.	Private	Peasland, Cyril.
Private	Hill, George James.	L/Corporal	Peasland, Eric William.
Sergeant	Hill, Horace.	Private	Pendered, Walter.
L/Corporal	Hodgson, Henry Percy.	Private	Phipps, William.
Private	Holmes, John Aubrey.	Private	Phipps, William Charles.
Corporal	Holt, Henry Alfred Harold.	Private	Prigmore, John Charles.
Private	Hooper, Archibald.	Private	Pulley, Joseph Henry.
L/Corporal	Horsman, Dennis Hughes.	L/Corporal	Ralph, Thomas Alfred.
Private	Howkins, Arthur William.	Private	Rattan, Cyril George.
L/Corporal	Humphrey, William Robert.	Private	Reynolds, Oliver Frank.
L/Corporal	Hunt, William Frank.	Private	Rice, George Felix.
Corporal	Hutchings, Sydney George.	Private	Rickard, Harry John.
Private	Jeyes, Alfred Leonard.	Private	Ringrose, Thomas.
Sergeant	Jeyes, Frederick William.	L/Corporal	Riseley, William.
Private	Jeyes, James Albert.	Private	Roberts, Charles Harry.
Private	Jonas, Archibald.	L/Corporal	Roberts, Edward Arthur.
Corporal	Johnson, Alfred James.	Private	Robbins, John Richard.
Corporal	Jones, Horace Ralph Henry.	Private	Robins, Ronald Moore T.
Private	Keil, George Wm. Thomas.	Private	Robinson, Archibald R.
Sergeant	Kennell, Sidney Thomas.	Sergeant	Roddis, Harry Wallis.
Corporal	Kidney, William Alfred.	Private	Rogers, Henry Leonard.
Private	Kingham, Herbert Wright.	Private	Row, Eric Driver.
Private	Knight, Harold George.	Sergeant	Rush, Albert Reginald.
Lieutenant	Lawley, Percy.	Private	Russell, Arthur Harry.

Private	Sabey, Leslie.	Private	Spinner, John Vigor.
Private	Sampson, James Tindall.	Lieutenant	Spires, John William.
Private	Scott, James Bernard.	Private	Tibbles, Eric Walter.
Private	Scott, Samuel Ernest.	Private	Tibbs, Edward Lewis.
2nd/Lieut.	Seago, George.	Private	Tipler, Thomas Frederick
Private	Seaman, Reginald Stanley.	Private	Tootell, William Drewe.
Corporal	Secker, Arthur.	Private	Toseland, John Henry.
Corporal	Sharman, Harry.	Private	Turland, Lawrence Wm.
L/Corporal	Sharpe, Frank.	Lieutenant	Turner, Edward Gordon.
Private	Shaw, William Harold.	Private	Turnock, Walter Edwin
Lieutenant	Sherwell, Victor Roy.	Private	Tysoe, Ewart William.
Private	Short, Ernest Harold.	L/Corporal	Tysom, Eric Raymond.
Private	Squire, Philip Henry.	Private	Veitch, Robert Samuel.
Private	Stanton, Herbert George.	L/Corporal	Wales, Leslie Herbert.
Sergeant	Stockford, Herbert.	Private	Walker, Douglas Harry.
Private	Summerfield, Edward.	Corporal	Wallington, Frank.
L/Corporal	Sykes, Ben.	L/Corporal	Ward, Frederick.
Private	Tarry, Norman Wilfred.	Private	Ward, Horace.
L/Corporal	Thomas, Peredur Wynn.	Private	Watkins, Ronald George.
Private	Shortland, John James.	Lieutenant	Watts, Ernest Frederick.
Private	Shrive, Tom.	L/Corporal	Webb, George William.
Private	Simons, Samuel.	Sergeant	Wheatcroft, Albert Edward.
Private	Simpson, Alfred John.	Private	White, Bernard Harry.
Sergeant	Simpson, Reginald Chas.	Private	White, Herbert Cecil.
Corporal	Smith, Charles.	Private	Whiteman, Arthur.
Private	Smith, Eric John.	Private	Whitsey, George Thomas.
Private	Smith, Frederick George.	Private	Willars, William Albert.
L/Corporal	Smith, Roland Cecil.	Private	Williams, Eric Cecil.
Private	Smith, Sydney George.	L/Corporal	Wills, Charles.
Corporal	Soden, William Thomas.	Corporal	Wood, William Jacob.
Private	Spencer, Edwin Worley.	Private	Wrigley, Wallace Fredk. J.
Private	Spicer, William James.		

D COMPANY

Private	Alibone, Albert Victor.	Captain	Beeston, Eric.
Private	Allen, Joseph William.	Sergeant	Bland, William George.
Private	Antliff, William Belmont.	Private	Blundell, Frederick Harry.
Private	Arthur, Leonard.	Private	Botterill, Albert Oldham.
Sergeant	Ashby, Alfred George.	Private	Bourne, Walter Frederick.
Corporal	Ashford, Walter.	Sergeant	Bradbury, Arthur.
L/Corporal	Bailey, Frank Cyril.	Private	Bradshaw, Albert Edward.
Corporal	Baines, Walter Charles.	Private	Briggs, William Eric.
Corporal	Baker, Eli Frederick.	L/Corporal	Brock, Alfred Falkland.
Private	Baker, Reginald Frank.	Sergeant	Bruley, Charles Reuben.
Corporal	Ball, Albert James.	Private	Burt, Donald William.
Sergeant	Banks, Harry.	L/Corporal	Butlin, Albert Edward.
Private	Barcock, Frederick Frank.	Corporal	Butlin, John Edward.
Private	Barker, William James.	Private	Cadd, Englebert Alfred.
Private	Barnes, Henry James.	Sergeant	Campin, Alfred.
Private	Battison, Arthur B.	Sergeant	Cannon, Albert William.
Sergeant	Bawcutt, Harry.	Private	Carr, Leonard Ewart J.
Private	Bayes, Alfred John.	Private	Chambers, Frederick Geo.
2nd/Lieut.	Bayly, Leonard Marshall.	Private	Childs, Harry.
Private	Bazeley, Kenneth.	C.Q.M.S.	Chown, William Charles.

Private	Clark, Alan Arthur.	Private	Judkins, Alfred William.
Private	Clarke, Bert.	Private	Judkins, Jack.
Private	Clarke, Reginald Wilfred C.	Private	Kightley, William Victor.
Private	Clifton, Thomas Henry.	L/Corporal	Kilborn, Percy Thomas.
Private	Coley, John Arthur.	Private	Kirby, William Bert.
2nd/Lieut.	Cox, Edward Albert Regent.	Private	Kirk, Reginald.
Private	Curry, Richard Frank.	L/Corporal	Lack, Reginald John.
Sergeant	Day, Stanley Ernest.	L/Corporal	Lack, William Charles E.
Corporal	Delamare, Peter John.	Lieutenant	Lansman, Harold Fred.
Private	Desbrow, Joseph.	Private	Lee, Arthur William.
Private	Dilley, Arthur William B.	L/Corporal	Leigh, Thomas James.
Private	Doeg, George William.	Corporal	Lyon, Sidney James.
Private	Douglas, William John.	Private	Macfarlan, Parlan James.
Private	Dunkley, W. L. George.	Sergeant	Mallard, Alfred.
Private	Dunmore, Ernest.	Corporal	Mann, Vincent Spurgeon.
L/Corporal	Dunmore, Ernest William.	Private	Mathews, Joseph Trevor.
Sergeant	Fitzhugh, Reginald Arthur.	Sergeant	Messenger, Charles Horace.
Private	Flavell, Walter.	Private	Mineards, Charles.
Sergeant	Foll, John Edward Linnell.	Corporal	Morris, Arthur Frederick.
2nd/Lieut.	Freeman, Reginald.	Private	Muddiman, Percy.
L/Corporal	Freeman, Robert Edmund.	Private	Munnings, James Daly Lee.
L/Corporal	French, Frank Edward.	Private	Overton, George William.
Private	Frost, Thomas Albert.	Private	Page, Horace George.
Private	Gardner, Francis Edward.	Sergeant	Page, John.
Private	George, William.	Lieutenant	Parker, Frank.
Private	Green, Frederick Arthur.	Corporal	Parsons, Edward.
Lieutenant	Griffin, Stanley Russell.	Private	Partridge, Fredk. Robert.
Private	Hanwell, Frank Thomas.	Corporal	Paterson, Arthur James.
Private	Hargrave, Cyril.	Corporal	Payne, Stanley William.
Private	Harris, William Thomas.	Sergeant	Penn, Frederick.
Private	Harrold, Dennis Frank.	Private	Perryman, Patrick Arthur.
Private	Harte, Frederick Robert.	Corporal	Pettit, Bert.
Private	Hawkes, Ronald Frederick.	Private	Pollard, John William.
Private	Hawkins, Charles Wm. K.	Private	Price, Arthur Joseph.
Private	Hewitt, John.	Corporal	Redley, Frederick Thomas.
Private	Hibbitt, Wilfred Faulkner.	Private	Reynolds, Walter James.
Corporal	Hoar, Reginald Charles.	Private	Richards, Reginald Walter.
Private	Hodges, Robert Richard.	Private	Rickerd, George Campion.
Corporal	Hodgkiss, Alfred John.	Private	Roberts, Alfred Samuel.
Lieutenant	Holland, Arthur.	Private	Roe, George Brown.
Private	Holmes, Philip Edward.	Private	Rogers, Charles Ernest B.
Private	Hornby, Ronald.	Private	Rolfe, William John.
Private	Hornby, Thomas George.	L/Corporal	Ruff, John Francis.
Private	Hornsey, Albert Eli.	Private	Saunders, Edgar George.
2nd/Lieut.	Horwood, John Robert.	C.S.M.	Saunders, Robert William.
Lieutenant	Howard, Harold Holt.	2nd/Lieut.	Sharman, George Harold.
Corporal	Howe, James Alfred.	Private	Simons, Robert James.
Private	Hubbard, Leonard Harry.	Private	Sly, Reginald Herbert.
Private	Irons, John William.	Private	Smart, William Samuel.
Private	Jeffery, Gordon Bertram.	Private	Smith, Sydney Vivian.
Private	Jennings, Harold Edwin.	Private	Spencer, Cyril Arthur.
Private	Jones, Charles William.	Private	Spicer, Arthur Frank.
Private	Jones, Horace William.	Corporal	Squires, Edgar James W.
Major	Jordan, Frankham.	Private	Stinson, George Albert E.
Private	Jordan, George Frank.	Private	Stroud, William Frank.

Private	Stubbs, William Herbert.
Private	Swallow, Ernest.
Private	Tero, Arthur William.
Private	Thompson, James.
Private	Thorneycroft, Peter Geo.
L/Corporal	Tite, Frank Eusby.
Private	Tooms, Leslie Thomas.
Private	Tyson, George.
Private	Wade, Raymond.
Private	Walker, Ronald John.
Private	Walker, Thomas Fredk.
Private	Watson, James Ernest.
Private	Watson, John Maclaren.
Sergeant	Wesley, Walter William.
L/Corporal	Westley, Thomas Charles.
L/Corporal	White, Arthur John.
Private	Whiting, William George.
Private	Wilkins, John Albert.
Corporal	Willford, Thomas.
Private	Williams, John Richard.
Private	Wills, Walter Nelson.
Sergeant	Wilson, Leonard French.
Private	Woolmore, Thomas Leslie.
Private	Wright, Harold Geoffrey.
Lieutenant	Wright, Thomas Collins.
Corporal	Wright, William Arthur.
Private	Young, Herbert.

F COMPANY

Sergeant	Akers, Bert.
Sergeant	Allbright, Thomas.
L/Corporal	Allen, Frederick Ernest.
L/Corporal	Arthur, Leonard.
Private	Ashard, Alexander.
Corporal	Askham, Albert Edward.
Private	Askham, Thomas.
L/Corporal	Atkinson, Harold.
Corporal	Austin, Horace Alfred.
Private	Austin, Walter George.
Private	Avenell, Harry Callow.
C.S.M.	Bailey, Francis Walter.
Private	Ball, Cyril George.
Private	Bamford, Albert.
Lieutenant	Barratt, John Russell.
Private	Barrie, William.
Private	Bason, Aubrey Albert.
Private	Battison, Bertram Charles.
Major	Baxter, Arthur Spencer.
Private	Bayliss, Roland Leslie.
L/Corporal	Bishop, Herbert.
Private	Bishop, Norman.
C.Q.M.S.	Boddington, Charles Wm.
Private	Bonham, Frederick James.
Private	Brawn, Albert George.
L/Corporal	Brenton, Leonard Charles.
Private	Brown, Ronald Joseph.
Private	Brown, Walter James.
Private	Bruce, Charles.
Private	Bruley, William.
Lieutenant	Burton, Alan Jocelyn.
Private	Buthee, George Ernest.
Private	Campbell, Herbert.
Private	Carpenter, John James.
Sergeant	Care, Arthur.
Corporal	Chick, Kenneth James.
Private	Church, Peter Wilfred.
Private	Davies, Thomas John.
Private	Clarke, Stanley.
Private	Clarke, Thomas.
Private	Collier, William George.
L/Corporal	Collins, Reginald John.
Lieutenant	Cooch, John Henry.
Private	Cotton, William Charles.
Private	Coulson, Leonard Thomas.
Private	Cox, Sydney.
Sergeant	Crofts, William Frank.
Private	Cross, Albert.
Private	Cross, Sidney.
Private	Cross, Walter Edward.
Private	Curtress, Alan Charles A.
Private	Dennis, William Francis.
Private	Dexter, Willie Arthur.
Sergeant	Dickens, Reginald Charles
Private	Doherty, Patrick.
Private	Drummond, John.
Corporal	East, Albert Edward.
Lieutenant	Evans, William Alfred.
Sergeant	Facer, William Alfred.
L/Corporal	Finch, Reginald.
Private	Fletcher, Reginald Wm.
Private	Foster, Edwin.
Sergeant	Frisby, John Francis.
Private	Gardner, William George.
Private	Garland, Walter E.
L/Corporal	Griffin, Percy Frederick.
Captain	Harris, Cecil George.
Private	Harrison, Walter Harold.
Lieutenant	Harrold, Arthur Edward.
Private	Healey, Bertie Osborne.
Private	Heath, Jack Alfred.
Private	Henman, Alwyne Aubrey.
Private	Herbert, Arthur George.
Private	Hicks, Harry Charles.
Private	Hobson, Benjamin Alfred.
Private	Howard, John Herbert.

Private	Isaac, Joseph Thomas.	Private	Sargeant, Robert George.
Private	Jackson, Walter Raymond.	Private	Scarlett, Frederick Wm.
Private	Jeffery, George William.	Private	Sheffield, Douglas Henry.
Private	Johnson, George John.	Private	Shipton, Walter Joseph.
Private	Jones, Ernest Eric.	Private	Short, Stephen James.
Private	Jones, Philip.	Private	Smith, Frank.
L/Corporal	Lambert, Aubrey James.	Private	Smith, Sidney Harry.
Sergeant	Lambert, Thomas George.	Private	Smith, Victor.
2nd/Lieut.	Lawrence, Harold James.	Private	Smith, William James F.
Private	Leach, Ronald Cyril V.	Private	Solari, Peter.
Lieutenant	Leach, Sidney George.	Sergeant	Spanton, George Alfred.
L/Corporal	Lee, John Frederick.	Private	Spencer, Nat.
Sergeant	Lee, William.	Private	Stallard, Arthur William.
Private	Legg, George Frederick.	Private	Stephenson, Charles.
Private	Lewis, Frederick.	Private	Stutley, Joseph.
Private	Linnell, Reginald John.	Private	Suter, Russell.
L/Corporal	Luck, Ronald.	Private	Swannell, George Joseph.
Corporal	Lyon, John.	Private	Tarry, William George.
L/Corporal	Malin, Stanley Thomas.	L/Corporal	Taylor, Edward James.
Private	Mann, Henry Joseph.	Private	Thorpe, William Ferguson
Lieutenant	Manning, Thomas Edgar.	L/Corporal	Tew, Ernest Arthur J.
Corporal	Markie, Arthur.	Corporal	Turner, George.
Private	Markie, Ernest Leslie.	Private	Underwood, Cyril.
Sergeant	Marlow, Ernest James H.	Private	Warboys, William Walter.
Private	Morris, Edward William.	Private	Ward, Raymond Henry.
Private	Mundin, Samuel Thomas.	L/Corporal	Warnes, Leonard.
Private	Murton, Robert George.	Private	Warren, George.
Private	O'Driscoll, Timothy.	Private	Weatherall, Bert Fredk.
Private	Onley, George Henry.	Private	Webb, Raymond George.
Private	Opas, Samuel.	Private	Wheatley, Frederick.
Private	Packer, William George T.	Private	Whitaker, Charles John.
Sergeant	Parker, William Charles.	Private	White, Albert Edward.
L/Corporal	Parsons, Dudley Richard W.	Private .	White, Charles Frederick.
Sergeant	Payne, Wallace.	L/Corporal	White, George Henry.
Sergeant	Penn, Sydney Gray L.	L/Corporal	Wilby, Frederick James H.
Private	Pettitt, Richard.	Private	Williams, David Brynman.
Private	Poole, Ernest Maurice.	Private	Winter, Leonard Arthur.
Private	Prentice, Ernest Charles.	Private	Withey, Albert.
Private	Rain, Thomas Calvert.	Private	Wixon, William.
Private	Reynolds, Richard.	Private	Wrighting, Arthur John.
Private	Robinson, Christopher.	Private	York, Frank.
Private	Rowett, Edgar.	Private	Young, John Richter.
Private	Sanders, Harry Bertram.	Private	Young, William Henry.

G COMPANY

L/Corporal	Abraham, Harold Richard.	Private	Battison, Frank H.
Lieutenant	Allinson, Vincent Birkett.	Private	Battison, Victor.
Private	Arnold, Herbert Henry.	L/Corporal	Beasley, Henry Charles.
Private	Atkinson, Frederick James.	L/Corporal	Bee, William.
Corporal	Atterburn, George.	L/Corporal	Bell, Percy.
Private	Bailey, William.	Private	Bennett, Herbert Russell.
Lieutenant	Barker, Francis William.	Sergeant	Billing, Reginald Wilfred.
Private	Barrett, William Charles.	Sergeant	Billingham, Arthur Wm.

Private	Billingham, Geoffrey H.	Private	Gibson, Keith.
Private	Birch, Jack.	Private	Giddings, Geoffrey Donald.
Private	Bird, Frederick Arthur.	Private	Gillham, Ronald.
Private	Bland, Stephen H.	Corporal	Goffe, Frank.
Private	Blunt, Frederick.	Private	Golding, George Peter.
L/Corporal	Bodsworth, Thomas Brice.	Private	Goodman, Israel.
Private	Bonham, Mark.	L/Corporal	Goodridge, Albert.
Private	Boswell, Henry.	Private	Gookey, John Edward.
Private	Bosworth, Herbert.	L/Corporal	Gribble, Horace Herbert.
Private	Botterill, Charles William.	Private	Harris, Frank Thomas.
Private	Briggs, Reginald George.	Private	Harrison, Alfred J.
Corporal	Brooks, Percy.	Private	Hart, Percy Albert James.
Private	Brough, Francis Mark.	Private	Haynes, Cecil Frederick.
L/Corporal	Broughton, Sydney.	L/Corporal	Hill, Arthur.
Sergeant	Brown, Frederick Thomas.	Private	Hill, Ronald Arthur E.
L/Corporal	Burton, William Percy.	Private	Hodges, Dennis William M.
Private	Butler, Kenneth Rush.	Private	Holland, Stanley George.
Corporal	Button, John.	Private	Horsley, Walter Herbert.
Private	Campbell, Daniel.	Private	Hutchins, Frank.
Sergeant	Chambers, Albert Edgar.	Private	Jackson, Albert.
Corporal	Chapman, Samuel R.	L/Corporal	Jarman, Ernest.
Private	Clarke, Cyril George.	Private	Judge, John B.
Private	Clarke, Malcolm Owen S.	Private	Kershaw, Alfred.
Private	Clarke, Thomas Eric.	Sergeant	Kersting, Phillip Eric.
L/Corporal	Clayson, Arthur.	Corporal	Kimberley, Stanley Francis.
Private	Clayton, Desmond Cyril.	Private	Kingston, Raymond S. L.
Captain	Cleaver, Alfred Ernest.	L/Corporal	Kirkton, Sydney George.
Private	Coles, Arnold.	Private	Langford, Alan L.
Sergeant	Collings, Cyril Reginald.	L/Corporal	Lawman, Harold S.
Private	Cook, Norman Ellis.	Private	Lawrence, Chas. Rowland.
Private	Crowson, James F.	Private	Lawrence, Wm. Richard C.
Private	Cummings, Albert Arnold.	Private	Lee, Grahame Kelsey.
L/Corporal	Davis, Frederick George.	Private	Letts, Henry Harry.
Private	Day, Francis Alfred.	Private	Lewis, Frederick Walter.
Private	Dazeley, Francis.	Private	Lineham, Cyril.
Private	Dickens, Richard Oliver.	Corporal	Lines, Alfred Ernest.
Private	Dommett, William Arthur.	Private	Lloyd, David James Walter.
Private	Downing, Stephen Edward.	Private	London, Max.
Corporal	Dyett, John.	Private	Love, Lionel Leonard.
Sergeant	Edmonds, Thomas George.	Private	Lyon, Frederick.
Sergeant	Edmunds, John Phillip.	Corporal	Mackenzie, Kenneth.
L/Corporal	Edwards, Albert William.	Private	Malin, William.
Lieutenant	Edwards, Cyril Muschamp.	L/Corporal	Malpas, Frederick.
Corporal	Edwards, Thomas.	Private	Marlow, Frank.
Private	Ette, Stanley Martin.	Sergeant	McCallum, Malcolm.
Private	Falkner, Frederic S. Neil.	Corporal	McLeod, James.
Corporal	Finch, John.	Private	Metcalf, Walter Ernest.
Private	Finn, Harold M.	Private	Mickley, Sydney.
Private	Fitzhugh, Lawrence Henry.	L/Corporal	Mills, William Walter.
Private	Flynn, William James.	Sergeant	Morgan, Walter Blatchford.
Private	Frear, James Arthur.	Private	Moring, Albert Vincent.
Private	Freeman, Arthur William.	Private	Morris, William Edward.
Private	George, William E.	Corporal	Norfolk, Harry Spencer.
Private	Gibbins, Albert.	Private	Notton, Cecil Leonard R.
Private	Gibbins, George.	Corporal	Oldham, William Henry.

Corporal	Oxborough, Ernest.	Private	Stonebanks, Christopher E.
Private	Pack, Frederick.	Private	Stones, George Edward.
Private	Panther, Rupert Thomas.	Corporal	Streeter, William James N.
Corporal	Parker, Christopher Fred.	Private	Swallow, Walter John.
Private	Parsons, Reginald.	Private	Tear, Reginald.
Major	Patrick, Stephen Berrill.	Private	Thomas, Arthur Frederick.
Lieutenant	Pearce, Christopher Chas.	Private	Thorpe, William Arthur T.
C.Q.M.S.	Pepper, Thomas Isaac.	Corporal	Towers, John A.
Sergeant	Perry, Frank Edward.	Private	Vernon, Arthur.
Corporal	Pittam, Robert.	Private	Wade, Harold.
Private	Powell, Arthur William.	Private	Wakeling, Henry William.
Corporal	Powell, William Percival.	Private	Walker, Robert.
L/Corporal	Press, Henry.	Private	Walker, William Barratt.
Lieutenant	Purdy, Victor Horner.	Private	Ward, Leslie Ernest.
Private	Ramsey, Stanley Clifford.	Private	Warden, George.
Private	Rathbone, Edgar.	Lieutenant	Watts, Jess.
Private	Redgrave, Wilfred.	L/Corporal	Watts, Joseph Thomas.
L/Corporal	Relf, Henry John Ronald.	Private	Webb, Cyril John Fredk.
Private	Rhead, Harry.	Private	Webb, James Thomas.
Private	Richards, Arthur.	Sergeant	Welch, Harry Ernest.
Private	Robinson, Peter.	Private	Welsh, Reginald Joseph.
Corporal	Rogers, Griffith William.	Private	Westell, George.
Lieutenant	Rowe, Ralph Herbert.	Sergeant	Westley, Charles.
Private	Saffer, Maurice.	Lieutenant	Wheeler, Reginald Leslie.
Corporal	Savage, Bernard Arthur.	Private	White, Reginald.
Sgt.-Major	Savage, Herbert Arthur.	Captain	Whiting, Fredk. Charles.
L/Corporal	Scrivener, Robert Henry.	Sergeant	Wilde, Claude Cecil John.
Corporal	Sherwin, Walter.	Private	Wingrove, Eric.
Private	Shipley, James.	Private	Wood, Leslie Edward.
L/Corporal	Shortland, Frank.	Private	Worley, Albert G.
Lieutenant	Simon, Horace Leslie.	Private	Wright, Anthony John.
Sergeant	Spencer, Horace Frederick.	Private	Wright, Percy John S.
Private	Steel, George Arthur.	Corporal	Yoxall, George Henry.

H COMPANY

Private	Adams, John George.	Private	Bird, Howard George.
Private	Allibone, Arthur.	Sergeant	Bland, Philip Henry.
Private	Anderson, Gordon Percy.	Major	Blason, Alfred William.
Private	Ansell, Edward John.	Sergeant	Blason, Arthur Charles.
Private	Appleton, William Charles.	Lieutenant	Blason, Frank Ernest.
Captain	Armitt, Reginald Burbidge.	Corporal	Block, Horace Edgar.
Private	Austin, William.	Private	Bond, John William.
Private	Banks, Frederick George A.	Private	Boyes, Charles William.
Private	Banks, William Robert.	Private	Brazier, George.
Private	Barden, Herbert Thomas.	Private	Breavington, William Fred.
Sergeant	Barford, Stanley.	Private	Briggs, Alfred Sidney Geo.
L/Corporal	Barker, Francis Joseph.	Private	Brown, Arthur John.
Private	Barnard, Robert Woolfrey.	Sergeant	Bullard, Albert George.
Corporal	Barnett, John William.	C.S.M.	Butcher, Alfred Alphonso.
Lieutenant	Barrett, Arthur George.	Private	Carpenter, David John.
Private	Baubutt, Stanley Edward.	Lieutenant	Cattell, Herbert.
Sergeant	Bayes, Kenneth George.	Private	Chambers, Cecil.
Corporal	Beesley, Harry.	Private	Chapman, Charles Henry.
Private	Bell, Albert.	Private	Chick, Frank.

Corporal	Clarke, Frank.	Private	Masters, Alexander Frank.
Private	Clayson, Francis Henry.	Private	Mills. Norman Frank.
Private	Coe, William Charles F.	Private	Moody, James William.
Private	Collier, Eric Richard.	Private	Morgan, Peter William.
2nd/Lieut.	Collier, John Veasey.	Private	Morgan, William Ronald.
Private	Cooper, S. G.	Private	Morris, Daniel Robert.
Corporal	Cory, Charles Samuel.	Private	Moseley, Albert Edward.
Private	Darlow, William Thomas L.	Private	Mott, James Thomas.
L/Corporal	Davies, Archibald Curtis.	Private	Moyes, William.
Sergeant	Davis, Leslie Victor.	Private	Munroe, Ernest.
Private	Davis, William Thomas.	Private	Nobbs, John Herbert.
Private	Deutsch, Leopold.	Private	Oakey, Ronald.
Sergeant	Downing, Fredk. William.	Private	O'Dell, Joseph Stewart G.
Private	Dunce, William Edward.	Corporal	Ogborn, Stephen William.
Private	Farey, Walter Thomas.	L/Corporal	Osborne, Harry Bray.
Private	Figg, Alan David.	Private	Page, Leslie Henry.
Private	Ford, Arthur James.	Sergeant	Passey, Edgar Robert.
L/Corporal	French, George James.	Private	Pickerill, Edwin Fredk. W.
Private	Goldman, Abraham.	L/Corporal	Poole, Bertie Horace.
Private	Goodman, Sidney B.	Private	Preece, Alfred E.
Private	Green, Francis Horace.	Private	Prior, Frank.
Corporal	Green, Robert Leslie.	Private	Reynolds, Charles Samuel.
Private	Greenfield, Walter.	Private	Reynolds, Sidney Albert.
Private	Hambilton, Charles W.	Private	Richards, Walter George.
2nd/Lieut.	Hancock, William Eastlake.	L/Corporal	Richardson, Edwin R.
Private	Harrison, Raymond Geo.	Corporal	Rootham, Harold Alwyne.
Sergeant	Harvey, Charles Ernest.	Private	Rosier, Alfred.
Private	Harvey, Robert.	Private	Rowell, John William.
Corporal	Harwood, Reginald Chas.	L/Corporal	Rowell, Thomas Whiting.
Private	Hawes, James William.	Corporal	Sharman, Herbert Brand.
Private	Hembrough, Alec Edward.	Sergeant	Sharman, William George.
Private	Henderson, John Vincent.	Private	Sheffield, Robert William.
Private	Henson, Ronald Andrew.	Private	Sheppard, Archibald W.
L/Corporal	Hill, Harold Edward.	Private	Sibley, George Edward.
2nd/Lieut.	Hollowell, Clifford James.	Private	Simons, William.
Private	Hope, Robert.	Private	Slack, Leonard.
Private	Horsley, Clement John.	L/Corporal	Smith, Cyril.
C.Q.M.S.	Jeffery, Arthur.	Private	Smith, Philip Brodie.
Private	Jennings, Albert.	Private	Smith, Walter.
Sergeant	Johnson, Alfred Henry.	Private	Smith, William Henry.
Corporal	Johnson, William.	Private	Spevock, Max.
Private	Knight, William Edward J.	Private	Staley, Albert Charles.
Sergeant	Langton, William.	Private	Stevens, Albert.
Private	Latimer, Hugh.	Private	Stevens, Albert Lewis.
L/Corporal	Law, Gerald Austin.	Private	Stubley, Leslie George.
Private	Lees, Alan Brian.	Private	Swift, William Walter.
Private	Limbert, Thomas Sydney.	Private	Thornton, Edgar.
Private	Little, John Thomas.	Private	Tingey, Cyril William.
Private	Lockett, Michael Anthony.	Private	Tobutt, William Ernest.
Corporal	Mallard, George Thomas.	Private	Tunley, Albert.
Sergeant	Manger, Arthur George.	Private	Vennervald, Sidney R.
Private	Manger, Jack Frank.	Sergeant	Wade, George.
L/Corporal	Mapstone, Fred Tom Jas.	Corporal	Wait, William Charles.
Corporal	Marshall, George.	Corporal	Walden, William Arthur.
Private	Mason, Richard.	Private	Walker, John George.

Corporal	Warren, Arthur.	Private	Wedgwood, Gordon Josiah.
L/Corporal	Warner, Frederick George.	Corporal	West, Albert Luke.
Sergeant	Watts, Frank.	Sergeant	Wheatcroft, Arthur.
Lieutenant	Watts, Herbert Arthur.	L/Corporal	White, Ernest Joseph.
Private	Wayman, John Mackness.	Private	Youngs, Derek Martin.
2nd/Lieut.	Webber, Harold Frederick.		

LADY MEMBERS

Mrs. S. B. Patrick   (G Company)
Miss Margaret Tench (F Company)

RECORD OF OLD MEMBERS WHO JOINED H.M. FORCES

When I was getting toward the end of this history, I began to have letters from old members of the Battalion who were serving in all parts of the world. The thought then struck me that it would be interesting to have a record of all those who had left us for H.M. Forces, or of as many as we could obtain. The collection of this material has involved much work and has taken much time, but I think that the effort was worth while. Much of the information has been obtained from old members themselves or their relatives, who responded to appeals in the local Press, but the bulk has been collected by boys of the Town and County School and of Modern Secondary Schools in the town. To these lads I am greatly indebted for their kind assistance.

I am aware that this list is by no means complete, for as I have said elsewhere, our first job in those days of 1940 was to get out on the Observation Posts and to train ourselves hurriedly for the expected invasion. It was impossible, with no staff, to keep a record of those who left us to join the Forces. However, from various sources, information has been obtained showing that 1,172 members left the Battalion to enlist in the Army, Navy and Air Force. Particulars have been received of 724 of these, but of the remaining 448, owing to various causes such as removal, the only fact known about them is from the Battalion Part II Orders showing that they joined up in one of the branches of the Services.

As will be seen, 37 old members of the Battalion will never return; their graves are in all parts of the world. We shall never forget them, for the majority of these lads were those who stood out with us on the Observation Posts in 1940, when the call came for us all to defend this country. It has been said that " our battles are won by the men who fall," and we who are left owe a great debt to all those who will not come back.

One surprising feature of the record is the number who enlisted in the Royal Navy, especially as Northampton is a town remote from the sea. They have served in all units of the Army and on many ships in all parts of the world. Many have interesting stories to tell. A large number were in the D Day landings in Normandy; others were at Arnhem. We like to recall that most of these received their first military training in our Battalion, and we hope to see them all at the various reunions that will no doubt be held. One of the most interesting stories is that of Flying-Officer Edmund H. Pack, an old L.D.V. member of A Company and the son of C.Q.M.S. Tom Pack (afterwards Q.M. of the 15th). Previous to July, 1944, he had taken part in 47 operational raids over Germany, including nine over Berlin, and had been in the historic bombing of Peenemunde. On July 5th, 1944, he was engaged in " straffing " V-bomb sites in Northern France when his machine was shot up, and he only of the crew managed to bale out. He landed safely some miles from Dunkirk and evaded capture although a German patrol car on the look-out for survivors passed quite close. He was no doubt undetected by the fact that he dropped among a herd of cows, among which he hid After some time he was able to move and, after burying his kit, took refuge in a cornfield. Here he remained for two or three days, when a peasant boy passed whom he contacted. Fortunately the boy's father was a member of the underground movement and, although unable to hide Pack owing to the close watch of the Germans in this area, supplied him with bread and beer. For eight days he wandered from the V-bomb site area towards the interior, and this day reached a farmhouse, where he was hidden by a French farmer, who supplied him with civilian clothes. Here he received a French identity card from the Maquis, and here " Jean Duquesnay " lived until September 10th, when he was freed by the liberating armies. All this time 200 Germans had been stationed in the village, and a battery was positioned at the rear of the farmhouse, but Pack managed to escape detection and was finally flown back to England on September 14th.

I have no doubt that many more have had their adventures, and it has been a pleasure to include their names and records in the history of the Battalion in which they started.

WALL CLIMBING — CRISPIN STREET   (Photo: J. Wright)

ROAD BLOCK (Abington Park).

(Photo: J. Wright)

OLD MEMBERS KILLED OR DIED ON ACTIVE SERVICE

BATTALION HEADQUARTERS

DESPATCH RIDERS

Clarke, Ivan Trevor, 38, Weedon Road; R.A.F.; Flight-Sergeant. Killed in action, B.N.A.F.

Yarde, Samuel, Kettering Road; R.N.V.R.; Sub-Lieutenant. Presumed killed in air operations in Eastern Waters.

MESSENGERS

Lineham, William A., 2, St. James' Mill Road; R.A.F.; Flight-Sergeant, attached Pathfinder Force. Killed on operational duties over Bochum, September 29th, 1943.

ELECTRIC LIGHT PLATOON

Pullen, David L., 17, Beech Avenue; Fleet Air Arm; Sub-Lieutenant. Took part in the bombing attack on the Tirpitz. Later shot down off Norway, May 6th, 1944, during attack on German south-bound convoy. Buried at Kristiansund, Norway.

EXPRESS LIFT PLATOON

Amberg, A. V.; R.A.F.; Flight-Lieutenant. M.E.F. Killed on operations.

GAS COMPANY PLATOON

Snape, Ronald H., 23, Tanner Street; 3rd Royal Tank Regiment; Private. Went to France shortly after D Day. Killed in action July 18th, 1944.

A COMPANY

Beale, R. W., 23, Sandhills Close, White Hills; Royal Navy. Accidentally drowned at sea.

Beer, J. A., 7, Brookland Road; R.A.F.; Warrant Officer. Killed in operations over France.

Corsby, D. E., 157, Ashburnham Road; Royal Field Artillery; Major. Killed in operations in France.

Dodd, Sidney J., 77, Ashburnham Road; Royal Artillery; Bombardier. Killed in Burma, February 6th, 1944.

Hussey, Albert John, 107, Kenmuir Avenue; 5th and 2nd Bns. Northamptonshire Regiment; later transferred to Royal Fusiliers. Served in Madagascar and Tunisia. Wounded in the invasion of Sicily; later fought at Anzio Beach-head, and killed in action September 9th, 1944.

Wilson, Geoffrey, 3, Birch Barn Way; Queen's Royal Regiment; Lance-Corporal. Killed in action in Normandy, August 9th, 1944.

York, G. H., 46, Cedar Road; R.A.F.; Flying-Officer, 144 Squadron. Reported missing from raid on Egersund, Norway, 24th March, 1945.

B COMPANY

Barden, W. H., 113, Southampton Road; 2nd Bn. Lincolnshire Regiment. Took part in D Day landings. Killed in Holland.

Barker, Donald, 228, Billing Road; 1st Bn. Queen's Own Royal West Kents. Killed in action in Italy, July 28th, 1944.

Barker, R., 30, Blenheim Road; 2nd Bn. East Yorkshire Regiment; Lance-Corporal. Died of wounds in Holland, October 19th, 1944.

Chambers, A. A., 14, Stevenson Street; R.A.F.; Sergeant Air-Gunner. Killed in air crash.

Crofts, D. A., 21, Pleydell Road; R.A.F.; Sergeant Air-Gunner. Killed over Occupied France.

Cross, C. F., 32, Euston Road; R.A.F.; Sergeant-Pilot. Killed in action.

Cross, Ronald, The Spread Eagle, Wellingborough Road; R.A.F.; Flight-Sergeant. Killed on operations over English Channel.

Greaves, C. G., 40, Towcester Road; 2nd Bn. Lincolnshire Regiment. Killed in the Ardennes, September, 1944.

Harrison, Eric G., 40, St. James' Street; Army Reconnaissance Corps. Killed in France.

Jeyes, B. J., 86, Cedar Road; 1st Bn. Leicestershire Regiment; Lieutenant. Served in N.W. Europe. Killed in action two days after his 21st birthday.

Kinns, R. E. J., 93, Abbey Road; 2nd Bn. Northamptonshire Regiment. Killed in Italy.

Plowman, Cecil, 61, Whitworth Road; 3rd Recce Regiment, attached Northumberland Fusiliers. Landed Normandy June 18th, 1944. Died of wounds July 2nd, aged 20. Buried at Hermanville Beach Cemetery, Calvodos.

Whitbread, P., 55, Pleydell Road; R.A.F.; L.A.C. Died in hospital.

C COMPANY

Skey, Derek N., 38, Sandiland Road; R.A.F.; Flight-Officer. Died while on service.

Stevens, John H., 152, Ashburnham Road; Coldstream Guards and Glider Pilot. Killed in action.

D COMPANY

Coles, Terence, 5, Sulgrave Road; Northamptonshire Yeomanry. Served in North Africa. Accidentally killed, February 8th, 1944.

F COMPANY

Bailey, F. E.; 28th Dragoon Guards, R.A.C.; Trooper. Killed in North Africa, December, 1942.

Battersill, C. W., 19, Lawrence Street; 2nd Bn. Lancashire Fusiliers; Fusilier. Killed in action in Italy, November 23rd, 1943.

Cotton, William E., 49, Brunswick Street; Duke of Cornwall's Light Infantry. Died of wounds in France, August 3rd, 1944.

Tompkins, P. R., 24, Military Road; Grenadier Guards; Guardsman. Killed in action, N.W. Europe, April, 1945.

G COMPANY

Chandler, Horace, 96, Adams Avenue; Army. In Normandy landings; killed in wood near Wessels.

Pepler, Sidney G., 81, Kingsley Road; 1st Bn. Northamptonshire Regiment. Killed in action in Burma, June 14th, 1944.

Rowe, Clarence L., 5, Craven Street; The Royals, R.A.C. Took part in the Normandy Campaign. Died of wounds, April 22nd, 1945. Buried Celle Cemetery, near Hanover.

Walton, Charles, 40, Arthur Street; Northamptonshire Regiment. Died of wounds, March 15th, 1944.

RECORD OF SERVICE OF OLD MEMBERS

BATTALION HEADQUARTERS

DESPATCH RIDERS

Adams, Michael O., 68, Derngate; Inniskillins; Lieutenant. Served in India.

Addington, Bryan, 141, Welford Road; R.A.F. Home Bases.

Catt, Warwick M., 337, Billing Road East; Army.

Coker, Alfred, 46, Christchurch Road; R.A.F.; F./O. Pilot, seconded to J Squadron, Glider Pilot Regiment.

Coker, Edgar, 46, Christchurch Road; R.A.F.; Pilot-Officer. Trained at Arizona, U.S.A.; Home Bases.

Copson, Alan A., 8, Cotton End; Royal Corps of Signals. India, Burma and Malaya; Indian Special Wireless Section; joined first road convoy Kuala Lumur to Singapore.

Dickens, S. L., Merchant Navy.

Featherstone, John, 310, Devon Parade; Royal Navy; Sub-Lieutenant. Motor Torpedo Boat No. 617, operating off the Dutch and French Coasts. Mentioned in Despatches.

Felton, Raymond, 55, Upper Harding Street. R.E.M.E. India and Singapore.

Freeston, E. J., R.A.F.

Gibbins, A., Royal Navy.

Gubbins, Robert E. G., 14, Park Way; Royal Navy; Sub-Lieutenant. Torpedo and Motor Boats; Home and Foreign Waters.

Gubbins, R. John W., 14, Park Way; R.A.F.; Flight-Lieutenant Pilot. Trained in Canada. Served at Gibraltar, etc.

Hawtin, Douglas, St. George's Avenue; Royal Corps of Signals; Captain. Served with 4th Indian Division in North Africa and Italy; wounded and mentioned in Despatches at Monastery Hill, Casino; later served in India.

Houghton, C. R.; R.A.F. Home Bases.

Leach, Jack, 102, Hunter Street; Royal Navy; H.M.S. Assistance; P.O., R.M. India and Ceylon; present at Bombay at time of Indian Naval Mutiny, February, 1946.

Leachman, Jack R., 70, Ridgeway; R.A.F. Pilot; Flight-Lieutenant. M.E.F., later Aden Command.

Lewis, Edward, The Avenue, Dallington; R.A.F. Rescue Service. Served English Channel, Atlantic and North Sea, later in Far Eastern Waters.

Needle, Ivor W. J., 31, Victoria Gardens; R.A.F.; W.O. Air Gunner on operations over Germany and Italy; later served in Burma.

Reynolds, R. W., R.A.F.

Stokes, Norman W., 23, Cecil Road; R.N.V.R.; Sub-Lieutenant, L.C.T., H.M.S. Quebec. Combined operations and Normandy.

Tinsley, W. G., Army.

Welch, Peter T., 126, Penrhyn Road; R.A.F. Home Bases and N.W. Europe.

A.F.C. MESSENGERS

Barber, C. D., 7, The Broadway; R.A.F.

Barnell, Frank, 73, Ivy Road; R.A.F.

Brewster, Peter, 81, Ashburnham Road; R.A.F.; Warrant Officer. Coastal Command; completed tour of duty in Atlantic, Dutch and German Waters; Anti-U-Boat Patrols on flanks of convoys during invasion of Normandy.

Dunnett, Stanley C., 17, Ryland Road; Royal Marines. H.M.S. Indefatigable, Aircraft Carrier, Aircraft recognition Gunlayer and Duck Driver. Home and Pacific Fleet.

Evans, Alec W., 16, Woodford Street; R.A.F. Home Bases.

Facer, Douglas K., 47, Harlestone Road; R.A.F.

Freestone, Bernard J., 58, King Edward Road; R.A.F., Bomber Command; W.O., 1st Bomber Group. 35 missions as air-gunner in Lancasters.

Kirsch, J., 16, Wheatfield Terrace; R.A.F. Home Bases.

Markie, Leonard W., 162, Broadway East; R.A.F.; Warrant Officer Pilot. Trained U.S.A. Home Bases.

Stevenson, Richard H., 4, The Fairway; R.A.F., M.T. Section; Corporal. Landed in Normandy after D Day; attached to American A.F.; later passed out as parachutist; in German break-through at Aachen.

Thompson, Bernard G., 48, Moore Street; 112 Provost Company, C.M. Police; Lance-Corporal. C.M.F., Africa and Italy.

Warren, Thomas C., 9, Harlestone Road; R.A.F.

York, Kenneth H., 27, Wantage Road; R.A.F. Home Bases.

BATTALION BAND

Brown, Frank, 20, Cottarville; R.A.M.C. North-West Europe.

Judd, J., 42, Queen Eleanor Road; Royal Navy. Mediterranean, etc.

No. 3 (MOBILE) PLATOON

Emery, Frederick E., 33, Alliston Gardens; R.A.C., transferred to 7th Queen's Own Hussars. Served with 8th Army in North Africa.

Hylands, J. R.

Johnson, Frank, 55, Naseby Street; 2nd Bn. Buffs. India, Java and Malaya; served with the Chindits in Assam.

Manning, P. L.

Richardson, Raymond, 71, Eastern Avenue; R.A.F.; L.A.C. India.

Smith, A.

Whitsey, G. F.

Wyton, A. F.

No. 4 (BOROUGH WATER) PLATOON

Askham, W. H.

Bull, Charles Edward, 4, St. Andrew's Road; Royal Artillery; Gunner, V.M. Served in North Africa and Italy, later in Austria.

Dolling, A. J.

James, R. G.

McMahon, M.

No. 6 (UNITED COUNTIES BUS) PLATOON

Duke, Edward, 42, Lowick Terrace, Moulton; Royal Navy.

Freeman, E.

Stewart, D. L. A.

BATTALION HEADQUARTERS STAFF

Barton, Ronald David (son of the Adjutant), St. Giles' Hotel; Royal Fusiliers; Second-Lieutenant. Cyprus and Egypt.

ELECTRIC LIGHT PLATOON

Aldridge, R. L.; R.E. Palestine.

Ayres, L. G., 86, Kingsthorpe Grove; R.A.F.; Flight-Lieutenant. North Africa and India.

Baldwin, D. A., 7, Cowper Terrace; R.A.F. Home Bases; crashed and grounded.

Bennett, W.; R.E. North-West Europe and Far East. Wounded in leg.

Betts, S. H. F., 37, Gloucester Avenue; R.A.F.; Sergeant. North-West Europe.

Clark, D. I., 39, Bush Hill; R.A.F. M.E.F.

Cosford, J.; H.M. Forces.

Cross, J. E., 22, Malcolm Drive; R.A.F. M.E.F.

Crossley, C. H., 3, Birchfield Road; R.A.F. Far East.

Denney, J. L., 12, Warren Road; R.A.F.; Flying-Officer.

Eyre, Geoffrey A., 35, St. Edmund's Road; R.E. Joined L.D.V. when only 15½. Took part in D Day landings and went through safely from Caen to Bremen; afterwards sent to Singapore.

Fidgett, J.; Army; Second-Lieutenant.

Foster, Ernest G., Hillcrest, Wootton; R.A.F. Regiment. M.E.F.

Gammons, L.; H.M. Forces.

Gardiner, R., Friars Crescent, Delapre; Royal Navy. Mediterranean.

Jeyes, F. E., 144, Adnitt Road; R.A.F.

Larkin, F., 26, Wycliffe Road; R.E. Far East.

Lessells, W. J., 57, Stimpson Avenue; R.A.F.; Flight Officer.

Markie, George, 58, Hervey Street; Royal Engineers. North-West Europe.

Pell, D. A., 26, Cecil Road; R.A.F. Gibraltar.

Pinney, Sidney W. L., 57, Kenmuir Gardens; R.A.F. Regiment; Sergeant. B.W.E.F., Denmark.

Rickerd, F.; R.A.P.C.

Smith, C.; Royal Navy. Ceylon and Eastern Waters.

Snedker, H. H., 169, Bush Hill Road; R.A.P.C.; Sergeant. North-West Europe.

Taylor, Norman S., 21, White Hills Way; R.A.F. Served in West Africa.

Timpson, A. D.; H.M. Forces.

Toseland, G. W., 4, Newland Square; R.A.S.C.; Sergeant. India.

Williams, W. A., 109, Lea Road; R.A.F.; Corporal.

Wright, Ronald, 16, Semilong, Road; R.A.F. B.W.E.F.

GAS COMPANY PLATOON

Askham, W. H.; Royal Armoured Corps. North Africa. Wounded.

Bradshaw, K. J.; Royal Corps of Signals; Lieutenant. · Wounded in Italy.

Cox, A.; Royal Artillery. Iceland and North-West Europe.

Darby, R. H.; Royal Corps of Signals. India.

Dixon, F. C.; Royal Engineers; Sergeant. M.E.F., 8th Army and France.

Harding, R. A.; Grenadier Guards; Sergeant. B.A.O.R.

Henson, S. T.; Royal Artillery; Corporal.

Hobbs, W. F.; Northamptonshire Regiment.

Hodges, P. H.; R.A.F. India.

Hopkins, R. L.; R.A.O.C.; Sergeant.

Hull, H. G.; R.A.F.; Corporal.

Lines, J.; R.A. India.

Oxley, L. A.; R.A.F.; Corporal. North Africa, Sicily and Italy.
Parry, F.; R.A.F. Egypt and Palestine.
Swingler, J. J.; Fleet Air Arm.
Sykes, A. J.; Royal Navy.
Tebbutt, J. E.; Northamptonshire Regiment; Corporal. Italy.
Tuck, L. C.; Fleet Air Arm; Lieutenant. Middle East, Ceylon and India.
Turland, A. R.; R.A.F. Iraq and Aden.

EXPRESS LIFT WORKS PLATOON

Andrews, R. J.; R.E.M.E.; Craftsman. C.M.F.
Ansell, J.; Royal Signals. B.L.A.
Bates, A. C.; R.A.F.; Sergeant.
Britton, W. A. A.; H.M. Forces.
Britton, W. K.; Fleet Air Arm; AM/OI.
Brown, D.; Royal Tank Regiment. C.M.F.
Botterill, S.; Fleet Air Arm; AF/E.
Burton, S. E.; Anti-Tank, R.A. B.M.A.F.
Cox, A. E.; Fleet Air Arm; AM/A.
Fairey, H. G.; Fleet Air Arm; AF/L.
Ferrar, C.; Derbyshire Yeomanry. C.M.F.
Gamble, G.; R.A.F.; Sergeant. M.E.F.
Garner, R. A.; Northamptonshire Regiment. S.E.A.C.
Gossage, S.; Royal Navy.
Heap, R.; Royal Navy; Stoker.
Henderson, R. J.; Royal Engineers. Overseas.
Herbert, F.; R.E.M.E. India.
Hopewell, C. W.; R.A.F.; A.C.1.
Hutchins, C. E.; R.A.O.C. C.M.F.
Hutt, C.; H.M. Forces.
Hutt, C. J.; R.A.O.C.; S.Q.M.S. India.
Jesson, G. A.; Grenadier Guards.
Jones, G. A.; R.A.F.; L.A.C.
Kidsley, H. E.; Cheshire Regiment. B.L.A.
Lemon, S. E.; Royal Artillery. India.
Loveland, W.; R.E.M.E. M.E.F.
Mason, A. E.; Army.
Newmarch, D.; East Yorks.
Powell, R. J.; Royal Artillery. India.
Ryder, J.; Grenadier Guards; Sergeant. B.L.A.
Salt, H. J.; Gordon Highlanders. B.L.A. Wounded.
Sanders, J. G. D.; R.A.F.
Shipman, W. W.; Royal Lancers. M.E.F., C.M.F.
Simons, R. J.; Fleet Air Arm; AM/L.
Smith, A. A.; R.E.M.E. Home Service.
Stevenson, H. H.; Northamptonshire Regiment. C.M.F.
Strike, A. F.; Fleet Air Arm; AF/MW.
Sutton, J. J.; R.A.F.; Flight-Sergeant. M.E.F.
Thompson, R. H.; Royal Tank Regiment; Corporal. B.L.A.
Tompkins, L.; R.A.O.C. B.L.A.
Vaughan, L. B.; Royal Engineers; Corporal.
Webb, W.; Grenadier Guards. M.E.F.
Wells, G.; Royal Navy; A.B.
White, K. W. J.; R.E.M.E.; Sergeant. India.

A COMPANY

Abrams, Albert W., 50, Balmoral Road; R.A.F.; Flight-Lieutenant. British Bases.

Abrams, Edwin H., 50, Balmoral Road; Royal Corps of Signals; Lance-Corporal; M.E.F. and B.L.A.

Afford, Roger A., 94, Birchfield Road; R.A.F.; Flight Lieutenant. Home Bases and Africa.

Alibone, Alfred J., 1, Shelley Street; R.A., 616 Battery; Gunner. Germany.

Allinson, J. G., 49, Park Avenue North; Royal Corps of Signals; Captain. Served in B.A.O.R.

Arscott, W. G., 6, Wheatfield Terrace; R.A., 26 L.A.A. Regt. Home Service.

Ashton, Frederick, "Rose Garth," Booth Rise; Royal Navy.

Austin, Francis St. John, 15, St. Matthew's Parade; Army.

Baker, F., 82, Boughton Green Road; R.E.M.E. Served in Germany.

Bamford, Charles, Boughton Green Road; Army.

Barltrop, Donald E., Moorlands, Kingsthorpe; Royal Navy; Sub-Lieutenant. Minesweeping, Eastern Waters.

Barringer, J., 8, Cranford Road; 2nd Field Regiment, R.A. M.E.F.

Beaumont, Leslie A., 18, Romany Road; R.A.O.C., 9th and 10th Battalions; Lance-Corporal. Home Service.

Berwick, Arthur B., 108, Kingsland Avenue; R.A. Italy and India.

Bird, Ernest, 19, Masefield Way; R.A.F.; L.A.C. Middle East.

Bishton, Reginald, 71, Cedar Road; 5th Northamptonshire Regiment; Sergeant. Italian Campaign; first troops to enter Agenta.

Blincowe, Edward, 21, Kingsley Road; 2nd Lincolnshire Regiment. Egypt, Palestine and North-West Europe; landed D Day with 3rd Division and fought at Caen, Falaise Gap and on to Bremen.

Block, Arthur E., 52, Boughton Green Rd.; Royal Engineers; Lance-Corporal. North-West Europe.

Botterill, George W., 20, Briton Gardens; R.A.S.C.; Lance-Corporal. B.A.O.R.

Brabbins, John E., 138, Eastern Avenue; Royal Corps of Signals. North-West Europe. Commended.

Brawn, Stanley R., 16, Monks Hall Road; R.A.F.; Corporal. Home Bases and Northern Island. Mentioned in Dispatches.

Brown, Frederick J., 107, Lutterworth Road; Army.

Budd, H. M., 3, The Bungalows, Great Billing; R.A.F. Regiment.

Bullimore, John A., 38, Langdale Road; R.A.S.C.; Driver. Germany.

Busby, Walter, 16, Ennerdale Road; Army.

Buswell, H., 17, Chestnut Road; R.A.F.; A.C.1, Armourer. West Africa. Discharged ill-health.

Butler, Leslie, 17, Langdale Road; Essex Regiment. B.L.A.

Cave, Tony G., 27, Hawthorn Road; Royal Navy; H.M.S. Kingsmill and H.M.S. Formidable; Petty Officer Motor Mechanic. Atlantic, Home Waters and S.E.A.C.

Chapman, William, 59, West Ridge; 145 R.A.C. Through African Campaign with 1st Army; slightly wounded in arm; later served in Italy.

Chappell, George A., 124, Lindsay Avenue; Royal Navy; A.B., Gunner. Served on defensively-equipped Merchant Ships; India and Burma.

Clifton, R., 10, Wallace Road; Army.

Collins, Cyril, 17, Junction Road; R.A., H.A.A. (Radar); Gunner O.F.C. South Wales.

Cooke, Herbert C., 13, Clarence Avenue; 5th Northamptonshire Regiment. Italy, Austria and Greece.

Dakin, William J., 75, St. Matthew's Parade; R.A.F.; L.A.C. India.

Davenport, Harry, 131, Eastern Avenue; R.A.M.C. Egypt.

Davison, Dennis J., 16, Newington Road; R.A.S.C.; Private. B.L.A., B.A.O.R.; in D Day landing and at Antwerp. Wounded in Holland.

Deacon, Raymond B., 61, St. Matthew's Parade; R.N.V.R.; Petty Officer. Home Service.

Deacon, William J., 411, Kettering Road; R.A.O.C.; Private. Home Service.

Dexeter, Raymond, 125, Beech Avenue; R.A.S.C.; Driver. Normandy to Germany.

Doggett, George C.; 107, Lindsay Avenue; Pioneer Corps. Landed Normandy D Day.

Downes, Leonard C., 12, The Fairway; Royal Navy. L.C.F. 37. In Normandy and Walcheren landings; survivor when ship was sunk at Walcheren.

Draper, C., 276, Birchfield Road East; R.A.F.; Flight-Sergeant Air-Gunner. Operations over Norway and Germany; later served in India.

Dunkley, Arthur, 125, Harborough Road; R.A.F.; A.C.1. Home Bases.

Durran, Harry H., 6, Chestnut Road; R.A.P.C. Home Service.

Earl, Raymond, 88, Ruskin Road; Royal Navy; Petty Officer. Italy and India.

Eaton, John S., 54, Compton Street; R.A.F. Regiment; L.A.C. Home Service and India.

Ellis, William V., 149, Ruskin Road; Royal Navy; A.B., Asdics. Africa and Mediterranean.

Evans, Richard Arthur, 50, Exeter Road; R.A.F.; Flight-Sergeant, Navigator. Trained in Canada; operations with Mosquitos from Home Bases; later served in India.

Eyton Jones, J. A., 20, Rushmere Road; Army.

Finn, Kenneth C. A., 109, Ennerdale Road; Royal Navy; H.M.S. Woolwich. Ceylon and Eastern Waters.

Flowerday, H. R., 74, Broadmead Avenue; R.A.O.C., 15 Tech. Stores Company. North-West Europe.

Flowers, Kenneth, 9, Queensland Gardens; Royal Navy; A.B. H.M.S. Wolfhound and H.M.S. Balfour. Service in Atlantic Ocean, etc.

Freeman, E. J., 75, Kenmuir Crescent; R.A.; Lance-Bombardier. M.E.F.

Freeman, Edwin J., 75, Kenmuir Crescent; Ayrshire Yeomanry, 152 R.A., 6th Armoured Division. North Africa, Italy and Austria.

Frost, William, 46, Kenmuir Avenue; Royal Navy. Home Waters.

Fulthorpe, Albert E., 2, Cranford Road; Northamptonshire Regiment.

Gardner, Leslie S., 56, The Drive; Royal Marines; Captain. Home Service.

Gardner, Stanley, 36, Malcolm Road; Army.

Gayton, George A., 34, Moore Street; Army.

Gasson, Albert E., 17, Alpha Street; Royal Navy. Mediterranean; Wounded. Coastal Force Craft and Minesweeper. Visit to Pope at Vatican.

Gray, C. A., 146, Lindsay Avenue; C.M.P. and Northamptonshire Regiment; Sergeant. M.E.F.

Green Dennis V., 153, Milton Street; Royal Navy; H.M.S. Ajax; Leading Seaman. Sicily landings and Salerno.

Halford, Colin, 21, Ashburnham Road; R.A.F.; L.A.C. India.

Harman, Jack G. W., 4, Danefield Road; R.A.F. Home Bases.

Hartop, P. W., 36, Foxgrove Avenue; R.A. B.A.O.R.

Hocknell, Walter R., 72, Milton Street; Royal Navy; H.M.S. Duke of Wellington. In D Day landings and at Antwerp.

Holton, Thomas, 65, Chestnut Road; R.A.S.C. India and Malaya.

Hope, Leslie R., 2, Kenmuir Crescent; Army.

Hopper, John W., 12, Chestnut Terrace; Royal Navy. H.M.S. Emerald. In D Day landing; also Mediterranean and Pacific.

Howard, Michael H., 61, Queen's Park Parade; Royal Navy; Stoker 1; H.M.S. Sarka. Home Waters and Mediterranean; Minesweeping in Aegean and Duodecanese.

Howe, Clifford, 30, Ruskin Road; Royal Navy; A.B. L.C.I. (L.) 118. Java.

Howe, Kenneth, 125, Lindsay Avenue; Royal Navy. Mediterranean.

Hussey, Charles, 107, Kenmuir Avenue; Royal Navy; A.B. H.M.S. Anson with Russian Convoys, and H.M.S. Pretoria Castle.

Hutchins, Ernest, 9, Elmhurst Avenue; R.A.F.

Jeyes, Alfred J. L., 57, Moore Street; Royal Berkshire Regiment. India and Burma; wounded gunshot wound in neck.

Jones, Albert, 76, Nursery Lane; Royal Navy; A.B. Australian Waters.

Jordan, G., 35, Chestnut Road; 5th Northamptonshire Regiment. Austria; posted to C.M.P. in Italy.

Judkins, Fred, 3, Vicarage Lane; Royal Engineers; Sapper. Germany.

Kightley, Stanley W., 21, Ashcroft Gardens; Royal Navy, Combined Operations; Petty Officer (E.R.M.). In D Day landings, Norway and Holland.

Knight, Frank C., 13, Reedway; Royal Navy; Sub-Lieutenant. Served on Russian Convoys, in D Day landings, and in Far East.

Langford, C., 40, Hastings Road; R.A.S.C. Airborne Division. Wounded in 6th Airborne Division landing on the Rhine; invalided out.

Lester, Edward A., 10 Watkin Terrace; Army.

Lucas, Raymond, 67, Kingsland Avenue; K.R.R.C. North-West Europe; Wounded, February, 1945.

Mains, Edwin A., 58, Rosedale Road; R.E.; Sapper. S.E.A.C.

Mann, Bernard J., 35, Broadmead Avenue; R.A.O.C.; Major. Home Service and India.

Marshall, H. F., 58, Kingsland Avenue; R.A.F.; Sergeant. Home Bases.

Mayle, Alexander D., 73, Bective Road; Royal Navy; A.B. On H.M.S. Kent on Russian Convoys and patrol work in Atlantic; badly frost-bitten and discharged.

Mayle, John G. N., 73, Bective Road; Maritime R.A.; Gunner. Served in landings in Sicily, Anzio and on D Day. Wounded in London Docks by V1.

Mayle, R. S., 73, Bective Road; Royal Navy. H.M.S. Benbow. Joined Naval Commandoes and took part in Normandy landings.

McGibbon, William, 40, Kingsthorpe Grove; Army.

Mead, Frank H., 1, Rosedale Road; R.A.F., 640 Squadron; Flight-Sergeant. Based in England; shot down over Germany, September 12th, 1944; Prisoner of war till released by Russians from Stalag IIIA, near Berlin.

Meredith, Walter, 6, High Street; R.E.M.E. Germany.

Miller, Ralph C., 105, Broadway East; R.A.F.; L.A.C. North Africa, Italy, and S.E.A.C.

Mineards, Norman C., 26, Langdale Road; 1st Northamptonshire Regiment; Corporal. In Burma Campaign.

Minty, Charles N., "Nantfield," The Avenue, Spinney Hill; R.A.F.; L.A.C. Home Bases, Cyprus and Egypt.

Mitchell, Frank J., 10, Brunswick Place; Royal Navy. Home Waters.

Morton, Sydney J., 18, Lime Avenue; R.A., S/L. North-West Europe.

Munroe, Walter, 67, Yelvertoft Road; Army.

Nutter, George, 35, Addison Road; Royal Marines, Plymouth Division. Italy and Egypt.

Oliver, Percy, 49, Eastern Avenue; R.A.F.; L.A.C. Home Bases.

Osborne, Donald H., 35, Lincoln Street; Royal Navy. Home Waters.

Osborne, William P., 56, St. David's Road; Royal Engineers. Home Service.

Pack, Edmund H., 80, Trinity Avenue; R.A.F. Pathfinder Force, Squadrons 97 and 635.

Page, Frank, 13, Kingsland Avenue; Royal Navy; Leading Stoker; H.M.S. Boy Philip. Mediterranean Waters.

Page, Kenneth, 13, Kingsland Avenue; Royal Navy; H.M.S. Florizel. Mine Sweeping, Home Waters.

Patrick, Frank, 56, Bective Road; Gloucester Regt. Wounded in Normandy.

Payne, Bernard C. E., "Rozel," Queen's Park Parade; R.N.V.R.; Sub-Lieut., Fleet Air Arm; H.M.S. Formidable. Served in Pacific Ocean and was over Nagasaki soon after the fall of the atom bomb.

Payne, Sydney H., 117, The Drive; R.A.C.; Lance-Corporal. Home Service.

Pearson, Bernard F., 11. Greenfield Avenue; R.A.F.; L.A.C. Home Bases and North-West Europe.

Pell, T. W., 140, Beech Avenue; R.A.P.C., 38 Bn.; Sergeant. Home Service.

Pettitt, Herbert W., 100, Nursery Lane; R.A.F.; L.A.C. B.A.O.R.

Pidd, Dennis, 68, Ashburnham Road; R.N.V.R.; Petty Officer. India.

Piggott, Leonard S. E, 261, Kettering Road; Northamptonshire Regiment; Captain. Home Service.

Riley, James A., 6, Kenmuir Gardens; R.E.M.E.; Craftsman. In D Day landings; at Caen and Rhine crossing; Wounded.

Robins, Geoffrey S., 35, Fort Street; R.A.S.C. North-West Europe and later in India.

Robinson, Frederick J., 36, Nursery Lane; R.A.O.C.; Lance-Corporal. B.A.O.R.

Romain, Frederick C., 3, Norton Road; Royal Army Pay Corps. Home Service.

Roney, Charles T., 133, Colwyn Road; Army.

Sawford, Leslie A., 83, Junction Road; Army.

Scott, George, 142, Ashburnham Road; Royal Marines; Lieutenant. Served in North Sea area.

Shananan, James, 29, Windy Ridge; Royal Marines. Home Service.

Simons, George L., 148, Ruskin Road; R.A., A.A. Brigade. Home Service.

Skipp, Michael S., 93, Birchfield Road; R.A.F.; Flight-Sergeant. Home Bases.

Slinn, Eric, 200, Birchfield Road East; G.H.Q. Liaison Regiment, Phantom. In D Day landings and throughout campaign to Germany.

Smart, Frederick J., 50, Raeburn Road; R.A.M.C. North-West Europe.

Smith, Alfred T., 60, Chaucer Street; Royal Coastal Artillery. England and Scotland.

Smith, Charles, 69, Stanhope Road; R.A.; Gunner. Palestine, N.W. Europe.

Smith, John H., 161, Bush Hill; R.A.F.V.R., Airfield Defence. Home Service and Isle of Man with American A.F.

Smith, Reginald, 64, Cranford Road; Army.

Spence, Leslie, 8, Manor Road; Cameronians; Lance-Corporal. M.E.F. and B.A.O.R.

Spittles, Dennis, 5, Knightley Road; Fleet Air Arm. H.M.S. Bambara. England and Ceylon.

Stamp, William H., 13, Boughton Green Road; Royal Navy. H.M. L.S.T. 413; 1st Class Stoker. S.E.A.C.

Stevens, Fred R., 5, Northumbria Gardens; R.A.M.C., Airborne Div. India.

Sudborough, A. J., 137, Beech Avenue; Royal Marines; Lieutenant. Landed in Normandy on D Day with R.M. Commandos; invalided out.

Talbot, John O., 16, Ryland Road; R.A.F.

Tee, Walter, 86, Stanhope Road; Royal Navy; A.B. H.M.L.C. In landings at Sicily, Italy, Normandy and Holland; survivor when ship was sunk off Westerpell, Holland, November 1st, 1944.

Tero, Robert A., 33, Ruskin Road; R.A.F.; Flight-Sergeant. Home Bases.

Thomason, D., 2, Northwood Road; Royal Navy; Submarine Service. Wounded, Pacific Waters. Met twin brother in Australia.

Thomason, L. F., 2, Northwood Road; Royal Navy; Submarine Service, Pacific. On Submarine Truant when attacked in Japanese Waters.

Thorneycroft, D. G.: Royal Navy.

Timson, Arthur E., 11, Clarence Avenue; Ist Royal Dragoons; Trooper. M.E.F. and B.A.O.R.

Tipplestone, Edgar C., 61, Harborough Road; R.A.F.; L.A.C. India.

Todd, John P. W., 18, Wakefield Road; Army.

Tyrell, W. G., 17, Pinewood Road; R.A.F.; Flying-Officer Navigator 44 operations on 2nd Tactical Air Force; Night-Flying Mosquitos.

Walden, Leonard, 27, Raeburn Road; R.A.O.C. Home Service.

Wallace, Charles R., 23, Knight's Lane; R.A.O.C. Italy.

Ward, Frank, 12, Newington Road; Army.

Warner, George, 148, Kingsland Avenue; R.A.S.C. Motor Boats. S.E.A.C.

Waterfield, Alfred W. G., 77, St. David's Road; R.E.; Lance-Corporal. B.A.O.R.

Watkins, Roy, 16, Albion Place; Army.

Watson, Peter F., 87, West Ridge; Royal Marines. Served with Pacific Fleet.

Westbury, R., 85, Ruskin Road; Royal Marines. Wounded in D Day landings.

Westley, Ronald J., 2, Wheatfield Terrace; Royal Navy.

White, John R., 67, High Street; Fleet Air Arm; Air Mechanic, 1st Class. Home Bases. Invalided out, and later in Manfield Hospital.

Whitehead, H. H. E., 93, Kenmiur Avenue; Army.

Whitehead, Ronald J., 93, Kenmuir Avenue; Army.

Williams, Thomas, 89, Cecil Road; R.A.F.; A.C. North-West Europe.

Wills, Leslie R., 129, Welford Road; R.A.F.; L.A.C. Home Bases.

Woodford John R., 145, Lindsay Avenue; Army.

Woolman, M., 72, Broadmead Avenue; Royal Corps of Signals. S.E.A.A.F.

Wright, R. C. B., 55, Pinewood Road; Royal Navy. East Coast Patrol.

York, Ernest C., 71a, Kingsley Road; Royal Navy; Telegraphist. Awarded D.S.M. for courage, skill and determination in successful actions with enemy forces off the coast of Italy.

Zissler, Lawrence J., 6, Alexandra Terrace; Army.

The following also joined H.M. Forces

Addington, G. D.	Davis, G. H.	James, A. B.	Sibley, R. B.
Andrews, G.	Dilley, N. H.	Jelley, R. G.	Smith, J. H.
Arthur, E. R.	Dilley, S. C.	Lack, S.	Smith, W. H.
Atkins, E. F.	Edgar, V. H. W.	Lee, F.	Tallett, E.
Atkinson, R.	Emery, J. H.	Lister, D.	Thornton, S.
Bailey, R. C.	Emery, R. A.	Manning, H. G.	Turner, R. G.
Barford, H.	England, S. A.	Maysmore, T. C.	Varley, J. C.
Bodsworth, R.	Fall, D. A.	Middleton, V. E.	Waterfield, H. W.
Bonnet, S. F.	Fall, F. W.	Palmer, C. W.	Waterfield, R. N.
Breavington, G. E.	French, T. W.	Parsons, D.	Watts, D. G. B.
Brown, P.	Gillies, J. C.	Perkins, J. E.	West, R. H.
Clarke, F. A.	Goldstein, A.	Robinson, R. C.	Witkiss, C.
Cochran, K.	Griffiths, S. H.	Rodhouse, D. A.	Woodward, M. W.
Collins, C.	Hanford, H. R.	Shelton, A.	York, R. E.
Cumberpatch, B.	Howells, R. D.	Shepherd, J. W.	York, R. F.

B COMPANY

Aldridge, Leonard, 34, Market Street; R.A. North-West Europe.

Ashby, W. J., 3, Delapre Street; Royal Navy. Home Waters.

Bailey, A. R., 19, Southfield Avenue; 8th Army H.Q. Signals, Royal Corps of Signals; Corporal. North Africa, Italy and Austria.

Barnatt, William, 31, Alfred Street; Royal Corps of Signals. Home Service; on communications G.O.R. to A.A. sites on coast.

Barnes, Albert R., 33a, Stanley Road; R.A.F. Home Bases.

Batchelor, Kenneth G., 38, Thirlestane Road; R.A.F. Home Bases, Bomber Command; later served in Iraq.

Batchelor, Ronald G., 21. Thirlestane Road; R.A.S.C. B.A.O.R.

Beasley, Ernest, 29, Brunswick Place; 122 Anti-Tank Regiment, R.A. North-West Europe and India.

Beech, F. E., 8, Western Terrace; Royal Norfolks; Corporal. N.-W. Europe.

Beech, S. N., 8, Western Terrace; Royal Corps of Signals. North-West Europe and India; landed in Normandy shortly after D Day.

Bignell, F. R., 80, Rothersthorpe Road; Royal Navy.

Blencowe, G. E., 64, Blenheim Road; Royal Corps of Signals; Signalman; 3 G.H.Q. Signals. Normandy and Egypt.

Booth, F. J.; Pioneer Corps.

Bosworth, Christopher W., 63, Wheatfield Road; Royal Navy. Atlantic and Pacific.

Bosworth, Harry L., 63, Wheatfield Road; General Service Corps. Home Service.

Britten, Frank W., 53, Wilby Street; R.A.F. Home Bases.

Brown, James G., 56, Sheep Street; Royal Navy; Acting Sto. P.O. H.M.S. Barcroft. North Atlantic, Russian Convoys and Mediterranean.

Brown, N. J., 5, Hereward Road; R.A.F.; L.A.C. Home Bases.

Bulleyment, D. J., Cattle Market House; Army.

Burke, John, 96, Adams Avenue; Army.

Carmody, C. J., 8, Prince's Street; Army.

Carroll, Thomas, 218, London Road; Army.

Carter, F. H., 49, West Street; Royal Engineers; Sapper. Dredging Coy., Hull.

Clancey, A., 26, Queen Eleanor Road; Northamptonshire Regiment. Wounded in France.

Clarke, F. W., 48, Cyril Street; R.A.F.

Clifton, Walter S., 19, Commercial Street; Army

Clout, A. G. J., 132, Market Street; Army.

Chennells, Frank, 62, Edith Street; R.E. India.

Church, J., 99, Queen Eleanor Road; R.A.F. Training Command. Home Service No. 8 S. of T.T., and Group Base Hospital.

Coldwell, Ronald F., 26, Briar Hill Walk; Army.

Coleman, G. F., 34, Queen Eleanor Terrace; Royal Irish Fusiliers. Italy and Austria.

Colledge, J. F., 206, London Road; R.A.F.; P.O. Home Bases.

Collins, Arthur W., 12, Rickard Street; Royal Corps of Signals. Attached to Base Air Force, India.

Collier, G. H.; Northamptonshire Yeomanry.

Collyer, L. L., 60, Clinton Road; Fleet Air Arm; Leading Air Fitter. United Kingdom and Malta.

Cousins, Norman, 41, Southampton Road; Royal Navy; A.B.; H.M.S. Stevenstone.

Crossley, Clifford H., 3, Birchfield Road; R.A.F.; Flight Sergeant. Canada, America and Bahamas.

Crowley, Anthony, The Exchange Cinema; Royal Engineers; Lieutenant. Royal Bombay Sappers and Miners, Poona, India.

Day, Walter H., 64, Euston Road; Army Dental Corps. Home Service.

Deacon, A. T. B., 37, Delamere Road; Army.

Deacon, Dennis, 31, Queen Eleanor Road; Fleet Air Arm. India and Ceylon.

Dean, A. D., 4, Court Road; 43rd Royal Tank Regiment. India. In rioting at Bombay.

Dewison, R. A., 69, Wheatfield Road; Merchant Navy. Overseas.

Digby, J. A., 4, Eastfield Road; R.A.F., later R.A.F. Regiment. France and Germany.

Digby, R. H., 4, Eastfield Road; R.A.F.; Corporal. France and-Germany.

Dix, Raymond, 142, Rothersthorpe Road; Royal Navy; Stoker 1st Class; H.M.L. C.Q. 390. In Normandy landings.

Eastaff, J. R., Stevenson Street; Royal Tank Corps; Corporal. Burma Campaign.

Edwards, Gilbert H., 28, New Town Road. Served in Germany.

Elliott, F. W., 60, Rothersthorpe Road; R.E.M.E. Home Service.

Elliott, H., 136, London Road; Leicestershire Regiment. Wounded in France.

England, D. G., 23, Lawrence Street; 61 B.S.D. North-West Europe from D Day to Germany.

Farmer, Leslie, 5, Weedon Road; R.A.F.

Fawdon, Thomas W., 25, Freeschool Street; Royal Navy.

Fleming, T. A., 8, Vernon Terrace; R.A.F.; Air Mechanic. Home Bases.

Fox, Ronald, 47, Queen Eleanor Road; R.A.F.; W.O. Navigator. Trained in Canada; Bomber Command, Lancasters, 166 Squadron. European theatre of Operations.

Freeman, Ernest G., 150, London Road; Royal Navy; H.M.S. Stevenstone. Atlantic and Mediterranean.

Fuller, H. S., 33, Rothersthorpe Road; R.E.M.E.; Lance-Corporal; V.M.II; attached 33 Field Regiment and 2nd East Yorks. In D Day landings, North-West Europe and Germany; also served in Egypt and Palestine.

Gibb, Thomas, The Lodge, Rush Mills; Army.

Giles, N., 15, Southfield Avenue; R.A.F. Regiment, 2809 Squadron; Flight-Sergeant. In D Day landings; North-West Europe and Germany.

Glasspool, Frederick C., 26, Clarke Road; R.A.S.C. Egypt.

Goodsir, James A., 31, Newland; Royal Navy.

Goodwin, Richard H., 46, Towcester Road; Royal Navy.

Green, Ronald, 153, Euston Road; Royal Navy. Home Waters.

Haddon, Stanley, 11, Briar Hill Walk; R.A.M.C. F.D.S., Scotland, and on S.S. Troopship Samaria.

Hall, A. F., 4, Victoria Promenade; Royal Armoured Corps; Corporal. Home Service; Instructor on Comet and Cromwells.

Hall, Kenneth F., 27, Forest Road; Royal Navy; A.B. (Radar Control). H.M.S. Caprice (destroyer). Home Fleet based at Scapa Flow; three Russian Convoys and several sweeps off Norway.

Harrold, Alfred J., 169, Wellingborough Road; 8th Bn. Parachute Regiment; Sergeant. France and North-West Europe. Twice wounded.

Hart, K. P., 15, Alton Street; Army.

Hill, Harold C.; 2nd Bn. Lincolnshire Regiment. North-West Europe; landed in Normandy with 3rd Division.

Hodges, George K., 5, St. James' Terrace; Royal Navy.

Hudson, Guy, 268, London Road; R.A.F. Served in North Africa as Sergeant Wireless Operator; later commissioned in Italy as Flying Officer.

Irons, Albert, 67, Queen Eleanor Road; Royal Marines. Home Service. Discharged medically unfit.

Jervis, Martyn A., 1, St. Peter's Gardens; Royal Navy.

Kent, Cyril, 5, Bouverie Street; Duke of Cornwall's L.I. Belgium and Holland. Twice wounded.

King, John A., Kettering Road, Moulton; Army.

King, Thomas, 5, Bouverie Street; Royal Marines. Germany.

Kinsley, Charles S., 73, Melbourne Street; Royal Navy; Stoker 1. H.M.S. Gabral Maria, B.MS. 76, and H.M.S. Loodswezen. Atlantic.

Lambourne, W. J. G.; R.A.F.

Lane, George R., 136, Penrhyn Road; R.A. (Field); Gunner. Home Forces.

Langwith, R. W., 2, Hereward Road; Army.

Linaker, Robert J., 16, Alfred Street; Pioneer Corps; Sergeant. Holland and Germany.

Luff, Leonard S., 170, Towcester Road; R.A.F. Home Bases.

Marlow, R. H., 73, Abbey Road; 2nd Bn. Northamptonshire Regiment; Corporal, Acting Sergeant. North Africa, Sicily, Anzio Beach-head; later in North-West Europe; finally served in Palestine.

Martin, Ralph E., 8, Ecton Street; 2nd Dorsets. In D Day landing with B.L.A.; also India and B.O.F., Japan.

McPherson, Alfred, 4, Thorpe Road; R.A.F. Home Bases.

Meads, Clifford J., 160, London Road; R.A.F.; Sergeant Pilot. India and Burma.

Mitchell, V. J., 12, Rockingham Road; Army.

Mitton, C. A., 12, Artizan Road; Royal Navy; Stoker. Home Waters and Atlantic.

Morley, L., 91, St. Edmund's Road; R.A.F.; L.A.C. S.E.A.A.F., Hong Kong.

Mortimer, C. A.; R.A.F.: F.O. Navigator. Ferry Service Canada and United Kingdom: later troop carrying England to India; flew Atlantic over twelve times. In two major crashes, May, 1942, and November, 1944.

Morton, Albert E., 22, Alfred Street; R.E.M.E.; attached 5th East Yorks; Sergeant. Served in Egypt, etc.

Mutton, Ernest A., 21, Langdale Road; Hampshire Regiment. Germany.

Oliver, R. J., 4, Albion Crescent; Army.

Osborne, Frank, 44, Melbourne Street; R.E.; Sapper. Italy.

Owen, Dennis H., 147, Station Road, Coventry; Army.

Parish, E. G., Drill Hall, Clare Street; R.A.S.C.; Lance-Corporal. Italv, Egypt, Palestine and Syria.

Patching, G. E., 38, Tanner Street; Royal Navy. Home Waters and Far East.

Patterson, George, 116, Euston Road; Royal Corps of Signals. 18th Air Formation and H.Q. 21 Army Group. Belgium and Germany.

Peach, Anthony J., 31, St. Edmund's Road; Royal Marines. France, Bombay, Malaya, Singapore; in several Combined Operations.

Peck, Reginald Arthur, 19, Thirlestane Road; Royal Navy; Leading Stoker; H.M.S. Tyne. Served in Eastern Waters.

Penn, George, 36, Louise Road; Army.

Phipps, Raymond, 37, Bearward Street; Royal Navy; A.B. 1st Gunner. M.T.B. Served in Mediterranean.

Potter, Cyril, 20, Blenheim Road; R.A.F.; Sergeant Pilot. India and Burma.

Potter, J. H., 20, Blenheim Road; R.A.F. Home Service.

Rennie, Alexander C., 44, Billing Road; Pioneer Corps; Captain. Home Service.

Roan, C. C., 16, Blenheim Road; Airborne Division; Paratrooper. Taken prisoner of war at Arnhem.

Robinson, A., 10, Vernon Street; R.A.F. Regt.; L.A.C. North-West Europe.

Robinson, Keith, 212, Kettering Road; R.A.F. Home Bases and Italy.

Rosen, J., 44, Parkfield Avenue; R.A.S.C. North Africa and Italy.

Round, R. V., 2, Pilgrim's Way; Leicestershire Regiment; Commando. Took part in raids on Lofoten Islands, St. Nazaire, Dieppe, and Sicily and Italy. Taken prisoner of war; escaped from internment and joined with partisans.

Smith, Leslie P., 34, Forest Road; Royal Navy. Minesweepers; Home Waters.

Smith, Ronald, 126, Market Street; Royal Navy; A.B. Radar rating; H.M.S. Vindex (aircraft carrier). On Russian Convoys.

Stafford, George K., 100, Wycliffe Road; Royal Navy. H.M.S. Venerable. Malta, Ceylon and Pacific.

Stamps, Gordon T., 27, Briar Hill Walk; R.A.S.C. North-West Europe.

Stevens, Leonard C., 19, Cambria Crescent; R.E.M.E.; Sergeant. Germany and India; went to Normandy two weeks after D Day; later in Rhine Crossing.

Stratton, Stanley A., 46, Bouverie Street; R.A. Landed in France six days after D Day; later driver with Royal Ulster Rifles in Germany; served with North German Coal Control.

Strike, Sidney W., 198, St. James' Park Road; R.A.S.C. Egypt.

Sturgess, A. H., 67, Lower Thrift Street; South Staffs, South Lancs, and R.A.S.C. Served in North Africa, Italy and Greece.

Tebbutt, L. C., 65, St. Edmund's Road; R.A.F.; 137 M.U., Malta Force; L.A.C. North Africa and Malta.

Travill, William F., 97, Green Street; Northamptonshire Regiment, Sherwood Foresters and D.L.I. Served in Italy. Twice wounded—at Solara Beach and Cassino.

Truish, H., Ransome Road; Royal Corps of Signals, Airborne. France and Germany.

Tunks, B. G., 156, London Road; Leicestershire Regiment.

Underwood, William, 46, Melbourne Street; Leicestershire Regiment, also Heavy A.A.; Instructor I.T.C. Home Service. Discharged through accident with 3-inch mortar.

Walden, Dennis Robert, 151, Wycliffe Road; 2nd Lincolnshire Regiment; Corporal. North-West Europe and M.E.F.

Wann, D. A., 23, York Road; 1st Airborne Division. North Africa, Sicily, Italy (Taranto); was in the first wave to land at Arnhem and was one of the last six to get away.

Warwick, Arthur J. W., 136, Wycliffe Road; Army.

Watts, Alfred, 39, Euston Road; Royal Navy; A.B. Stoker. H.M.S. Escapade (destroyer) on Convoy duty in Atlantic; later served on H.M.S. Moorson on D Day.

Watts, W. B., 87, Abbey Road; R.A.F.; L.A.C. Home Bases.

Wesson, R. C., 18, Stevenson Street; R.A., later Argyll and Sutherland Highlanders. Sergeant. Served in North-West Europe.

Whittaker, W. V., 142, Wellingborough Road; Army.

Whyborn, Ivor H., 16, St. Michael's Avenue. Greece.

Wimpress, G. F., 12, Pleydell Road; Royal Marines.

Wolf, K., 133, Towcester Road; Royal Navy; A.B. Served on H.M.S. Blenheim, Ryde, Peacock and Cawsand Bay; Home Waters and Atlantic. In D Day landings.

Wootton, R. G., 17, Queen's Street; R.A.S.C.; Lance-Corporal. 5th Division; North-West Europe and B.A.O.R.

Wright, John A., 18, Wheatfield Road; Royal Navy; L/MM. H.M.S. Pembroke. Home Fleet. In Normandy landings.

Wrighton, J., 65, Pleydell Road; 294 Coy. (Inf. Brigade). North Africa, Sicily, Italy and Austria.

Yates, Arthur E., 19, Stenson Street; Royal Navy. Home Waters and Atlantic.

York, John W., 3, Briar Hill Road; R.E.M.E.; Corporal Home Service.

The following also joined H.M. Forces

Alibone, J.	Denton, S. G.	Fruish, R.	Mortimer, C. A.
Ashton, P.	Dobson, G. J.	Hancock, G.	Muddiman, F. G.
Barnhope, H.	Dunkley, D.	Harris, S.	Payne, L. F.
Beech, W. S. J.	East, P. J.	Horner, H. G.	Richardson, H.
Berwick, E.	Eastaff, J. R.	Johnson, H. F. W.	Rogers, C. A.
Clancy, A. M.	Eaton, E. W.	Lack, S.	Taylor, A. H.
Clarke, N. L.	Emery, R. F.	Marlow, A. H.	Turner, A. J. C.
Church, J.	Farnell, R. F.	Mayes, L.	Wilkes, J. W.
Cockayne, A. C.	Farrell, S. E.	Moore, G. A.	

CAMOUFLAGE SUIT.

(Photo: J. Wright)

(Photo: J. Wright)

HOME GUARD FETE FOR HOSPITALS (September 9th, 1944).

C COMPANY

Arnold, Douglas J., 15, Abington Grove; R.A.F. India.

Ash, L. A., 51, Brunswick Street; Royal Navy; A.B., Q.O. Home Waters and Channel Islands.

Bage, James B., 45, Clarke Road; R.A F. Operations over Germany.

Barker, Herbert J., 182, Broadway E.; Royal Corps of Signals. Home Service.

Barron, Reg., 56, Fullingdale Road; Royal Engineers. Home Service and Java.

Billington, John W., 105, Lea Road; Royal Navy; Petty Officer. H.M.S. Saltburn and H.M.S. King George V. Atlantic, 1942 and 1943; Far East, 1945.

Blundell, G., 29, Stockley Street; Army.

Blunt, C. T., 28, Perry Street; Royal Engineers; Sapper. Docks, Home Bases.

Bradshaw, Thomas W., 85, Ivy Road; 1st Bn. Royal Irish Fusiliers. Egypt, Italy and Austria. Wounded June 24th, 1944.

Brame, Ernest J., 26, Norman Road; Queen's Bays (Royal Armoured Corps); Corporal. North Africa and Italy.

Brownsell, Alan G., 23, Portland Street; Royal Marines, transferred to 5th Devons; Lance-Corporal. Austria.

Bryant, Charles W., 12, Hunter Street; R.A. France and Germany.

Campbell, John J., 330, Birchfield Road; Army.

Chambers, Edward R., 260, Birchfield Road East; R.E.M.E.; Lance-Corporal. Home Service, including 18 months at Dover, Hellfire Corner.

Clark, Ralph, 10, Portland Street; R.A.C. Landed in Normandy July 1st, 1944; in break-through at Caen; in campaign to Holland, and German thrust in Ardennes.

Clarke, T., 28, Norman Road; Royal Corps of Signals; Lance-Corporal. C.M.F., in North Africa with 8th Army.

Clayson, William E., 96, Purser Road; Army Dental Corps; Dental Orderly Clerk, Class 1. Home Service.

Clayton, W., 67, Monks Park Road; Royal Tank Regiment. 8th Army; North Africa.

Coates, Leslie S., 35, Bush Hill; R.E.; Corporal. Egypt.

Cosford, George E., 15, Charles Street; K.R.R.C.; Rifleman. North-West Europe. Wounded by bomb.

Curling, Leslie F., Court House Farm, Weston Favell; R.A.F.

Davis, George R., 103, Market Street; Army Catering Corps. Served in North-West Europe. Wounded.

Deacon, Lionel K. L.; Royal Navy; Petty Officer. H.M.S. Landrail; F.A.A. Base; Maintenance work.

Denton, Ronald A., 63, Market Street; Royal Navy; A.B. Radar rating. H.M.S. Vindex (Aircraft Carrier). On Russian Convoys.

Denton, Sydney H., 27, Cambria Crescent; R.A.O.C.; Corporal. M.E.F.

Dickens, Albert G., 133, Milton Street; R.A.F. Home Bases.

Elliott, William F. D., 170, Cedar Road; Northamptonshire Regiment; Lieutenant. Home Service and Middle East.

Ellis, A. T., 42, Florence Road; R.A.F. Home Bases.

England, R., 46, Saxon Street; Royal Navy; Leading Sick Berth Attendant. India.

Epps, John, 298, Birchfield Road East; Royal Corps of Signals; attached to 2nd Tactical Air Force. North-West Europe.

Ette, Clifford A., 37, Adnitt Road; Northamptonshire Regiment. Home Service.

Farndon, D. J., 21, Wellington Street; Royal Marines. India.

Freeman, Eric F., 50, Fullingdale Road; Durham L.I. North-West Europe. Twice wounded.

Freeman, Frederick, 3, Lindsay Avenue; R.E.M.E. India and Japan.

Gale, Thomas J. B., 126, The Headlands; Royal Navy; Coder. Served with H.M.S. Neon and H.M.S. Cleopatra in the Atlantic and with H.M.S. Manxman in the Pacific.

Goodridge, Richard H., 10, Abington Cottages; Royal Navy. Home Waters.

Goodson, John F., 37, Cleveland Road; Royal Navy. H.M.S. Rajah.

Goom, Bert E., 13, Colwyn Road; Army.

Hemmings, Frederick G., 14, The Vale; Pioneer Corps. Holland and Belgium.

Hitchcock, R. A., 52, Church Way, Weston Favell; Royal Marines. H.M.S. Anson, Australia and Hong Kong.

Houghton, Frank E., 20, Briton Road; Royal Corps of Signals. Went to France in July, 1944, and in campaign to Germany; helped to clear up Belsen Camp of both dead and living.

Inwood, Cyril R., 67, Purser Road; Royal West African Frontier Force; Lieutenant. Served in India.

James, Stanley E., 2, Lea Road; Army.

Jeyes, Sydney, 36, Cleveland Road; Royal Marines. Iceland and Australia.

Kelly, Robert H., 31, Ardington Road; R.A.F.; L.A.C. Home Bases.

Knighton, J.; Northamptonshire Regiment. India and Burma.

Lankshear, Alan F., 375, Billing Road East; Army.

Lenton, Sydney, 59, Bush Hill; R.A.F. Home Bases.

Luck, F. R.; Royal Artillery.

Marriott, John E., 46, Cyril Street; Royal Navy; Stoker 1st Class. Mediterranean and in D Day landings with H.M.M.L. 1301.

Marshall, Ernest W., 66, King Edward Road; R.A.S.C.; Lance-Corporal. North-West Europe.

Mason, Robert W., 115, Holly Road; R.I.A.S.C.; Captain. India.

Mason, W., 55, Adams Avenue; R.A.F. India.

McDowell, Richard G., 64, Purser Road; Royal Marines. Home Service.

Meakins, Donald E., 182, Broadway East; Royal Navy; A.B., Gunner rating A.A.III (L.C.). Service in the North Sea, the Italian Campaign, and D Day; present at the surrender of the German Adriatic Fleet at Ancona.

Merrifield, G. D., 26, Saxon Street; Royal Navy; A.B. H.M.S. Chaser-Aircraft Carrier; Russian Convoys and Far East; off Japan on V.J. Day.

Merrifield, W. J., 26, Saxon Street; R.A.; Lance-Bombardier. North Africa, Anzio Bridgehead and Italian Campaign.

Miller, N. J., 113, Derby Road; Royal Navy. Africa and Sicily.

Morgan, Peter, 10, Monks Hall Road; R.A.C. France and Germany.

Muddiman, Leslie, 3, Melville Street; R.A. Home Service.

Newman, William C., 35, Randall Road; R.A.F. France and Germany.

Oldham, E. T. E., 168, Beech Avenue; R.A.S.C., Air Despatch. Home Service.

Osborn, Frederick T., 14, The Headlands; D.L.I.; C.Q.M.S. In D Day landings, Normandy and North-West Europe.

Payne, Sidney, 51, Manfield Road; Army.

Pell, W. T., 140, Beech Avenue; R.A.P.C. B.A.O.R.

Phillips, A.; Northamptonshire Regiment. France and Germany.

Plowman, R., 61, Whitworth Road; R.A. France.

Plumley, Thomas J., 20, Norman Road; Royal Corps of Signals; Sergeant. North-West Europe and Austria.

Ponting, C. H., 130, Adnitt Road; A.C.C. Home Service.

Prickett, Arch. E., 7, Wessex Way; Royal Navy. H.M.S. Octavia. Mediterranean and Atlantic.

Rees, David M., 2, Bush Hill; R.A.O.C.; Lieutenant. Home Service.

Roberts, C. O., 146, The Headlands; R.A.O.C.; Sergeant. North Africa and Egypt.

Roberts, P.: Northamptonshire Regiment.

Rowe, Reginald, 95, Alcombe Road; Royal Navy.

Sale, A. P., 118, Adnitt Road; Royal Irish Rifles, later Royal Ulsters. Landed in Normandy D Day plus 2. Wounded in Normandy fighting.

Self, Peter B., 41, Saxon Street; R.A.S.C.; Corporal. 5th Armoured Bridging Coy., B.A.O.R.

Sharpe, C. R., 65, Headlands; Royal Navy.

Sheppard, Richard, 3, Dover Street; Fleet Air Arm. H.M.S. Implacable.

Skinner, R. T., 88, Derby Road; R.A.O.C. 8th Army.

Smart, G. J., 31, Norman Road; R.E.M.E. A.A. Command Research Workshop.

Smart, Leslie A., 41, Fullingdale Road; R.E.M.E.; Craftsman. India.

Smart, Reginald, 27, Melville Street; Royal Corps of Signals. India.

Smith, K. A., 58, Stimpson Avenue; 7th Bn. North Staffordshire Regiment; Lance-Corporal. C.M.F. and Italy.

Smith, Reginald W., 44, Beech Avenue; Royal Navy; A.B. (Asdics). R.N. Station, May Island. Submarine hunting.

Spencer, E., 7, Kingswell Terrace; 3rd King's Own Hussars; Sergeant. 6th Airborne Division. Invasion of Normandy and North-West Europe; also served in Palestine.

Stevens, Thomas G., 34, Roe Road; Royal Navy. H.M.S. Dittany and Berwick. North Atlantic, West Africa and Australia.

Thorneycroft, Eric G., 25, Briton Road; R.A.C. France and Holland.

Tillson, M. B., 102, Bush Hill; Army Signals; W.O.2. After 1945 transferred to Army Educational Corps. Served in M.E.F. and later at Asmara, Eritrea.

Tornberg, J., 6, Florence Road; R.A.F. North Africa.

Twist, A., 4, The Crescent; R.A.F. Africa and Italy.

Valentine, T. H., 14, Burwood Road; R.A.F.; Wireless Operator. Captured in Duodecanese Islands, October, 1943; prisoner of war Stalag IVb, Germany

Walton, Reginald G., 94. Market Street; D.E.M.S. defensive equipping Merchant Ships, including Queen Mary. Home Waters and Atlantic and Pacific Bases.

Warnes, John M., 27, Bushland Road; Royal Navy: Petty Officer Motor Mechanic; Landing Craft Maintenance. South India.

Wastell, William G., 223, Birchfield Road East; R.A.S.C. Home Service.

Westley, John H., 42, Lindsay Avenue; R.A.F.; A.C.1. Home Bases.

Williams, Keith, 12, Robert Street; Army.

Wills, W., 53, Adnitt Road; R.A.F. India.

Wright, Edward W., 44, Lindsay Avenue; Royal Navy; A.B. H.M.S. Amethyst. Pacific Ocean.

The following also joined H.M. Forces

Andrews, A.	Doolan, S. R.	Juffkins, G.	Smith, P. H.
Asbrey, J.	Downing, A. J.	Kent, J.	Smith, R. A.
Baker, A. W.	Dunmore, A.	Kirby, D. F.	Spokes, H.
Barrows, R. A.	Ellard, G. A.	Lee, A. J.	Stevenson, H. M.
Bates, C. H.	Ellis, A. T.	Lee, E. W.	Stuckey, J.
Bates, H.	England, D. G.	Littlewood, E. A.	Swannell, W. H.
Baxter, W.	Etheridge, A. J. E.	Littlewood, J.	Utley, D. H.
Bridge, H. A.	Freestone, R. W.	Loveridge, E. T.	Ward, E. F.
Boxall, J. E.	Garnett, R. F.	Mickley, E. E.	Webb, R. W.
Brooks, J. L.	Haddon, W. F.	Mosley, A.	White, H. R.
Brown, H.	Hall, A.	Ouless, J. M.	Whiteman, H.
Burrows, H.	Harris, W. H.	Parker, A. V.	Wilkinson, F. G. D.
Childs, R. D.	Harrod, L. W.	Peasland, S.	Wills, A. E. L.
Coles, F. J. S.	Harrod, R. A.	Pebody, A. G.	Wilson, D. H.
Coley, P. W.	Hawley, S.	Pettitt, W. A.	Wilson, G. D.
Collier, R. J.	Hill, R. L.	Reeves, F.	Wilson, G. G.
Cook, F. T.	Inglis, R.	Robinson, R. V.	Wilson, R. J.
Cook, M.	Jacklin, N. S.	Skinner, R. T.	Wright, F. C.
Davies, T. A.	Jelleyman, R. S.	Smith, J. P.	Wright, N. F.
Davis, C.	Jones, D. T.	Smith, P. A.	

Abington Mill Platoon

Baker, Roy, 32, Victoria Road; Royal Navy.

Beale, John R., 73, Vernon Street; R.A.C. Reconnaissance Corps; Corporal. North Africa, Italy, Palestine, Egypt and Syria.

Brooks, Frederick, 59, Stanhope Road; 6th Northamptonshire Regiment and 2nd Cameronians. Served in North Africa, Italy, Palestine and Germany.

Butlin, Kenneth, 1, Semilong Road; 5th Northamptonshire Regiment. Italy and Austria.

Cockburn, Matthew T., now living at Wishaw, Scotland; Pioneer Corps. Sicily, Italy and North-West Europe.

Edwards, W., 67, Ashburnham Road; Royal Navy. H.M.S. Kaluga. Pacific Waters, Cochin and Ceylon.

Ette, Charles, 7, Barry Road; 7th Cameronians. Holland, Rhine Crossing and Germany.

Haseldine, Ernest A., 132, Broadway East; R.A.F.; L.A.C. North Africa and Italy.

Hewitt, Sidney, 52, Wheatfield Road; 9th Cameronians, Scottish Rifles. In Normandy landings; taken prisoner at Falaise.

Latimer, Stanley, 11, Abington Grove; R.E.M.E.; Sergeant, Sudan Defence Force. Egypt and Sudan.

Lines, Ronald, 105, Raeburn Road; Royal Navy; A.B., Stoker. Minesweeping English Channel, North Sea, Scheldt Estuary and European Waters.

Morrison, John R., 17, Alcombe Road; Duke of Wellington's Regt. Wounded in North Africa.

Patching, Albert, 47, Danefield Road; Royal Field Artillery. North Africa and Italy.

Perkins, Ronald, 32, West Ridge; R.A.F.; L.A.C. North Africa, Italy, Syria and Palestine.

Pettitt, William, 56, Gray Street; Royal Corps of Signals; Lance-Corporal. North Africa, Italy and Palestine.

Reeves, F., 17a, Monks Hall Road; R.A.F.; W.O. Home Bases. Did 23 operational flights by night, Berlin, Hanover ,etc.; also flights supplying French Maquis, and minelaying, Bay of Biscay.

Robinson, W. C., 6, Talbot Road; Ist Northamptonshire Regiment. S.E.A.C., Burma.

Smith, A. G., 27, Victoria Gardens; Royal Ulster Rifles. Palestine.

Snell, Ernest, 30, Haseldene Road; Royal Corps of Signals. North Africa and Italy.

Surridge, George, 91, Grafton Street; Royal Field Artillery; Corporal. Burma.

Surridge, John, 91, Grafton Street; Royal Artillery; Corporal. Home Service.

Swingler, Robert C., 25, Exeter Road; 3rd Bn. Grenadier Guards. Palestine.

Towers, Tom; Royal Ulster Rifles; Sergeant. North Africa, Sicily, Italy, Iran and Palestine.

Ward, Frederick, 61, Cowper Street; R.A.S.C. North-West Europe and Egypt.

Whiteman, Harry, 6, Lindsay Terrace; Royal Navy; A.B., Radar. Atlantic and Home Waters, Minesweeping; took part in D Day landings, and also dummy Commando Raids on France.

THE OLD D COMPANY

Ablett, J. A., 61, St. George's Street; Royal Corps of Signals. North Africa, Italy, Palestine and Egypt. Later member of E.N.S.A. Concert Party in M.E.F.

Anderton, J., 16, Arundel Street; R.A.S.C. and Royal Navy. M.E.F.; took part in D Day landings with Royal Navy.

Ansell, John E., 111, Raeburn Road; Army.

Barker, Reginald, The Crescent. Weedon Road; Army.

Barron, J. P., 32, Bants Lane; Army.

Blinco, Fred, 11, Willesden's Cottages; Royal Navy; Stoker 1. H.M.S. Teazer. Minesweeping in Mediterranean. Joined H.G. when 15.

Blinco, William, 11, Willesden's Cottages; Royal Corps of Signals; Corporal. North Africa, Sicily, Italy, later in Palestine.

Bliss, Cyril J., 54, Horsemarket. Landed with 154 Leicestershire Yeomanry at Anzio and went through Italian Campaign; later served with Anti-Tank Regiment in Greece.

Botterill, Sidney, 13, Charles Street; Fleet Air Arm. H.M.S. Venerable. Australia and Pacific.

Brooks, Ernest, 66, Lovat Drive; Army.

Burchall, Kenneth G., 15, Leslie Road; Royal Navy. Home Waters.

Burdett, Charles D., 15, Inkerman Terrace; Army.

Burton, Stanley E., 40, Kerr Street; Army.

Bushell, Leslie F., 81, St. James' Park Road; R.E.; Sapper. N.-W. Europe.

Causby, John T., 4, Lewis Road; Grenadier Guards. Joined H.G. when 15 years old. Served in Africa, Italy and Germany. Twice wounded.

Chapman, Daniel W., 25, Cartwright Road; Army.

Chapman, L., 120, Spencer Bridge Road; Army.

Coles, Stanley E., 5, Sulgrave Road; Northamptonshire Yeomanry, also R.A., attached R.M. In D Day landing, North-West Europe and Germany.

Cox, Roland W., 26, Stanley Street; R.A.O.C.; Sergeant. India and Burma.

Craddock, H. C., 94, St. James' Park Road; Royal Corps of Signals. Europe and India Command.

Culley, S. R., 13, Stanley Road; Queen's Royal Regiment. Italy and Germany. Wounded January 21st, 1944, in M.E.F.; taken prisoner of war July 4th, 1944.

Darby, Reginald, 40, Euston Road; Royal Corps of Signals. North Africa, Italy and Burma.

Davies, Eric E., 46, Streatfeild Road; R.A.F.

Day, J., 123, Gladstone Road; R.A.S.C., 3rd Inf. Brigade. France, Palestine.

Drinkwater, K., 24, Duston Road; R.A.F.; Corporal. Home Bases, Belgium and India.

Dove, Jack R., 22, Stenson Street; R.A.O.C.; Lance-Corporal. East Africa.

Ekins, George L., 30, Spencer Street; Army.

Faulkner, Cyril B., 9, Semilong Road; Royal Inniskillin Fusiliers. Sustained shell-shock in Italy.

Ferrar, Cecil C., 46, Wantage Road; 44th Reconnaissance Corps; Corporal. With 5th Army in Italy, and then with 8th Army. Slightly wounded January, 1944. Transferred to 1st Derbyshire Yeomanry, serving in Egypt and Tripoli.

Finch, John, 142, Gladstone Road; Northamptonshire Regiment, later 2nd Lincolnshires. In D Day landing, wounded in foot; later served in Italy and Austria.

Frost, Arthur F., 55, Salisbury Street; Fleet Air Arm, 802 Squadron; Seafires; Petty Officer. H.M.S. Queen (escort aircraft carrier). Home Waters and air cover on D Day; in action against V.1's.

Fryatt, Frederick A., 138, Gladstone Road; Pioneer Corps. Normandy D Day plus 2, and North-West Europe.

Fryatt, Thomas, 138, Gladstone Road; R.A.S.C. Normandy and N.-W. Europe.

Gamble, Gordon P., 55, Ashburnham Rd.; R.A.F.; Flight Sergeant Navigator. Gained wings in South Africa.

Gardner, Roy, 141, Beech Avenue; Northamptonshire Regiment; Corporal. Germany.

Gibbs, W. A., 52, Sheep Street; Army.

Gibson, C. H., 5, St. James' Park Road; Army.

Heap, R., 24, St. James' Street; Royal Navy. H.M. Submarine Shalimar. Served in Far East, and assisted in sinking Jap tanker and landing craft.

Hillery, R., 5, Streatfeild Road; Fleet Air Arm; L.A.F. (E.) 824 and 791 Squadrons. H.M.S. Initer and Vindex. Singapore, India and Ceylon.

Hobbs, William T., 38, Kingsway; Northamptonshire Regiment. Italy and Belgium.

Hodges, William S., 80, Alma Street; Royal Navy; Stoker 1st Class. H.M.S. Dornoch. Minesweeping in Atlantic, Mediterranean and Cherbourg (D Day).

Hunter, Arthur, 33, Greenwood Road; Royal Navy. H.M.S. Garuda. India.

Illing, Leslie A., 18, Tintern Avenue; R.A. B.L.A.

Ingham, Arthur W., 23, Alma Street; Royal Sussex Regiment. Italy. Twice wounded.

Inwood, Albert, 28, Streatfeild Road; Royal Navy.

Inwood, Arthur R., 1, Dryden Road; Army.

Knight, Raymond G. C., 26, Tintern Avenue; R.A.S.C., Airborne. North Africa, Italy and France.

Marriott, R. W., 32, Lower Priory Street; Green Howards. Home Service.

Masters, F. W., 62, Lower Hester Street; R.A., 1st L.A.A., S.L. Battery. B.A.O.R.

May, P. J., 19, St. Andrew's Road; R.E.M.E.; Sergeant. India.

Muddiman, James W., 37, Monks Pond Street; Army.

Munroe, F. W., 24, Knightley Road; Royal Navy; A.B. H.M.S. Wilton, Camerton and Howe. Served in Mediterranean and Far East. Wounded at Anzio Beach-head.

Nutt, Alfred R., 3, Sulgrave Road; 2nd Bn. Lincolnshire Regiment. Landed in Normandy on D Day. Badly wounded by shell-burst.

Osborne, Victor, 17, Sulgrave Road; R.A.C. Home Service.

Parker, D. W., 162, Semilong Road; Royal Corps of Signals. Served with 4th Indian Division, 8th Army, in North Africa, Syria, Italy and Greece.

Parker, Frederick C., 1, Abbey Terrace; R.A.M.C. India and S.E.A.C.

Perkins, Roy F. A., 46, Dallington Road; Duke of Wellington's Regiment. Home Service owing to broken ankle received while practising for D Day Invasion.

Robertson, Wallace J., 4, Lincoln Road; R.A. Italy and M.E.F.

Robinson, Jack E., 2, St. Andrew's Road; 2nd Bn. Northamptonshire Regt. North Africa, Italy and B.A.O.R.

Rymer, John A., 20, Wood Street; Army.

Salt, Harold G., 28, Spencer Bridge Road; Gordon Highlanders. Went abroad on D Day. Wounded by shrapnel February 20th, 1945.

Sanders, Hugh, 74, Wheatfield Road; Army.

Shipman, Walter W., 68, Cambridge Street; R.A.C. Italy, Austria and Middle East.

Shirley, William E., 2, Gladstone Road; R.E. Home Service.

Smith, Arthur E., 7, Monmouth Road; R.E.M.E. Home Service.

Smith, Donald K., 19, Sulgrave Road; Royal Marines. H.M.S. Dicto. Rammed twice. Was in first Naval Squadron to visit Denmark since time of Nelson.

Smith, George, 25, Uppingham Street; R.A.M.C. B.F.I.F.

Smith, J. V., 14, Gladstone Road; R.A.F.; Sergeant Cook; 621 Squadron. Mombassa, Aden and Middle East.

Stapleton, Peter F., 65, St. James' Park Road; R.A.S.C.; Driver. With first landing craft on D Day; served in North-West Europe and Palestine.

Stockwell, Frank, 11, Horsemarket; Army.

Strike, Archie F., 7, Parkfield Crescent; R.A.F.; L.A.C. Home Bases.

Suter, William, 23, Bearward Street; R.A. and P.C. Landed D Day plus 2; North-West Europe and Germany. Present at Belsen Trial in Lununburg.

Tebbutt, J. E., 239a, Wellingborough Road; Army.

Tero, Bernard K., 36, Aberdare Road; Royal Navy; A.B. H.M.S. Phoebe. Mediterranean and Pacific.

Thompson, Reginald H., 6, Thirlestane Road; 5th Royal Tank Regiment; Corporal. North-West Europe.

Tompkins, Lionel T., 45, Greenwood Road; Army.

Tredwell, G., 42, Muscott Street; Fleet Air Arm; Leading Air Mechanic. H.M.S. Chitral, Unicorn and Newcastle. Home Fleet and Foreign Service, India, Burma and Far East.

Turner, Charles, 105, St. Andrew's Road; Fleet Air Arm. Home Bases.

Vaughan, Leonard B., 29, Trevor Crescent; R.E., Movement Control Section; C.Q.M.S. Home Service.

Verrecchia, Michael, 2, Cooper Street; R.A.M.C. In D Day landings.

Wells, Geoffrey J., "Firwell," Weedon Road; Army.

Williams,E. T., 6, St. Edmund's Road; Army.

Wright, F., 12, Mill Road; 2nd Northamptonshire Regiment. Italy and North-West Europe.

The following also joined H.M. Forces

Andrews, W. T.	Day, J.	Inwood, R. L.	Roe, P. A.
Barnes, F. W. T.	Day, R. A.	Jack, D. W.	Scotney, W. J.
Barringer, J.	Day, R. V.	Jackson, W. H.	Simpson, R.
Bending, W.	Fleming, A. R.	Jarrett, H. W.	Slinn, J. G.
Blackett, A. G.	Gasson, E. G.	Jelleyman, W. W.	Smith, F. C.
Brittain, R.	Gillham, J.	Joyce, S.	Smith, T. A.
Britten, W. G.	Goodman, R. T.	Knight, C.	Sorrell, L. A.
Brown, K. F.	Green, T. G.	Onley, R. A.	Terry, P.
Burman. F. S.	Gribble, A. G.	Page, R. D.	Toseland, R. W.
Burrows, L. J. W.	Hancock, R. W.	Page, S. J. E.	Wakeling, E.
Chappell, A.	Hefford, J.	Parker, D. W.	Warner, R.
Clarke, D. A. J.	Hughes, M.	Perkins, E. H.	Whiteley, J. F.
Clarke, P. J.	Hughes, M. J.	Price, A. L.	Whitworth, W.
Coe, L. W.	Inwood, D. W.	Reeve, H.	Wilkins, R. P.
Curtis, G. T. G.	Inwood, H. C.	Robinson, E. J.	Wilson, H.
Davis, G.			

THE NEW D COMPANY (Coastal Reinforcement)

Atkinson, William, 55, Norton Road; Army.

Barcock, Leslie B., 43, Hastings Road; Royal Navy; A.B. H.M.S. Pique. On convoys from Africa and America; later served on minesweeper.

Davis, Charles H., 47, Norton Road; Army.

Dixon, Benjamin, 77, Cecil Road; R.A.F.; L.A.C. Home Bases.

Draper, Colin, 276, Birchfield Road; R.A.F.; Flight Sergeant Air-Gunner. Operations over Germany and Norway; later in India.

Gardner, John S., 160, Beech Avenue.

Garratt, Harry G., 116, Kingsland Avenue; Pioneer Corps. Germany.

Hasnip, Edward W., 48, Whiston Road; R.E.; Corporal. Basra, Iraq.

Hickerson, Frederick W., 9, Langdale Road; R.E.; Sapper. Java.

Hope, William, 117, Welford Road; Army.

Langford, Cyril, 40, Hastings Road; R.A.S.C., Airborne Division. Rhine Crossing and Palestine. Wounded in Palestine.

Pettitt, Cyril H., 22, Balmoral Road; R.A.F., 608 Mosquito Squadron, Pathfinder Force. Home Bases.

Redford, Frederick E., 6. Balmoral Road

Snedker, Harry G., 112, Kingsland Avenue; Royal Navy. H.M.S. Sultan II. Eastern Waters.

Timms, Dennis, 79, Bective Road; Royal Navy; Seaman. H.M.S. Bermuda. Pacific.

Timson, Arthur D. T., 155, Kingsland Avenue; R.A.F. Served in Iraq.

Warwick, Fred, 57, Cranford Road; R.A.O.C. Egypt.

E COMPANY

Ambidge, George A., 76, Somerset Street; Royal Navy. Far East.

Bentley, John L., 34, Charles Street; R.A.F.
Blincow, John L., 57, Colwyn Road; R.A.F. Home Bases and B.A.O.R.
Brown, Arthur, 92, Delapre Street; Royal Navy. Minesweeping, Atlantic and Iceland.

Coulson, Peter B., 5, Hawthorn Road; Royal Engineers. B.A.O.R.
Cox, Frederick A., 56, Cyril Street; Army.

Daniells, William L., 20, Seymour Street; Army.
Dawkins, A., Far Cotton; R.E. North Africa, Italy, and D Day landings.

Gadsden, Ronald P., 58, Euston Road; Royal Navy.

Hall, William J., 35, Parkfield Road; Army.

Kent, Frederick, 29, Pleydell Road; Army.
Kilsby, Jack, 62, Bants Lane; Royal Navy; Sick Berth Steward.

Littlemore, George R., 2, Albion Crescent; Army.

Mabbott, Walter S., 56, Dallington Road; Army.

Richardson, Frank M., 23, Briton Road; Royal Navy.
Rudd, Leonard A., 89, Delapre Park Crescent; Royal Navy.

Sewell, Reginald C. A., 36, Bailiff Street; Royal Navy. Aircraft Carrier. Far East.
Short, Percy G., 44, St. David's Road; Army.
Smith, Sidney B., 8, Abbey Park Terrace; Army.
Spokes, Francis T., 108, Rothersthorpe Road; R.A. and R.E.; Movement Control. Home Service.

Washington, Donald, 8, Salcey Road; Army.
Webster, Herbert, 1, Whitford Terrace; Royal Navy.

The following also joined H.M. Forces

Cousins, N.	Griffiths, J. B.	James, F. G.	Phillips, R.
Davis, D.	Hallett, F. J.	Lewis, F. W.	Pragnell, F. C.
Dawson, E. C.	Humphreys, B.	Manning, F.	Shorthouse, N.
Day, C. J.	Humphrey, W. H.	Mawby, L.	Smith, S. G. A.
Drinkwater, J. W.	Idill, H. T. W.	Merritt, J. A.	Taylor, R. J.
Fisher, A. C.	Jackson, P.	Oliver, A. E.	Teasdale, W. H.
Flynn, P. J.			

F COMPANY

Ager, William A., 53, Palmerston Road; Royal Corps of Signals. North Africa and Italy.

Amos, Stanley G., 8, Briton Gardens; Royal Navy.

Austin, Leslie H., 13, Overstone Road; R.A.F.; L.A.C. Flying Control. North-West Europe

Austin, P., 39, Palmerston Road; Royal Marines. Home Bases.

Barker, William R., 54, Hood Street; R.A. (Radiolocation). N.-W. Europe.

Bounds, George R., 15, Northwood Road; 1st Dorset Regiment. 8th Army in North Africa, landings in Sicily and Italy; also in D Day landings in Normandy.

Brittain, Charles H., 1, Ryland Road; R.A.F.

Butlin, Frederick A., 27, Overstone Road; Royal Marines; Corporal. At Walcheren landing in Holland.

Chester, K. J., 5, St. Michael's Avenue; Army.

Chesworth, James, 66, Colwyn Road; Army.

Childs, Lionel E., 53, Ethel Street; 229 Coy. R.A.S.C., 6th Guards Armoured Brigade; Lance-Corporal. North-West Europe.

Clarke, Eric P., 36, Hunter Street; R.A.O.C. Home Service.

Clifford, D. J., 105, Alcombe Road; Army.

Cookson, Reginald, 6, Overstone Road; Army. Served in Italy.

Derbyshire, Henry R., 21, Great Russell Street; Royal Navy. Home Waters.

De Turville, Serge, 87, Bailiff Street; Army.

Dunlop, Leslie H., 42, Market Street; Grenadier Guards; Corporal. Italy and Germany. Prisoner of war.

Dunlop, W. G., 40, Watkin Terrace; Army.

England, Raymond R., 21, Hunter Street; Royal Navy (Landing Craft). D Day Invasion and Rhine Crossing.

England, Walter, 21, Hunter Street; R.A.F.; Corporal. With 146 Squadron, forward areas, Bengal; later with 200 Squadron, Liberators, Coastal Command and Supply Dropping.

Finch, F. J., 6, Merthyr Road; A.C.C., attached Royal Signals. Landed in France with Patton's First Army. North-West Europe and Germany.

Flavell, John, 75, The Headlands; Royal Navy; A.B. (Radar). Served with 2nd and 4th Submarine Flotillas, British East Indies Fleet. Patrols in Indian Ocean and Malacca Straits with H.M. Submarine Statesman.

Freeman, R. G., 23, Inkerman Terrace; 2nd Northamptonshire Regiment. Palestine and Germany.

Frisby, John W. D., 2, Wallace Gardens; Royal Marines (Escort Vessels). Home Waters.

Green, J. J., 50, Hazelwood Road; Army.

Gibbins, Ernest W., 85, Hood Street; Royal Navy. H.M.S. Loika. Mediterranean and Aegean Seas.

Halsey, Eric T., 54, Craven Street; R.A.F.V.R.

Hammond, A. L., 153, Clare Street; R.E.M.E. North-West Europe, Germany and Egypt.

Harris, R. S., 13, Poole Street; Army.

Harvey, S. H., 12, Alcombe Road; Army.

Hillyard, William H., 13, Somerset Street; R.A.F.; Corporal. Home Bases and India.

Hood, B. B., 11, Briton Road; Northamptonshire Regiment and C.M.P. India.

Hutchings, Walter, 43, Lawrence Street; R.A.F.; A.C.2 Home Bases, B.L.A. and B.A.O.R.

Jennings, A. J., 22, Wellington Place; 1st Fife and Forfar Yeomanry and R.A.C.; Lance-Corporal. Germany.

Jones, Claude B., 63, Park Avenue South; Royal Navy.

Kendall, Ronald K., 41, Cloutsham Street; Army.

Knighton, Frederick E., 79, Hunter Street; Pioneer Corps; Sergeant. Home Service.

Leach, Arthur L., 17, Monks Park Road; Royal Navy. Atlantic and Home Waters.

Manton, Richard J., 5, Masefield Way; Royal Marines. Coastal Patrol on Western Approaches.

Marchant, Harold R., 24, Watkin Terrace; R.A.F.; W.O. Air-Gunner. S.E.A.C., India and Burma.

Markham, Peter, Ram Hotel, Sheep Street; R.A.F. Home Bases

Merrill, J. E., 14, Bull Head Lane; R.A.O.C., 38 V.R.D. Home Service.

Milne, Alan, 3, Abbey Park Terrace; The Chamar Regiment, Indian Army; Lieutenant. Served in India and Burma.

Mineards, Ronald W., 96, Hood Street; Royal Navy; A.B. H.M.S. Lamont. Australian Waters.

Phillips, Frederick C., 38, Lawrence Street; Pioneer Corps. In London Blitz.

Picking, John, 23, Maple Street; Army.

Poole, Ronald G., 6, Danefield Road; Royal Marines. North-West Europe.

Price, Wilfred, 14, Margaret Street; R.A.F.; L.A.C. Home Bases and Ceylon.

Redding, H., 26, Margaret Street; 72 Primary Training Centre; Cook.

Richards, Reginald H., 33, Abington Avenue; Army.

Roberts, Leslie J., 5, Lorne Road; Army.

Roberts, R. O., 7, Victoria Terrace; Royal Navy.

Roberts, Walter, 42, Kerr Street; Royal Navy.

Rowland, William J., 46, Balfour Road; Pioneer Corps. In D Day landings; at Falaise and later at Rhine Crossing.

Shipley, Arthur, 41, Salisbury Street; Royal Navy. H.M.S. Birmingham. Escort work.

Simpson, Alfred, 39a, St. Paul's Road; Royal Navy; A.B. (Gunner). Atlantic Ocean.

Simpson, G. H., 6, Pike Lane; Royal Navy. Home Waters.

Taylor, Kenneth W., 21, Brook Street; Leicestershire Regiment. North-West Europe and Austria. Wounded in Holland. January 18th, 1945.

Thompson, J. K. S., 53, Cloutsham Street; Army.

Warburton, J., 27, Gray Street; Pioneer Corps. N.-W. Europe and Germany.

Welland, Walter, 25, Cooper Street; Army.

White, W. J., 12, Little Cross Street; Army.

Wilson, G. W., 84, Hunter Street; Army.

Wood, George J. C., 31, Lorne Road; Royal Navy. Home Waters.

G COMPANY

Adams, William P., 23, Queensland Gardens; Royal Navy (D.E.M.S.); A.B. (Gunner). Atlantic, North Sea and Indian Ocean.

Allinson, G. V.," Vigoria," St. George's Avenue; Royal Artillery, attached No. 3 M.P. and B.B. B.A.O.R.

Andrews, Walter H., 31, Norton Road; Royal Engineers; Staff Sergeant. India and S.E.A.C.

Bament, John R., 175, Abington Avenue; R.E.M.E. Home Service.

Bamford, William, 12, St. Paul's Road; Rifle Brigade; Rifleman. Italy and Greece.

Barnes, Frank, 158, Kingsland Avenue; Royal Navy; A.B. H.M.S. Golden Hind. Australian Waters.

Barrick, Raymond A., 13, Clare Street; R.A.S.C.; Driver. Landed with B.L.A. and went through campaign to Germany.

Baucutt, Raymond, 3, Cranford Road; Royal Navy. H.M.S. Robertson. Home Waters.

Bex, Basil F., 132, Cedar Road; Royal Navy.

Bradshaw, Norman, 65, Lindsay Avenue; Royal Marines; Corporal. India, Malaya and Burma.

Braid, Melville, 56, West Ridge; 6th Black Watch. Italy and Greece.

Brooks, Thomas R., 11, Cranford Road; 15th Paratroop Regiment; Lance-Sergeant. India.

Brown, William T., 73, Salisbury Street; 1st King's Regiment. India.

Carvell, Robert, 82, Gordon Street; VIII R.R.I.H.; Lance-Corporal. B.A.O.R.

Collins, William, 106, Bailiff Street; Royal Marines. 682 Landing Craft Flotilla. Corporal (Landing Craft Driver). M.E.F. and Far East. With No. 7 V Force in Burma for special landings.

Crick, P. T., 25, Vernon Terrace; Army

Cumberpatch, Frederick C., 32, Shelley Street; Royal Marines. Shore Bases.

Deacon, B. J., 39, Adams Avenue; R.A.F.

Dixon, George E., 13, Greenfield Road (formerly I.O. to Company); Captain. On Claims Commission, Beirut, M.E.F.

Dugdale, Ronald R., 46, Alliston's Gardens; Royal Navy. Home Waters.

England, R. R., 21, Hunter Street; Royal Navy; A.B. Home Waters.

Fox, James, 78, Newland; Army.

Freeman, Kenneth, 36, Raeburn Road; Royal Marines

Frost, Arthur C., 90, Hood Street; R.A., 232/114 Field Regiment. S.E.A.C.

Golding, George P., 51, Spencer Street; Fleet Air Arm. Ireland and Scotland Bases.

Goodger, Leslie G., 167, Milton Street; Royal Marines. In D Day landings in Normandy, and in Japanese Campaign.

Goosey, R., 15, Maple Street; R.N.A.S.; Air Mechanic. Home Service.

Grimes, Raymond E., 59, St. Leonard's Road; R.E.M.E.; Tele. Mech. India, Java and Singapore.

Haddon, Herbert, 18, Cranbrook Road; R.E. London Docks.

Hadwin, John, 13, Wycliffe Road; Army.

Hanson, Peter H., 5, Lime Avenue; Northamptonshire Regiment, later transferred to 7th North Staffs. Belgium and Italy.

Hawker, Gordon L., 3, Ardington Road; Army.

Heeley, George D., 23, Austin Street; Royal Navy. Home Waters.

Hollowell, Ronald, 20, Murray Avenue; R.A.F.; A.C. Home Bases.

Howes, Noel, 6, Warren Road; Paratroop Battalion. India, Sourabaya, Batavia and Malaya. Among first British troops to enter Singapore after liberation.

Isaac, Walter, 53, St. David's Road; Monmouthshire Regiment. North-West Europe and Germany. Prisoner of war.

Jafkins, Donald W., 6, Junction Road; 7th Bn. Argyll and Sutherland Highlanders. Landed in Normandy with 51st Division. Wounded at St. Sylvian. Rejoined unit January, 1945.

Johns, Derek O., 62, Cedar Road; 5th Royal Gurkha Rifles; commissioned at 19 years of age. India.

Jordan, James R., 42, Kingsley Road; Royal Navy.

Kendall, Robert T., 20, Cranstoun Street; 2nd Recce Regiment. Malaya.

Knight, Reginald, 45, Ruskin Road; R.A.F.; L.A.C. Home Bases and Egypt.

Lee, Charles, The Gables, Spinney Hill; Army.

Lilford, Donald, 76, Cloutsham Street; Army.

Lilleyman, William, 8, Doddridge Street; Army.

Lines, John G., 128, Kingsland Avenue; R.A.S.C.; Corporal. Singapore.

Lovell, Ronald G., 32, Raeburn Road; Royal Marines. H.M.S. Saloween. India, Burma and Java.

Lloyd, David J. W., 32, Bush Hill; Army.

Marriott, Peter J., 37, Danefield Road; 6th Bn. Royal Welch Parachute Regt. North-West Europe and Palestine. Took part in 6th Airborne Division dash from Rhine to Lubeck to link up with Russians.

Mason, Albert H. G., 14, Cooper Street; Fleet Air Arm. Home Bases.

Merrick, F. E., 62, Cranford Road; Army.

Moore, John S., 90, Windsor Crescent; Royal Engineers; Officer Cadet. India.

Morbey, H. L., Rowan Avenue, Booth Rise; Army.

Munday, Dennis, 14, Randall Road; Royal Navy. Leading Wireman, Landing Craft; Combined Operations; India and the Pacific.

Peach, Herbert J., 58, St. Edmund's Street; Royal Navy; Leading Seaman. H.M.S. Vernon II. Mediterranean and North Sea. In Combined Operations. Wounded at Walcheren landing, Holland.

Phipps, John J., 37, Bush Hill; R.A.F. Fighter Command; Flying Officer (Spitfire pilot). Home Bases.

Pittam, Robert, 54, Hood Street; 8th Field Regt., R.A.; Bombardier. India.

Price, John A., 69, Abington Park Crescent; Royal Navy; Sub-Lieutenant. Legal Aid Department, Chatham.

Pyne, Frederick A., 56, Kingsway; R.A.F. Home Bases.

Reeves, William H., 39, Roe Road; Mobile Operations Naval Air Base. Home Service and Australia.

Reynolds, John F. D., 126, Loyd Road; R.A.M.C., Civil Affairs Service, Burma, S.E.A.C.; later Sergeant with Central Medical Stores, Rear Section, C.A.S.(B.), H.Q., Burma Command.

Roberts, Albert T., 103, Milton Street; R.A.O.C. Home Service.

Russell, T. B., 54, St. Michael's Road; Army.

Shaw, Bernard, 3, Pike Lane; Royal Navy.

Shrive, John, 54, Balfour Road; Royal Navy; A.B. H.M.S. Nelson. Atlantic and Pacific.

Smith, C. W., 20, Rothesay Road; R.A.F.

Soames, Leslie W. F., 12, Raeburn Road; Army.

Starmer, Harry, 50, New Town Road; Royal Navy. H.M.S. Birmingham. Mediterranean.

Storrier, P. J. G., 150, Kingsley Road; Army.

Swainsbury, W. H., 133, Eastern Avenue; Army.

Thompson, William, 35, Henry Street; Army.

Tilley, Edwin H., 26, Somerset Street; Army.

Tiplady, A. C., New Road, Rushmere Estate; Army.

Turner, Ernest G., 54, Lawrence Street; 2nd Field Regiment, R.A. Palestine.

Turner, Richard H., 37, Hazeldene Road; R.A.M.C. Took part in D Day landings; helped in liberation of Norway; received certificate of thanks from Norwegian authorities.

Vickers, Eric G., Weedon Road; Army.

White, Donald, 79, Rosedale Road; Royal Hussars. North-West Europe.

Williams, Owen J., 13, Prince's Street; Army.

Williams, R., 88, Bostock Avenue; R.A.F.

Wilson, Leslie J., 52, Northcote Street; Royal Navy. S.S. Fort Brandon. Served in Atlantic and D Day landings.

Wingrove, Eric, 37, Northcote Street; 5th Bn. Northamptonshire Regiment. Served in Austria.

Wright, John A., 3, Junction Road; R.A.S.C. M.E.F. and Austria.

Wright, John C., 33, Clare Street; R.A.O.C.; A.C. Sergeant. North-West Europe. Toured C.M.F. with "Stars in Battledress."

Young, Stanley, 17, Scarletwell Street; Royal Marines.

H COMPANY

Andrews, Herbert G., 1, Highfield Road (former Platoon Commander of No. 27 Platoon); A.E.C.; Lieutenant. M.E.F.

Banks, William G., 134, Milton Street; Army.

Botterill, Peter F., 17, Beaconsfield Terrace; R.E.M.E.; Craftsman. Mentioned in Despatches. Worked on tanks of vital importance for D Day.

Clark, Norman F., 13, Salisbury Street; Fleet Air Arm. Palestine and Malta.

Coleman, Frank W., 47, Raeburn Road; Army.

Dickens, Reginald H., 2, Agnes Road; Royal Navy; A.B. Atlantic.

Driver, Bert E., 58, Stanhope Road; R.E.M.E.; Craftsman. Home Service.

Farmer, Robert E., 16, Baker Street; R.E.M.E.; Corporal. Egypt.

Hickman, D. R., 7, Randall Road; Manchester Regiment. Home Service.

Jarman, Horace H., 15, Gordon Street; R.A.O.C. Home Service.

Lee, Frederick E., 151, Kingsland Avenue; R.A.S.C. North-West Europe.

Luck, Robert F., 9, Wellington Place; R.A.F. Home Bases.

Manning, Thomas L., 21, Cranford Road; 6th Northamptonshire Regiment and 1st Duke of Wellington's. Three times wounded, once in North Africa and twice in Italy.

May, John A., 129, St. Andrew's Road; Royal Navy. Home Waters.

Mayes, Ronald, 8, Brookfield Road; Royal Navy.

Moore, James W., 34, Randall Road; Royal Navy. Landing Craft. North Africa, Sicily and Italy.

Oldham, Raymond G. H., 8, Waverley Road; Army.

Payne, Philip T., 68, Balmoral Road; Army. Home Service.

Pearson, Norman, 114, St. Andrew's Road; Royal Navy. H.M.S. Indefatigable (Aircraft Carrier). Atlantic and Far East.

Randall, George A., 35, Murray Avenue; Grenadier Guards; Lance-Corporal. Home Service.

Robinson, Harry, 65, Kingsthorpe Hollow; Royal Engineers. Italy.

Robinson, L. T., 29, Elmhurst Avenue; Army.

Shrives, Joseph C., 72, Byron Street; R.A., 133 Field Regiment; Gunner. Landed D Day plus 14; in campaign to Germany.

Simons, Leslie Walter, 122, Adelaide Street (late Drum-Major, Band); R.A.S.C. B.A.O.R. and M.E.F.

Spittles, Harold F., 5, Knightley Road; Pioneer Corps. Germany.

Spokes, Henry F. J., 81, Semilong Road; Army. Home Service.

Stamps, Montague; R.A.C., 57 T.R. Experimental and Test Driver on Tanks.

Throssell, Herbert D., 37, Denmark Road; R.A.F.; Flight Lieutenant; 76 Squadron. Home Bases and India. Pilot, Halifax and Dakota. Participated in 41 attacks over Germany. Badly burned in crash, Sept., 1944, when on way to bomb Kiel.

Weaver, Walter C., 6, Birchfield Road; Army.

Whitaker, L. A. M., 21, Agnes Road; Army.

(Photo: Henry Cooper & Son).

THE BATTALION BAND.

REMOVING THE BLACK-OUT FROM WINDOWS AT MANFIELD HOSPITAL.

(Photo: Northampton Independent).

MEMBERS OF THE HOME GUARD WHO DIED WHILE SERVING WITH THE 12TH BATTALION

DIED WHILE ON HOME GUARD DUTY

G COMPANY: Private   A. H. Wimpress.

OTHER DEATHS

A COMPANY: Private   S. O. Voss.
                        Private   W. Jeyes.
                        Private   T. Bass.

B COMPANY: Private   F. J. Leddington.
                        Private   A. E. Faulkner.
                        Private   C. J. Fox.
                        L/Corporal J. Kean.

C COMPANY: Private   W. E. Newton.
                        Private   F. Wilson.

D COMPANY: Private   W. H. Barefoot.

E COMPANY: Sergeant   A. E. Graham.
                        Private   J. T. Fleming.

F COMPANY: L/Corporal W. T. Roberts.

G COMPANY: Private   R. A. Cox.

H COMPANY: Private   H. S. Burnhope.

No. 2 H.Q. PLATOON: Private   O. G. Wright.

2001 M.T. Company: Private   C. Toseland.

INTERESTING FIGURES OF THE BATTALION

Greatest Battalion strength, March 31st, 1943   2,776

Made up as under:—

Battalion Headquarters	52
A Company	455
B Company	417
C Company	299
D Company	451
E Company	440
F Company	203
G Company	212
H Company	124
Transport Company	123

Strength at Stand Down, December 31st, 1944   1,366

NUMBERS WHO SERVED IN THE BATTALION

Members who joined H.M. Forces	1,172
Discharged at Own Request before 1942	431
Failed to Report for Duty before 1942	77
Discharged Over Age	9
Discharged Under Age	4
Discharged Medically Unfit	195
Transferred to Other Home Guard Units	238
Discharged: Services No Longer Required ...	65
Discharged: Changed Conditions of Employment	186
Died While Serving	18
Transferred to 15th Battalion:	
D Company	462
E Company	408
Electric Light Platoon	117
Transferred to 2001 M.T. Company	184
Strength at Stand Down	1,366
Total	4,932

SPECIAL ARMY ORDER

The War Office.
14th November, 1944.

MESSAGE FROM HIS MAJESTY THE KING TO THE HOME GUARD

For more than four years you have borne a heavy burden. Most of you have been engaged for long hours in work necessary to the prosecution of the war or to maintaining the healthful life of the Nation; and you have given a great portion of the time which should have been your own to learning the skilled work of a soldier. By this patient, ungrudging effort you have built and maintained a force able to play an essential part in the defence of our threatened soil and liberty.

I have long wished to see you relieved of this burden; but it would have been a betrayal of all we owe to our fathers and our sons if any step had been taken which might have imperilled our Country's safety. Till very recently, a slackening of our defences might have encouraged the enemy to launch a desperate blow which could grievously have damaged us and weakened the power of our own assault. Now, at last, the splendid resolution and endurance of the Allied Armies have thrust back that danger from our coasts. At last I can say that you have fulfilled your charge.

The Home Guard has reached the end of its long tour of duty under arms. But I know that your devotion to our land, your comradeship, your power to work your hardest at the end of the longest day, will discover new outlets for patriotic service in time of peace.

History will say that your share in the greatest of all our struggles for freedom was a vitally important one. You have given your service without thought of reward. You have earned in full measure your Country's gratitude.

GEORGE R.I.
Colonel-in-Chief.

SPECIAL ORDER OF THE DAY
TO THE HOME GUARD

by

GENERAL SIR HAROLD E. FRANKLYN, K.C.B., D.S.O., M.C.,
Commander-in-Chief, Home Forces.

General Headquarters,
Home Forces.
November, 1944.

During the past few years I have had many opportunities of seeing the Home Guard in most parts of the country, including Northern Ireland. A high standard of efficiency has been reached, which has been made possible only by the keenness and devotion to duty of all ranks. I would like to emphasise the very special contribution of those who volunteered in 1940 and whose enthusiasm has never flagged since then; they have been the backbone of their units.

The Home Guard came into being at a time of acute crisis in our history, and for over four years has stood prepared to repel any invader of our shores. The reliance that has been placed on you during these years has been abundantly justified and it has enabled our Regular troops to go overseas in sufficient numbers to give battle to the enemy with the magnificent results that we have seen.

And now as to the future. I hope that Home Guardsmen will take every opportunity of preserving the friendships and associations that you have formed during these past years. You can continue to be a real source of stability and strength to the country during what may be difficult years ahead. I hope also that you will do all in your power to help the Cadets, even if only by encouragement. Here is a way in which you can continue to render valuable service for many years to come.

I am very proud to have had the Home Guard under my command. I have enjoyed meeting and speaking to thousands of you. Now you can stand down with every right to feel that you have done your duty and contributed very materially to victory.

The best of luck to every one of you.

Well done indeed the Home Guard.

H. E. FRANKLYN,
General.

MESSAGE TO ALL HOME GUARDSMEN
IN EAST CENTRAL DISTRICT

On handing over command of the District, I wish to thank all Home Guardsmen for the full and loyal support they have invariably given me during the past year. As a result, I have always felt the greatest confidence that come what might, we were ready for it.

I leave the District with a very high opinion of its Home Guard. Its keenness, its high standard of efficiency and its spirit of service merit, in my opinion, the highest praise.

It is greatly to be hoped that that spirit of service, as well as the comradeship and good will among men drawn from all walks in life, that has been such an outstanding characteristic of the Force, will be maintained in the future.

Its period of service to the country as a military force is now drawing to a close. But all Home Guardsmen may look back with great satisfaction on their efforts. The Home Guard deserves well of its country.

For myself, I shall look back on the past year spent in close contact with the Home Guard with the happiest recollections. It has indeed been a great honour to have such men under my command.

Goodbye to you all, and good luck in the future.

E. C. HAYES,
Major-General,
Commander, East Central District.

20th November, 1944.

NORTHAMPTONSHIRE AND HUNTINGDONSHIRE HOME GUARD

FAREWELL MESSAGE FROM THE COLONEL OF THE
NORTHAMPTONSHIRE REGIMENT

The time has come for the final " Stand Down " of the Home Guard, and I therefore wish to send you a message of thanks and good will on behalf of all ranks of the Northamptonshire Regiment.

Whilst the Battalions of your County Regiment have been away fighting the enemy in Africa, in Italy, in the Balkans, and in Burma, you, our comrades of the Home Guard, have guaranteed the defence of our home shores as a firm base.

I hope that the spirit of service and comradeship which has been such a marked feature of the Home Guard, will be kept up and preserved for the future good of our Country.

Goodbye and good luck.

G. St. G. ROBINSON,
Major-General,
Colonel, The Northamptonshire Regiment.

CHAPTER THIRTEEN

FINALE

" The Greatest Army mustered yet,
That never asked what it would get."
A. P. HERBERT.

A S I write this closing Chapter towards the end of 1945, the announcement has gone forth that on December 31st, 1945, the official disbandment of the Home Guard takes place and that large unpaid Army will be no more, except in memory.

It seems a long way off now since those early L.D.V. days of 1940 when bodies of eager volunteers donned what denims they had and gave up most of their leisure to training and observation patrols, usually after a hard day's work. In 1940 and 1941, when invasion appeared almost certain, it was a comparatively easy matter to arouse keenness and enthusiasm. It was later, when the danger of invasion seemed to have receded and when the strain of the years of war began to tell, that the Home Guard, to my mind, reached its height, in the perseverance with which it stuck to its task determined to see the job through. In 1940 such was the enthusiasm shown that in June of that year Sir Hereward Wake, the County Commander, considered it necessary to issue the following instruction: " I have no wish to damp the enthusiasm of the L.D.V., which I fully appreciate, but it is important that too heavy calls are not made upon them." The L.D.V. were setting a pace which it would be difficult to maintain.

The L.D.V. was formed in May, 1940, against invasion that was expected within weeks. It developed into something more, a well-trained army, and it speaks volumes for the spirit of the Home Guard that its enthusiasm was maintained to the end. In some areas Home Guard A.A. Batteries were formed, and these had at least the satisfaction of hitting back. This privilege, however, was denied to us in this area, but still we kept going.

I always found the Home Guard would do anything provided you explained why it was necessary. They would stand any discomfort if they knew that it could not be helped. They would be happy about anything if they saw that it was necessary to beat the Hun. But if you asked them to do something without them being able to see the reason, or in other words, if they thought they were being " messed about," heaven help you, for you were done, and could give up. When you had men living in their homes, putting in a full week's work at their civilian occupations, many working overtime, and giving voluntarily of their spare time to Home Guard duties, you could not expect, nor was it right to expect, all that you would from full-time Regular soldiers living in Army camps and barracks. It took a long time for some of the higher authorities to realise this; indeed, I believe some never did, but the Home Guard carried on in its own way to the end.

Before closing it would only be gracious and right to give our grateful thanks to all those who rendered much appreciated assistance to the 12th Battalion during its existence. Their names are legion, and if some are inadvertently omitted from this History I can only say that their kindly actions will always be remembered. To Sir Hereward Wake, the first County Commander, and to Colonel P. Lester Reid, who succeeded him, we owe special thanks. The latter was always present at all our Battalion parades and we were greatly indebted to him for his great interest in the Battalion. Personally, I shall always remember with gratitude his kindly and valued advice in the many difficulties that arose from time to time.

On the County Territorial Association fell a vast amount of administrative work necessitated by the Home Guard, and we received the greatest assistance in this sphere, first from Colonel R. M. Raynsford, and then on his retirement from his successor, Lieut.-Colonel O. K. Parker, not forgetting the Zone Quartermaster, E. H. Nelson, who successfully extricated us from the many tangles into which we got with deficiencies of equipment, etc.

On the operational side Colonel J. L. Short, of Sub-District, and his Brigade Majors, R. M. Jeffery and S. D. Bartley, were always ready to help us in whatever way they could. Although at times we did not see eye to eye with Colonel Short, yet we recognised his ability as a soldier, and had invasion taken place, we had the utmost confidence in him to cope with the situation in this district.

In the Summer of 1943, No. 4 Sector was formed, comprising the 9th, 11th, 12th and 15th Battalions, with Colonel G. S. Watson in command. Here we had a Home Guard officer who understood the Home Guard, something which was none too easy. With this change, matters proceeded much more smoothly and there was far more co-operation between the Battalions in this area. Our best thanks are due to Colonel Watson and his staff for all that they did for the 12th. When the Sector was formed, the Battalion made its contribution to the Sector Staff. We sent some of our best men for this purpose. On the Intelligence side, Lieutenant Dixon was in charge, and on his call-up for the Regular Army Lieutenant J. J. Wright took over. They were ably assisted by Sergeant J. D. Edwards and Lance-Corporal D. Plews, both from A Company. We supplied also Lieutenant Mobb (B Company), Sergeant A. H. Flack and Private W. J. Hartles (C Company), and Privates R. A. Shaw and R. G. Brewster (A Company) for the Signal side of the Sector work. We are much indebted to Jack Wright, late of C Company, an expert photographer, for the many pictures he took of the various phases of the Battalion activities, some of which are included in this book.

Our best thanks are due also to the local Press, for although much of our work had necessarily to be done without any limelight, yet Mr. W. Cowper Barrons, of the "Chronicle and Echo," and Mr. Bernard Holloway, of the "Northampton Independent," were always extremely helpful when we called upon them. The weekly Home Guard page in the "Independent" was looked forward to and read with the greatest interest by all the Battalion. Without their kind assistance much of the material for the Chapter on the record of ex-members would not have been obtained.

In the closing months of 1945 the 12th Battalion performed its last service before its disbandment. For a succession of Sunday mornings a happy band of some eighty members gave up their time in removing the black-out paint from the windows of the Manfield Hospital, a work for which no paid labour could be obtained at the time, and which in any case would have cost a considerable sum of money. What you get out of a society, a game, or life itself is just what you put into it. I believe that the chief recipe for happiness in this world is always looking out to see what you can give and how you can serve without thinking what you are going to get out of it. In war, self-sacrifice and unselfishness are experienced by all who serve. Would that we could carry on this spirit in the times of peace.

Although the Battalion sought no decorations or rewards for their service, yet in 1944 one award gave especial pleasure when Lance-Corporal P. F. H. Hickman, of C Company, received the B.E.M. An enthusiastic volunteer from the commencement, although suffering from a disability which would have excused him service, he performed his duties as a Lewis gunner with zeal and devotion and rarely missed a parade during the four and a half years. He was a typical example of the zealous Home Guard and his decoration was indeed well deserved.

The chief reason for the success of the 12th Battalion lay in the fact that all served without any thought of material gain, the only reward consisting in the knowledge that one was doing one's duty to one's country. One other reward came, a reward that is beyond price, the friendship of the many good fellows with whom one served, a friendship that will last a lifetime.

And so on this 31st day of December, 1945, we close this History and say farewell to the 12th Battalion Northamptonshire Home Guard. Thanks a lot for all the happy times which I have spent with you all.

THE LAST OF THE HOME GUARD (December, 1945). A party of "Black-out Scrapers" at Manfield Hospital.

(Photo: J. Wright)

21319337R00118

Printed in Great Britain
by Amazon